BLUE

BARRY FERGUSON

At the age of 29, Barry Ferguson is at the peak of his footballing powers and is the captain of both Rangers and Scotland, with a host of medals and 39 international caps behind him. With his kneecap wired together and his right ankle reconstructed, he is rebuilt and ready for what the final years of his career will bring. He lives in Lanarkshire with his wife Margaret, sons Connor and Kyle, and his daughter Cara.

IAIN KING

Iain King was born in 1967 and is the head of sport at the Scottish *Sun* and the current Sports News Writer of the Year. His travels round the globe representing Scotland's top-selling paper have taken him to almost 60 countries, covering the exploits of Scotland and our club sides and savouring the European Championships and World Cup finals. *Blue: The Life and Times of Barry Ferguson* is his fourth book. He lives in his home town of East Kilbride with journalist wife Lorna and their children Caitlin and Bruce.

BLUE

THE LIFE AND TIMES
OF BARRY FERGUSON

BARRY FERGUSON MBE
WITH **IAIN KING**

FOREWORD BY
DAVID MURRAY

MAINSTREAM
PUBLISHING

EDINBURGH AND LONDON

This edition, 2008

First published in Great Britain in 2006 by
MAINSTREAM PUBLISHING COMPANY
(EDINBURGH) LTD
7 Albany Street
Edinburgh EH1 3UG

ISBN 9781845962241

A catalogue record for this book is available
from the British Library

Typeset in Galliard and Univers

Printed in Great Britain by
CPI Cox and Wyman, Reading, Berkshire RG1 8EX

BARRY FERGUSON

This book is dedicated to my mum and dad, Maureen and Archie, who always made sure I had my three most-prized possessions: trackie, boots and ball.

Also to my wife Margaret, the strong woman I've needed behind me, and my kids Connor, Kyle and Cara – they all put up with me and my moods.

My brother Derek has always been there for me to lean on and ask advice, and I have to mention my in-laws Carol and Kanie, whose babysitting makes sure I can have a night out!

This book is also for all the friends I have found both inside the game and out – you know who you are.

IAIN KING

Being involved with this book got me through the hardest year of my life after the death of my father Matt; it is dedicated to him and the influence he had on me that never fades.

My mum Leila's belief in me has always been total – even when I don't deserve it – and my journalist wife Lorna has once more suffered with a smile and constant help while I mixed the writing of a book with my day job.

To my kids Caitlin and Bruce: thanks, as ever, for the smiles and for reminding me that the deadline is not always the most important thing.

Acknowledgements

BARRY FERGUSON

My first vote of thanks goes to three coaches: the late John Chalmers, John McGregor and John Brown. I truly believe that without them I wouldn't have such an interesting story to tell.

Thanks also go to Danny Cunning, now Livingston's kitman, who once had a far more important role coaching the narky wee No. 6 at Mill United – top man.

When Kingy interviewed me for the book, I needed food and drink to help me put up with his constant stupid questions, and we found two of the best restaurants and some of the best guys to put up with us: thanks to Aki, Col and the boys at Spice in Hamilton for the laughs and the nights out, and to Satty at Mr Singh's where we signed the deal with Mainstream to start out on this rocky road.

Also, a big shout out goes to JV for helping me get to where I am today and to Irene Logan for helping to run my life smoothly.

A special vote of thanks goes to Uncle Brian and Aunt Angela, who has been like a sister to me, as well as my cousin Kevin. Margaret and I will always value the friendship they give us.

Lastly, thanks to Elaine Dempsey at Premier Photography.

IAIN KING

The writing of this book required understanding from so many people; they have had to put up with me living and breathing it whilst also trying to conduct my normal everyday life at home and at work. That's why I'd like to thank Steve Wolstencroft, Andy Swinburne and all the boys at the Scottish *Sun* for their support and guidance throughout all my trials and tribulations. Also, to *The Sun*'s former sportsdesk coordinator Susan McLaughlin and her successor Collette Lynn: thanks for all your help with *Blue* and for ensuring that I don't turn up in the wrong city on the wrong day.

Aki, Col and the boys at Spice gave Barry and me a great environment in which to relax and do the interviews for the book, and they didn't laugh too much on the nights when I crashed and burned on the pool table.

At Mainstream, I would especially like to thank Bill Campbell for his support on the project, editorial coordinator Graeme Blaikie and my editor Paul Murphy, whose constant care and attention on the words helped no end.

You need a release when doing a job like this: mine has been helping to coach the would-be superstars of East Kilbride Burgh United, and my fellow José Mourinho wannabes Robert Terbit, Gus McDonald, Hugh O'Neill and Kenny Roden also helped to keep me sane as we led the kids to the last four of the Trofeo Mediterraneo in Barcelona at Easter 2007.

Finally, to my brothers Steven and Ronnie: thanks for getting me through the loss of the old man – and, yes, I will get your books signed!

Contents

Contents

Foreword

Sometimes you have to leave behind what you love to come to recognise how much it means to you – that is the story of Barry Ferguson and Rangers.

Barry's decision to walk away from Ibrox for Blackburn Rovers in August 2003 both puzzled and disappointed me, but there was never any question of bearing a grudge. I realised there was turmoil there at work inside of him. I had spoken to Barry on a Saturday pre-season and asked him if everything was OK, and he said, 'Yes.' Then, by the Wednesday, he wanted to leave, and for me, that was such a sudden change of mind. I was shocked and angered, and he knows that. Looking back now, though, it is not unreasonable to think that he had to leave Rangers to know what he had at this club.

These days you will seldom find a one-club man, but I know he wishes he was. He went to Blackburn, but after a very short period of time, I was getting the message that he wanted to come home to us. We had to play our cards close to our chest until the time was right, and we were fortunate to get him back. He is now playing football again where he belongs.

I first met Barry when we brought him in full time from school when he was around the age of 15. I was walking down a corridor inside Ibrox and decided to stick my head inside the boot room. This kid was there holding court amongst the rest of the boys, and when I asked him who he was, he puffed his chest out and said, 'My name is Barry Ferguson, Mr Chairman.' We had a little chat, and I just thought there was this spark about him from the off. I remembered that I'd been told he was special, and I could see the ambition in his eyes. I liked that.

I knew he was Derek's younger brother, but he made his own way at the club from the start, and it was recognised that he was an outstanding talent in his own right. He didn't have to trade on his brother's name.

The decision was always going to be when to launch a talent like Barry, and, in many ways, he was unlucky because of the pressures on the club at what was a unique time in Rangers' history as we went for nine in a row. That was not a time for breeding young players, and although Barry got his taste of it at 19, Walter Smith stuck with experience.

There were frustrations in that situation for Barry, which I could sense, but when Dick Advocaat came in, I had the Ferguson family through to my old offices at the South Gyle in Edinburgh. Barry's dad Archie is a solid man – a roofer who has given Barry the right values in his life. I knew Dick rated the kid highly, so I wanted his parents to have the reassurance of knowing how big a part their son was going to play in the Rangers of the future. We were making our plans for the following season, and I had Dick call the office from the Netherlands. He personally told Barry that he was going to be crucial, and we would build things around him. That was enough for Barry, and it intrigued me as to what Advocaat had spotted in the reserve-game videos he had been poring over.

I fully understood Walter's reasoning in keeping faith with the likes of Stuart McCall and Ian Durrant, because they had won so many big games for him. Now, though, it was Barry's time, and I could sense that the influence of someone like Advocaat at that point in this young player's career could be pivotal.

Barry is a Rangers man and a Rangers fan, but he doesn't have the captain's job simply because of that or some desperate hankering for us to hang on to our identity in these cosmopolitan times. We value that about him, but he must also be a great player and have the ability to lead – qualities he has in abundance. He has come through the media spotlight that was thrust on him at times early on at Ibrox and has matured as a man and a footballer.

There is a passion inside Barry, and that was no more apparent to me than at a meeting I called at Murray Park in November 2005 when things were going so badly for us. I wanted to find out why we were in such dire straits and called together Alex McLeish, Barry and Dado Pršo, the captain's choice as the other senior player. That meeting confirmed to me how much Rangers mean to Barry Ferguson – he was hurting so badly. He got that across to me, and I wish, in a way, every fan could have seen him that day. They should also know that he has pushed himself to the detriment of his own health at times for the benefit of the club. In Ferguson we have someone who is prepared to push himself beyond the normal limits for Rangers, and people should know that. He never puts himself first. He is a rare commodity when compared to the type of player we see in the modern game, dominated as it is by the Bosman ruling.

In Barry, we have a player whom I love to see most of all on the European stage. Judge him there, if you like, and you will see where he stands. There are times when I can understand that the motivation of players in Scotland drops a little when they face the same sides four times a season. But the real stars come alive and reach their peak in Europe. I have seen Barry as a young man against Parma and a mature man against Villarreal, and his performances have been exemplary. In particular, he was magnificent in the last 16 of the Champions League in Vila-real in 2006.

If I am being philosophical, I think you have to write off the decision to go to Ewood Park as part of his growing up and maturing as an individual. You have to be pragmatic in situations like that. I have always been close to him, and I was very disappointed that that was what he wanted to do. People, though, make mistakes in life, and I think the bright lights of the Premiership were glinting at him. I understand any player who wants to test themselves at a higher level, and that was the lure, but this is his club. I always knew that, and now he does too. I see no reason why he shouldn't finish his career at Rangers. He is our player until the summer of 2010, when he will be 32, and I think he will be here beyond that.

Sir David E. Murray
Chairman of Rangers Football Club
19 July 2007

1

Paul Le Gone

'I haven't won a war – Rangers have lost one.'

Barry Ferguson on 200 days of PLG.

'As long as I am manager here, you will not play for this club again. You are not the captain of Rangers any more.' New Year's Day 2007. Paul Le Guen had spoken just 24 words, but they smacked into me with the force of a hail of bullets.

I have a picture from one of my favourite movies hanging in my kitchen: Al Pacino as Tony Montana in *Scarface*. It makes me think of the moment when he trains a machine gun on his enemies as they raid his mansion: 'Say hello to my leetle friend!'

I know it is a surreal comparison, but Le Guen could have been Tony when he told me I was surplus to requirements. He'd opened fire, killed my career and shot my heart to pieces. I have honestly never experienced anything to compare with the pain I felt at that instant. I have come through a lot of things in this game, but that was the worst by miles: worse than when the bottle crashed into my face during 'The Battle of Bothwell Bridge' after having been beaten 6–2 at Celtic

Park; worse than the searing bolts of agony that surged through me when I bust my kneecap playing for Blackburn. Nothing compares to the way I felt when the Frenchman they'd brought in to revolutionise Rangers told me I was axed as his skipper and no longer wanted at Ibrox.

As 2007 dawned, most people were waking up and shaking off hangovers. I hadn't touched a drop, but I was wrecked. Le Guen had left me devastated. Emotionally and physically it was hellish. The first ten days of 2007 were the hardest ten days of my life.

Recounting this is not an attempt to stick a knife between the shoulder blades of Paul Le Guen now that he is gone. It's just my chance to put forward my side of a dramatic story that dominated the back pages – and occasionally the front ones – for the first two weeks of 2007.

The axe fell on me in Le Guen's office at Murray Park 24 hours before the Fir Park clash with Motherwell on 2 January 2007. That day will always live with me. If it had happened three years before, I would have done something very stupid. Instead, a force seemed to sweep me up and carry me out of the place. I felt like I was in a trance. I'm glad now that I kept my dignity.

I can hardly remember what happened after I spun on my heels and walked out of his office. I just knew that it was his club – he was the gaffer – and that I was finished. My feet somehow carried me down to the dressing-room to pick up my stuff, and emotion welled up inside me. I could hardly breathe. I picked up my gear and said, 'That's it. I'm done here.' A few of the boys getting ready for training looked up in stunned disbelief. They couldn't understand what was happening, and I knew I had to get out of there. 'Carry me feet,' I thought. 'Move.'

I was a wreck and didn't want my teammates to see me like that. They were asking me what was happening, but I just had to get out of there. Fast. I couldn't speak to them because I didn't want to show the depth of my emotion.

So many things went through my head: 'How did it reach this stage? Have I done something wrong? What could I have done differently?' I was hurting so badly and even now thinking back to that day kills me. I was cut to the bone, and those close to me know just how bad I was.

Then I was off again, walking down the corridor past all the photographs on the walls of our previous triumphs, past reception, where I pick up my letters from the fans, and out the revolving door to my car. 'Last time,' I thought. 'Last time I'll do that.' Then I got in the car, and it felt like a sanctuary for a moment. I'm not afraid to admit that this was when the tears came. I burst out crying.

I phoned my missus Margaret and got her to put my mum and dad on the phone, and I just blurted out to my old man, 'I'm not coming home. He's taken the captaincy from me. I can't play for Rangers again. I'm not coming home.' They were at my house for their New Year's Day dinner and now the place was in chaos.

I felt embarrassed and humiliated, and I phoned Iain King, who helped me write this book, to try and make sense of what was happening to me. He was on holiday in Blair Atholl with his wife Lorna and their kids. The mobile-phone reception is always awful there, and I had to keep shouting, 'He's taken the armband off me.' I said it three times before he believed me. There was no exclusive for him, though – this was a story that would never keep. By lunchtime, I was the lead story on BBC Scotland news.

I just didn't know what to do. It was in my mind to put

myself out of my misery and go out and get blind drunk. I gave myself ten minutes to compose myself a little, pulled into a lay-by outside Murray Park and sat there trying to gather my thoughts. 'How had it come to this?' I thought.

I'd prepared for that Motherwell game as normal. It was Ne'erday, and the family had been due to go to Margaret's mum and dad's house. I was missing out on all the festivities, as you do when you are a footballer – those are the sacrifices you have to make – but they had a power cut and all came to ours instead. I walked out that morning with my training bag and told them all to have a great day. I felt a pang of jealousy, but I got into my car for the journey to training anyway.

I left a party – and two hours later I walked back into a morgue. There was silence when I opened the door that day. My family was there to enjoy Ne'erday, but the atmosphere had been killed stone-dead. You could have heard a pin drop. They could see I was a lost soul. No one spoke to me – I went to our bedroom and sat alone.

Bile was rising in my throat, and I was shaking. I ran to the toilet and threw up. It was the first of three times that I was physically sick that day. My insides were churning. I was in a state of shock. But I knew I had to be strong and go and see my kids.

Little Cara was having fun, but my older son Connor knew what was happening and was deeply worried about his old man. His wee brother Kyle was bouncing around telling me I would be OK. He was playing *Pro Evolution Soccer* on his PlayStation and said he would get me moved from Rangers right away. He wanted me to join Everton!

However, I needed space that day – to be left alone so that I could come to terms with the enormity of what had just happened to me. My family and friends allowed me that, because they could see I was numb and shocked by the situation that I found myself in. I wasn't frightened to face people or cowering in shame, because I didn't think that I had done anything wrong. The media attention was huge, though. I was *front* page news again.

Looking back, I would change nothing. I am adamant about that. My crime? Well, in my eyes my crime was passion. I'd been brought up at Rangers to be a winner, reared alongside people like John Brown, Richard Gough, Ian Durrant and Ally McCoist. They would come in from training and fight each other if they lost, and I loved that. I looked at their commitment – at Archie Knox and Walter Smith, who led that band of brothers who won nine in a row – and believed that was the way to be as a Rangers man. I still believe that.

My dad and my brother Derek were steeped in that tradition, too, and I grew up training the way I play. Maybe that's why the cracks started appearing between me and Le Guen. Maybe that's where it all stemmed from, if I reason it out in the cold light of day. He felt that I was over-aggressive in training. He didn't like it that I hated losing so much. Well, show me a good loser and I'll show you a loser. He asked me not to shout at certain players because it hurt their feelings. I had to accept that his was a different mentality from mine, but it was very hard.

I'd seen other foreigners come into the club – guys like Dado Pršo, who bought into the way we were and had the same hatred of losing. It was always World War Three for him if he was beaten, and I loved that about Dado. If being like that is a problem for a manager, then I fear for football.

I was astonished to be told I shouldn't shout at certain players – staggered. Yet they were his rules, he was the boss, and I tried to abide by them at all times. I truly did. But we were in the midst of a season that needed turning around. I attempted to conform to what he wanted, but, if I am honest, I just couldn't. I should hold my hands up to that.

When I was 17, I had trained with Durrant and McCoist, watching them fly into tackles and compete and scrap. They were winners. Nights out to write this book were broken up any time my co-author won at pool. It didn't happen much, but it happened! Seriously, if you're a competitor, that's your mentality, and I didn't understand why Le Guen didn't like that about me. I tried to curb it all a touch, but I couldn't.

So there I was, done in, an outsider as I sat at home in Lanarkshire while my team, the one my heart and soul is with, were getting ready to play Motherwell a few miles away. The battle was just beginning.

The flak flew, and the whispering campaign got nasty. Before the French regime packed their bags and left, I even had to listen to leaked accusations from within their camp that I had celebrated the CIS Cup exit at home to St Johnstone when the manager chose to rest me. That more than anything else sickened me. The truth is that I left that game just after half-time with the score still at 0–0 before Stevie Milne's two goals, because I couldn't bear to watch us struggle so badly, and I feared that the worst was coming. To accuse me of glorying in my mates hitting such a low ebb at home to a First Division club beggars belief.

I might get embarrassed about badge kissing and all those flamboyant gestures that some players revel in, but I hope that I have never hidden just how much of a privilege I consider it to be captain of Rangers. To do it a second time meant the world to me, and I couldn't believe that it was now over. I am passionate about Rangers Football Club – and, as I say, if that is a crime, then I am guilty as charged.

That is the way I have been brought up. Those who don't rate me or hate me can have their views. But I'm not having that I celebrate Rangers losing slung at me. Never.

Even with all that was going on around me, I wanted to be at Fir Park, and at first it was my intention to sit amongst the fans and show how much I still cared. Yet it would have turned into a circus if I had gone to that game, and first and foremost I am a Rangers supporter. I would have been a sideshow to what really mattered on the park. I would have done more damage than good, and I couldn't have faced that. The media would also have been all over me if I had sat in the stand.

I texted the boys and wished them all the best. Yet for all the TVs in the house, I couldn't watch it on Setanta. I asked a pal to text me updates. I couldn't bear to see it and not play. All I wanted was for us to win. And it is crazy to suggest I would ever feel otherwise about any game, whether I am playing or not.

We did it that day – we won 1–0. Kris Boyd scored a penalty, and he cracked under all the strain that he too had been under due to his clashes with Le Guen. He reacted to all the mud that was being hurled at him. Boydy defiantly walked to the Rangers end and held up his fingers in a No. 6 salute – it was the back-page picture in every paper the next morning. I'll never forget the risk he took by doing that.

I had grown sick to the pit of my stomach of us being portrayed as the bad boys who were bringing down Paul Le Guen. Boydy was being painted as some kind of work-shy boozer who wasn't disciplined enough to be the next Ally McCoist. He was a young player making his way at Rangers, and some of the things published about him at that time were very low.

Yet he was battling through it, and when he scored I had

no idea he was going to do a salute. I was touched by what he did – it meant a lot. I don't like talking about him too much, because we have been singled out far too much as some kind of inseparable double act simply because we're pals and room-mates. All I'll say is this: he is a goal machine who would never have been out of my team had I been the manager back then. Can't run the channels? Perhaps you could have said that in the past, but the way he did it in Scotland's 1–0 friendly win in Austria at the end of the 2006–07 season showed that he was learning. Not fit enough? He can lose a little weight and work on it, and I know from his determination and the way he is relishing life under Walter Smith that he will. Can't score goals? He *always* scores goals. Look at the facts. He scored 39 in his first season at Gers when he finished top scorer for us *and* Killie in the same season after he moved to Ibrox in the January. Then, in his second season, he scored 27 goals, despite the fact that he went through so much turmoil under Le Guen and wore a sub's tracksuit far more often than he should. We ought to have been nurturing his talent, not trying to destroy his confidence.

Le Guen stuck the boot into me in his press conference after the Motherwell match, claiming that I had been a bad influence and was undermining him. It couldn't go on, he said. I heard this and boiled over with anger as my mind drifted back three months to September 2006 and something that bitterly disappoints me now, because it has been completely overlooked in almost every Le Guen v. Ferguson debate. I was rushed back too early after having my ankle reconstructed in the summer. After just 45 minutes in the reserves, I was thrown in against Hibs away. It is always a frantic fixture, but if the manager selects me, I don't say no. That's not in my nature. Le Guen needed me, and so did Gers, so I played.

I was 60 per cent fit, at the very most. I was nowhere near where I should have been, and I didn't play well. We lost, and I was slaughtered. The press wrote that Kevin Thomson had battered me, that it was the start of a new era of midfielders in Scottish football and that I was finished as a footballing force. For God's sake, I was only 28 at the time!

Still, I could look myself in the mirror and know that I had given Paul Le Guen 100 per cent. More than that, I had put my reputation on the line when others wouldn't have. Four months later, I was being branded a captain in charge of a drinking culture at Ibrox and a man who wanted the club to be ruled by player power. Those two phrases will be forever linked to Paul Le Guen and what went wrong for him at Rangers: drinking culture and player power.

Some of the things that were levelled at me were very wrong, but you would have to ask him if it was part of his exit strategy from Rangers with the vacancy at Paris Saint Germain, his next club, beckoning.

I look back to times like that day at Easter Road when I put myself on the line for him, and all the accusations of drinking, player power and disobeying tactical orders really get to me. Yes, if things were going wrong in a game, I'd drop deep and pick the ball up to try and make things happen. That's my job. I'm a midfielder and the captain. However, in Le Guen's eyes, the 1–1 draw with St Mirren at Ibrox just after Christmas marked the beginning of the end for me and him. He thought that I was disregarding his orders. Well, in my eyes it was down to interpretation – I was desperate to rescue yet another game that was running away from us, but he saw it as me undermining him.

It depends on whose camp you stand in which way you see it, but one thing puzzles me: we never once had a blazing row or fallout. That is the God's honest truth. Yes, I came in after games and shouted the odds at players and screamed at the ceiling in frustration – even at myself. I was dejected at the way the season was going. We would come in after another loss or draw, and there would be no reaction. I just kept thinking, 'This is Rangers here, Rangers. Do something.'

I kept hearing that Le Guen and I were at each other's throats every minute of every day, but it just wasn't like that. Maybe it would have been better if we had been. There was never a thundering row between us to clear the air, and I never knew where I stood with him. Maybe that's why they call him an enigma.

Whatever the problem was, I was never given a proper explanation as to why I was now surplus to requirements at Rangers, that's for sure. He always had the ultimate power, and I respected that – he was the manager. Someone, though, is going to have to sit me down and tell me how I undermined him, because I don't know what I did wrong. Whoever is standing in the technical area for Rangers or Scotland gets everything I have to give, even if it is sometimes not good enough.

The bottom line, however, was that a doomed relationship between a manager and his captain who just never clicked was now over. If Paul Le Guen was going to stay at Rangers, then I would have to leave. I sat in the kitchen of my house after the Motherwell game with my co-author and thought about the reality of that proposition. We were shell-shocked. Both of us. We sat watching Aston Villa v. Chelsea on the TV, had a glass of wine and tried to make it feel like the other nights when we'd had such a laugh writing this book. But it wasn't. The hardback version of the book was long finished by then and in the fans' Christmas stockings.

Now the subject of it was officially the former captain of Rangers.

I looked up at that screen, and we had a pop at the game, criticising the football. It was one of those horrible scuffling affairs that never got started. Then I glanced up and said, 'Better be quiet, eh? I could be playing for Villa soon.' He looked at me in surprise, and I nodded. I knew by that point that there was interest from Martin O'Neill at Villa, and Everton, Bolton and Newcastle United had been linked with me again. They'd all expressed an interest with my agent once they'd found out that I was damaged goods and unwanted by Paul Le Guen.

Then I received a mind-blowing offer from my old boss Dick Advocaat at Zenit Saint Petersburg. I hate talking about money, but let's just say the story that hit the papers of a £50,000-a-week contract was not an exaggeration. I had a little smile to myself when Dick signed Anatoliy Tymoschuk from Shakhtar Donetsk in a £10.3 million transfer. He got my contract. Well, the one I turned down. Lucky guy.

Seriously, though, can you see me in Russia? Since Garry O'Connor signed for Lokomotiv Moscow from Hibs, people have been aware of the money that can be earned over there. But it wasn't for me. I'd found it hard enough to settle in Blackburn! I knew Dick was loving it over there and that he had faith in me. He'd made me Gers captain at just 22, and now he had a vision of teaming me up with my former Ibrox teammate Fernando Ricksen. Fernando had settled there on a season-long loan after all the problems he'd had when Le Guen booted him off the pre-season trip to South Africa for drinking on the flight. Now Advocaat was offering me an escape route too, and the terms were just frightening. I think it worked out at £2.6 million a year

plus the use of a private jet for trips home if my family did
not make the switch with me.

I turned the offer down flat. Dick understood, because
he knows what Rangers mean to me. I was concerned only
with staying put, and that was that. I'd regretted going to
Blackburn and had been so lucky to get another chance at
Ibrox. Now there were even some people trying to link me
with *Celtic*! Come on, that certainly wasn't going to happen.
If I'd left the club, it would have to have been to England
or abroad. I couldn't have played against Rangers.

My first thought was to be flattered by all the interest
from managers I really respected: Martin O'Neill, Sam
Allardyce, David Moyes, Glenn Roeder and Dick Advocaat.
But my thinking was clear: I couldn't leave Rangers again,
because I had already made that mistake once before.

I vowed I would do everything in my power to stay put,
but as the days went by it seemed increasingly likely that
I would have to leave, and that was the hardest thing to
stomach. I couldn't face telling the kids again, because I had
fucked up their lives once before by going south. I began
to think of a life as a nomad player down there without my
family and contemplated commuting from Birmingham or
wherever it might be next so that the kids didn't have to
move schools and leave their friends again.

I was an outcast at Rangers, but I stayed professional.
I went into training and worked out with the players not
involved with the first team. But my routine changed,
because in the past I had always gone in early for training,
enjoying the *craic* with the lads. Now I would get there
bang on 10 a.m. to get changed, because I didn't want to
answer questions on how I was coping. The staff I am close
to were broken up about the situation, but I had to keep

my distance: train, have a shower, leave. I didn't want to cause friction, because the team had games to win.

There were always photographers outside the training ground. When I look at the pictures of me from back then, I am chalk white. I felt like a ghost, empty inside. I'd come out of training and phone my dad and brother. They kept me focused on doing the right thing and kept me working. Outwardly, I had to be strong, but inside I was falling apart, stressed out and in a world of woe.

That's when I was offered advice by a man who has seen so many football stars at their lowest ebb. Peter Kay of the Sporting Chance clinic helped former Arsenal skipper Tony Adams cope with alcoholism and his teammate Paul Merson with his gambling addiction. My own ex-Gers teammates Alex Rae and Fernando Ricksen faced up to their own drinking demons under his quiet guidance.

Of course, I realised that my own dejection at losing the captaincy and being dumped at Ibrox didn't compare with their problems. But when I had a chance meeting with Peter at Glasgow's Hilton Hotel, a helping hand was offered – and I'm not ashamed to say that I reached out and took it.

Peter was up in Scotland seeing the former Dundee United winger Andy McLaren, who has battled so bravely against alcoholism and is close to our former doctor at Rangers, Ian McGuinness. I sat and had a coffee with Peter, because he's an interesting guy and an expert in his field. He helped me, even if it wasn't a four-hour therapy session or anything like that. I just sat, listened and took on board certain things.

These days, if I need therapy I will go and talk to Coisty! But, seriously, speaking to someone like Peter is nothing to be ashamed of. I wasn't on my hands and knees crawling to his door pleading for help. I am a strong enough character to face all that goes with being a footballer in this country. I just felt that I was in a situation I couldn't possibly ever have imagined being in and that he might be able to help me get through it. I spoke to him and he helped – that was it.

He was part of my support network, but my real rock was my family. On holiday in Dubai in 2007, I had a little moment sitting in the sunshine watching Margaret and the kids as they played in the pool. I realised then that I couldn't have got myself through that time without them. When I needed them most, they were there for me. Along with my parents and in-laws, they helped me through the darkest spell of my career. Margaret especially was just great, and I owe so much to her and the kids. My family stepped up to the mark, and every one of my mates either came to the house or texted me. I was stressed-out and uptight, and I needed them. The letters from fans were also a big help. I will answer every one of them in time, because they helped me so much.

Day by day, my chances of staying at Rangers diminished, but there was always a little glimmer of hope inside me. Then came the bombshell news that Paul Le Guen was leaving. I was reeling like everyone else. But when the initial shock ebbed away, I couldn't help wonder where Le Guen's departure left me.

Almost right away, I knew that the rumours we'd heard inside the club as far back as November 2006 were right. Walter Smith *was* coming back. But would he want me to be his captain? Would I even be a Rangers player any more? Only one man at Rangers could give me the answer: Sir David Murray.

The chairman had seen the club lurch into a bitter crisis. It had been a back-biting mess, and he hated that. I was summoned through to his Charlotte Square offices in

Edinburgh. The newspapers always call these meetings clear-the-air talks. I'm not lying when I say that I thought they would be clear-out-your-locker talks. He could see faults on both sides and had tried desperately to make the Le Guen era work. Now it was over. Before the meeting, the chairman insisted to me on the phone that I'd better not think that I had won. I honestly didn't, because I was still in turmoil.

I can confess now that when I went to meet Mr Murray, I thought I was finished at Rangers and that he would clear the decks of me. I feared the worst, and it was a very long drive through. I didn't want to enter his office, because I thought he would tell me that my time at Gers was up. All the pressures of Le Guen dumping me had once more strained my relationship with a man I hugely respect.

There had been a rift when I left for Blackburn that was only healed by my coming home to Ibrox in January 2005. Now the bond between us was under severe threat once again after all that had happened. But we sat and chatted about things that will always remain confidential. I gave him my side of the story, and it was left to Walter Smith as to whether I would stay.

I had read all the headlines telling me that I would be stripped of the captaincy for good, but, as much as I cherish my armband, that was never my main concern. Instead, I was just worried sick that I wouldn't be given the chance to honour the deal that is designed to keep me at Rangers until I'm 32. It was down to Walter, but he hadn't rejoined the club yet. He'd become caught up in a war of his own with the SFA, which was battling for compensation.

Durranty was boss for our Scottish Cup tie at Dunfermline in the wake of Le Guen's departure. Just three days had passed since PLG had left, but I was back in the fold all of a sudden. Durranty wanted me to be his captain that day, but it was such a delicate situation that it would have deflected from what mattered most for the club: winning and rescuing our last chance of a trophy in a horrible season.

When I look back on that time, one of the biggest disappointments is that we lost the game 3–2 to the bottom club in the SPL. Dunfermline would go on to reach the cup final under their new boss Stephen Kenny but were still relegated.

The only reason I wanted to play that day was for Durranty. He's a Rangers diehard, and I knew that it might be the only chance he would ever get to take charge of the first team. He'd been there for me ever since the start of my career at Rangers, calling me 'Willie One Tie' and baffling all the foreigners. That nickname began when I was a YTS kid on £72.50 a week and I actually did only have one tie for every do we went to. It was all I could afford. He used to slaughter me back then and is still doing so 13 years on. Little wind-ups like that certainly make a football club bubble on, though. Now he was the gaffer for one game only, and even though my mind was scrambled by all that I had been through I just wanted to win for him.

But we were a defensive mess, as we had been far too often that season, and we fell two goals behind in the first half. Phil McGuire then made it 3–0 immediately after the restart. It was embarrassing. However, with the game just 34 minutes old, Durranty had been brave enough to change the central defence, hauling off Julien Rodriguez for Chris Burke and putting Brahim Hemdani back in beside Karl Svensson. That switch began to pay off in the second half. Boydy scored twice and gave it his all to try and win a replay for a guy who'd also inspired him at Killie. It wasn't to be.

We lost and tumbled out of the cup. I will always be gutted that we didn't get a win for Durranty at Dunfermline because he deserved it. In the build up to the match, he said that he'd die happy now he had been boss of Rangers. I wanted so much to win for him, and I just wish we had at least got a draw. For 45 minutes, though, I played like I was on a different planet. I was subdued, and I couldn't get on the ball to get things going. Durranty came in at half-time and bollocked us, and it woke me up.

I was happy with Gavin Rae as skipper. He had been given the armband by Le Guen, and it had put him in a really awkward position. But I knew it was a job he couldn't turn down. I just wish we had been able to give Durranty the result he deserved. In hindsight, I should have been on the bench, because my head was so messed up by all that had happened. The stubborn part of me, though, wanted to go out and win it for him. Instead, I had those 45 desperately poor minutes, until I got a grip of it when it was too late.

I went home that night to clear my mind and to face up to whatever fate awaited me when Walter came in. But even behind the gates of my house, where I can normally escape into my own little world, bad things were happening. Throughout my troubles with Le Guen, I'd had the solace of walking my Great Danes Homer and Holly round the grounds of my house to clear my head during the times I couldn't sleep. I'd usually have them out and about at 6.30 in the morning. But I'd recently noticed that the big fella was struggling a bit. He was passing blood and became a lethargic shadow of himself. He meant the world to me, and when he died the day before Walter's first game in charge against Dundee United I honestly thought that life couldn't get any worse. He'd had such a bad illness, and the vet tried so hard to save him. He was hooked up to drips, the lot, and I was devastated when I lost him. People who aren't dog lovers will sneer at me using a word like devastated; those who are will know exactly what I mean. I loved that big mutt. I'd walk around the grounds with him, thinking through what was happening to me. It helped a lot.

My other dog Holly has a bad back leg, and she'd walk slowly beside me when I was trying to get my head straight early in the morning. Homer always galloped ahead. Controlling him woke me up and cleared my thoughts. Then his weight tumbled down from 13 st., and I had to take the decision to have him put down – he was only five years old. He had an operation but an infection spread to his kidneys and I lost him. I know those people who don't love animals will say that he was just a dog and not a person, but I was in bits when he was put down. It just seemed to put the seal on a miserable time.

It was time to focus, though. Walter was back at Rangers, and we were flying again in training. He lifted the whole place with his presence. But in the background, in the newspapers and on TV and radio, the question remained: does Ferguson have a future and is he going to be reinstated as captain?

Nothing was said to me about the armband until the day of Walter's first game in charge at home to United. I was called into a meeting with the coaches at 1.30 p.m. The gaffer, Ally McCoist, Kenny McDowall and Durranty were all there. Walter looked up and said, 'You're captain again. Go out and do what you're good at. Be a player. Be a leader.'

That was that – a simple message from a straight-talking guy. It meant so much to me, and I just said, 'Thank you. From here on in I will run through fucking brick walls for you.'

I immediately bit my tongue. It wasn't the best response I could have thought of, but he just smiled and said, 'Good. Go and do it then.' Those words were like a rebirth for me. I felt like I had found my way again. That's Walter – no fucking around. If you don't do your work right, you get shouted at and left in no doubt what is expected of you. That's the way it should be.

It's seven years now since Dick Advocaat first made me captain of Rangers at the age of 22. I took over the job from Lorenzo Amoruso and was awarded the armband ahead of Arthur Numan, a true legend. Since then, I've won league titles, enjoyed the 2003 Treble and relished the job. The fact is, though, that when Walter returned to the fold I was more than happy simply to be a Rangers *player* again. I would happily have worked on under another on-field leader if that was what the gaffer wanted. When Walter came in, he had so much to cope with, and I was just happy to be playing. The captaincy would look after itself, I decided. All I wanted was to be a Gers player again.

Then he took me into his office and told me that I was his captain. A fourth Rangers manager had made me his skipper, and it pumped me up so much. All my sadness started to clear, knowing that he had such faith in me. There is an aura about the gaffer. That's why it means so much to me that he trusts me to be his skipper.

I believe that Rangers and Celtic are one-off monsters – two clubs steeped in history and tradition – and I think outsiders can underestimate the size of them. I have been to the Premiership, and I've been told that Newcastle United are massive, but they are nowhere near Rangers. This is an institution run by people who live for the club, and it needs people like Walter who understand it inside out.

He has been so clever with the way he has managed things the second time around. The 'Old Fox' is so strong-minded and has forgotten more about football than some inside the game will ever know. Behind him are the 'Hungry Ones': McCoist, McDowall and Durrant. People on the outside know all about Coisty and Durranty, because of what they did for Gers as players. But they shouldn't underestimate Kenny. He's a very shrewd man and a superb coach.

Between them they're rebuilding the togetherness. When there is a golf day now, it feels like a family again, right down to the physios and the masseurs, as we try to beat Charlie Adam off what he insists is an official handicap. That bond has to be re-esatblished, because Celtic have more money than we do at the moment. We can only bridge the financial gap by fighting for each other.

We are back to the days when every draw feels like a disaster, and that's the way it should be. Desire and hunger are the way forward, not no contact in training, as it was under the previous manager. Back then you would be told to stop putting in tackles during a session. Le Guen or his right-hand man Yves Colleu would shout, 'Hey, what are you doing?' I was brought up to go in with two feet during five-a-sides when I lost my place in the youth team to make sure that I won it back! I am not condoning going over the top, but John Brown and John McGregor turned us into winners because that's the way the nine-in-a-row squad was. That's the Scottish mentality. I'm sorry, but that's the truth. Look at the national team in recent times. Yes, we have some players with good technique, but every one of us battles our corner, and that's why we have been successful.

Before the Livorno game away in Italy in the UEFA Cup,

Le Guen told us that the team had been changed. Alan Hutton was back in at right-back and Phil Bardsley was out. Bardo wasn't a happy man as we went out to train. During a training match, he went into a tackle on Thomas Buffel, who went down on the touchline. I was 30 yards away, ready to play on again after the foul had been called. Then I looked across to see Phil walking to the dressing-room. I thought he had hurt himself making the tackle, but then I was told he had been *sent off.* Thomas was up and about by that point. He was fine and I couldn't understand the decision. I thought, 'Is this a contact sport or what?'

Again, PLG was the boss, and I had to bite my lip and respect him, even if I didn't agree with what was happening. I didn't mump or moan or shout about it. I got on with it but thought that life was becoming very strange if you couldn't tackle in training.

I rated Bardsley highly when he joined us on loan from Manchester United. However, Alan Hutton has been transformed under the new regime. He is a prime example of the effect Walter and the coaches have had. Kenny and Coisty are always on Alan, making him believe in himself, telling him to use the attributes he has as one of the best athletes about. What a transformation. He really deserved his first Scotland cap at the end of the 2006–07 season.

In time, I think that poaching Kenny McDowall from Celtic will be shown to be one of Walter's wisest moves. I love working with Walter and Ally, but we've hit the jackpot with Kenny. He is bubbly and full of knowledge, and every Rangers player loves being coached by him.

It's a fresh start now. I'm 29 and still at the club I love, whereas Paul Le Guen is not. I neither glory in that nor take any great pleasure from it. He is simply in the past now, and it's about Walter and ending the rot that led to two seasons without a trophy.

When the Gaffer came in, he set us the target of making second spot our own so that we could have a crack at the Champions League in 2007–08, and we went on an unbelievable run to qualify for the competition. He made a few changes, bringing in Davie Weir and Ugo Ehiogu for the experience and solidity we'd so badly missed in central defence under Le Guen, and we also spent for the future, paying £2 million for Kevin Thomson.

I am now drawing a line under PLG. I still find it hard to talk about those days, and I know that the stigma of what happened with Paul Le Guen will follow me to the end of my career. I get asked almost every day about what happened, and the fans have a right to pose the question. I have to reply that I don't know. Maybe he just didn't like me as a person – didn't like what I'm about or how I conduct myself.

It all spiralled out of control, and it became PLG v. the skipper in the eyes of many people. They thought that if I wasn't dropped, then the drinking culture and player power had won the day. It's nonsense, but I'll never be able to change some people's minds.

I am sick of those who don't even know me saying that I think I have won some sort of victory. I'm not strutting around thinking I am 'Billy Big Time'. It wasn't a competition. I just wanted Rangers to win games. If I'm guilty, then it is of being too passionate. I haven't won a war – Rangers have lost one. As a club, we went through a hellish time and finished a second season on the spin without a trophy, so who won? No one. No individual is bigger than this club. Rangers were all over the front pages, and so much mud was thrown. Did I want that? Not a chance.

2

Home

'You want a transfer? Fuck off out of my office.'

Mark Hughes, Blackburn Rovers manager.

Two years before Paul Le Guen told me that I was finished at Ibrox, I'd won the new start I had craved at the club I should never have deserted in the first place. The gates of Murray Park glided open; the door to Rangers that I feared had slammed shut on me for ever was unlocked again. I was home.

I will remember 31 January 2005 for the rest of my life. It was the night I made it back to the Gers with just 70 minutes to spare before the transfer window closed and left me facing the full force of Mark Hughes's gathering wrath and life languishing in the Blackburn Rovers reserves. The longest month of my career was over, and with one flourish of a pen at 10.50 p.m., I prayed that I could somehow score out 17 months at Ewood Park – draw a line through them and never look back. Life is not that simple, but in that fleeting moment, all the heartache, all the needless pain I'd caused my family and the club I love, ebbed away. Walking out on Rangers and joining Blackburn was the biggest mistake of my life, but, somehow, I'd won myself a second chance. I was back.

As I signed that contract, I just looked up at Martin Bain, the Rangers chief executive, and everyone else in the room with a huge idiotic grin on my face. I was a Gers player until 2010; I'd be 32 when the deal finished. I was now, in effect, a Ranger for life, and I felt whole again. My body might have left Rangers to go south to the Premiership but my heart and soul never did – that was the problem.

I walked outside into the icy night air as it approached midnight and was stunned to see about 50 punters there who had come out in the biting cold to our training ground on the outskirts of Glasgow just to welcome me home. The club opened the gates, and they swarmed in as the waiting press snappers clicked away. I was mentally drained, but I couldn't have been happier.

Across the city at Celtic, the drama of a fraught night for me was being mirrored as they won their own race against time and ushered in Craig Bellamy on loan from Newcastle United. I knew that deal was happening, but as I walked out to greet the fans I should never have left behind, I made a silent vow to myself. They wouldn't look back on Bellamy's signing as being the key moment in the title race. I'd give every shred I had to make sure I helped bring the trophy back to Rangers. If I thought 31 January was dramatic, though, 22 May would teach me what a true cliffhanger was!

I'd first learned of Rangers' interest on 2 January and wanted to come home there and then, but I knew that there would be a host of obstacles placed in my way by Blackburn. I'd gone in tentatively to raise the subject of a move with the gaffer Mark Hughes, and he glared at me and growled, 'Fuck off out of my office.' I took that as a 'No'.

For 48 hours, the thought of Hughes's anger at the prospect of me moving churned around inside of me, and I spoke to those I trust. For those two days, they were all sworn to secrecy, but I knew the story would come out and that the entire month of January was going to become a war of nerves between the two clubs. On 5 January, the back page of *The Sun* screamed 'Barry's Back!' Speculation of a return had surrounded me time and again since I'd moved south, but this time the story was based on fact. Now the chase was on, and the move was public.

From the minute I had turned my back on Gers to that first day when the deal to bring me home began to simmer, David Murray and I had not uttered a single word to each other. The chats between chairman and captain, all the guidance he had given me, was lost to me the day I walked out on his club. I understood that. I'd disappointed him – let him down. Now his voice was back on my mobile, and he confirmed it was true: what I had done would never be forgotten, but it had been forgiven.

The chairman said bluntly, 'We want you to come home to the club. I told you that you should never have left in the first place. We will forget that now. We'll do everything we can to bring you back here, but get yourself prepared for a long, hard slog.'

When the man who owns the club you love speaks to you in those terms, you listen. I told him, 'I will not let you down at my end, chairman. I will help you make this move happen.'

The fracture in our relationship had got to me badly, because he is a man I respect. He is more than your average football chairman. I am a boy from a council scheme in Hamilton, smarter than they'd have you believe but still earning money beyond my wildest dreams. You need guidance in how to invest it, advice from people you trust. The chairman is amongst the most important businessmen in Scotland. He is worth £650 million, and I am able to turn to him for tips on property, saving money and anything that affects my family's future. That relationship was lost to me when I split from Rangers, and I missed it.

That feud was always at the back of my mind all the time I was at Blackburn, because David Murray had done a lot for me. I hoped some day that whatever happened – whether I came back or not – we would be able to patch it up, share a bottle of his Château Routas red wine and bury the past. Now we have, and I think it shows the measure of the man that the past was forgiven.

Yet his hopes and my dreams meant nothing to Blackburn Rovers. I was Mark Hughes's captain, and he wanted to build a team round me. To him, the situation stank; it was a betrayal in his eyes. I understood his anger, every bit of it, but I was now consumed with the prospect of not living out a career regretting one wretched decision. Rangers were in for me; I *had* to make it happen.

I met with the gaffer and the Blackburn chief executive John Williams, and the ground rules were established. They told me there was no chance I was going to another Premiership club. They were adamant about that. The man who had signed me for Blackburn, Graeme Souness, could forget it. The offer from his new club Newcastle United was a non-starter in the club's eyes. Everton boss David Moyes, who'd chased hard when I made it clear I wanted to leave Ibrox in the first place, would also not be entertained. That didn't worry me. I said, 'I couldn't care less. I want to go home. I want to go to Rangers.'

Hughes and Williams looked at me as if I was stupid. I was in the Premiership, and although there is not a sliver of arrogance in either of those down-to-earth men, they felt I was already working in the 'Promised Land'. Why would I want to return to Scotland? Like many, they couldn't understand what my heart was telling me, but for all the desire I had inside me to see this through, the 26 days that followed the story breaking became sheer hell at times.

Blackburn offered me the chance to extend my contract until 2009 on improved wages – they just didn't want to lose me. But I was living a life of regret down there, constantly pushing the fact that I had made a mistake to the back of my mind. Now I could almost touch the chance to redeem myself, to be home and at the heart of Rangers again, and I clung to every last morsel of hope that it would happen.

Rangers signed Thomas Buffel for £2.3 million from Feyenoord, and they handed him the No. 4 shirt as he was paraded in front of the media. Watching *Sky Sports News* in my lounge in Lytham, I breathed a sigh of relief and smiled to myself: Jimmy Bell the kitman believed I was on my way back. My cherished No. 6 jersey – the one I'd worn since I was an eight-year-old kid playing for Mill United Boys Club in Hamilton – was still open, and he was refusing to hand it to any of the new signings.

I knew those inside the club wanted me to return – knew by now just how much Alex McLeish craved me coming home – but the support? What about the Rangers punters in the street? How would they feel? That haunted me.

During that time, it seemed as though the memories of when I'd been at my happiest at Rangers were stuck on a constant loop of action replays inside my head. For example, the 2002 Scottish Cup final when we beat Celtic and I scored a free-kick as we won 3–2. I remember the moment vividly: first, visualising the free-kick curling into the top corner before executing it, knowing it was the perfect hit, seeing it ripple the net; then I was gone, top off in front of the Rangers fans, going 'radio rental', losing it, loving it.

I get a feeling on days like that that I can't begin to describe. It's as if this is what I was put on the earth for. That's it; that sums it up. I feel fulfilled. Born to play for Rangers; lucky to captain them. On days like that, it's like there is a current of electricity running through me.

For those eighteen months when we won five trophies on the spin under Alex McLeish, I felt indestructible and so confident every time I tugged the armband on. Yet it was at the end of that spell that I somehow got my mind into a place where I felt that I had to leave. So how did I ever think I could give all that I had at Rangers up? I wish I could take the decision to leave and erase it like my son Connor does with the mistakes in his homework. But I can't.

There are things surrounding the initial deal that should be put to rest now. Rangers got money for me, and I suppose they were happy enough to do so. But I was never forced out of the door; it was *my* decision. To be honest, I used the fact that they had accepted an offer for me as an excuse. I could justify it to myself more easily if I did that.

I also had a grim feeling about the financial plight the club now found themselves in, and I was dejected that Arthur Numan had not accepted a new contract, because we had shared a room for five years. He was a footballing machine, a world-class left-back, a legend in my eyes and a gentleman who had taught me so much. Dick Advocaat making him my mentor was, in many ways, a master stroke. Numan rubbed off on me. I leaned on him so much, and now he was gone.

But the club were £68 million in debt, and they wanted him to take half his wages to stay on into his veteran years. He wouldn't accept that out of principle. He quit rather than take their offer, retiring from the game at the age of 33 when he could still be playing even now. He wasn't signing for Aston Villa, who had been watching him, he wasn't going home to the Netherlands, he just wasn't signing for Rangers again because we couldn't afford to pay him what he felt he was worth. It didn't make sense.

His departure affected me, no question about it. I was gutted and worried sick about the direction the club was taking. We'd just won the Treble, but it seemed like we were going backwards. Lorenzo Amoruso left for Blackburn, and Neil McCann – a player whose heart, skill and attitude I loved then and still do when we are together with Scotland – was out the door to Southampton. Looking back, all I can say is that the thought of where the club was going, with some of the top players leaving, was dragging me down. I felt lost.

In the end, the truth is that I listened to everything but my own heart. I heard every phone-in, and I read every article. Time and again, the same view was pounded home: 'Ferguson is living in a comfort zone at Rangers. He'll never test himself there. He's a waster and a no-mark if he doesn't try England.'

I had a brainstorm; I still don't know even now why I let it get to the point of no turning back with the club. I'd painted myself into a corner, creating a situation in which I was in conflict with Rangers and felt I had to go.

I beat myself up about it now, because I look at some Rangers fans and know they are thinking, 'OK, he is back, and we'll cheer him because he's the skipper, but that bastard left us in the lurch.' That cuts me to the quick and rips me up inside – I left the club I love. I still look at myself in the mirror and ask, 'Why?'

Believe me, I know that my leaving is always going to be an issue for some people, and I would never have a go at them. I knew I would have to take stick when I came back and that some Rangers fans would never forgive me for leaving in the first place.

But the way some fans look at me now goes beyond worries that the club should never go back to players who have left, beyond fears that I will toil the way the late, great Jim Baxter and Derek Johnstone did when they too walked into the marble hallway at Ibrox for a second time. Nah, this is down to some Gers fans seeing me as a traitor. You have to be honest about it. That's the bottom line, and I can accept that; I can't change the way they feel. In all honesty, I might well feel the same way in their shoes.

There's a reception desk at Murray Park on your way out the door to the players' car-park where the fan mail for every player is collected. When it became clear I was leaving, I had piles of it, and this time they weren't just looking for 'Barry Ferguson No. 6' autographs. People were pouring out their emotions to me in some of them. I opened those letters with dread, because I knew they would have me searching my soul. There was no hate really, no threats, they would just say things like, 'I thought you were a Ranger. I can't believe you've done this. You're one of us. I am just so disappointed in you. True Rangers men *never* leave.' It was a nightmare; those letters devastated me.

Even in the last game I played at Ibrox before I left when we beat Hibs 5–2, I was running round thinking, 'Christ, am I doing the right thing leaving here?' That's why there was no tearful farewell from me that day, no jersey chucked into the Enclosure. They'd probably have thrown it back at me.

Martin Bain brought me in after that game and pleaded with me to stay, but I was too far gone by then; my mind was away from Rangers. Even now, I can't explain how I got myself into that position, but it happened – it was my fault.

My last game for the club should have been one of those great nights. Shota Arveladze's goal clinched a 2–0 win in Denmark. We'd beaten FC Copenhagen, and the Champions League group stages beckoned. But instead of joining the party, I was leaving the club. Again, I couldn't indulge in any dramatics and pull a tearful farewell, throwing my jersey to the fans. Know why? I couldn't face them. I was *embarrassed* by what I had done; I was so disappointed in myself. I had pals in the Rangers end that night, and I couldn't face them. I had let everyone down.

I like to think that I'm not a footballer who is divorced from reality. I know how people in the pub regard me, because I still drink in the same places with the same faces I always did. I knew I was going to go in for a pint one day, and they would confront me and say, 'Why did you leave?' If my only answer was to turn to them and say, 'I don't know,' they'd tell me to fuck off.

I was 25 years old when I allowed myself to be sucked into the state of turmoil that saw me leave Rangers. It had never been an option that had crossed my mind before. Sure, when I was a daft kid of 18 begging Walter Smith for a game in the nine-in-a-row team, there were chances. I even once flew to France and went to Le Havre for talks. They were desperate to sign me, and I went with my brother Derek and my agent. The set-up in France was great, and they showed me their training ground and the stadium, but I never once thought I would sign for them. Deep down, I was never going to leave Rangers, but my contract was up at that point, so I thought I would assess the options. Playing abroad didn't appeal to me then, and it still doesn't now. There are those who claim they can't understand what I say in Scotland never mind France!

My mind was mixed up then. I wanted to play for Rangers, but the nine-in-a-row team were the lords of the manor, and it was so hard to break through. Morton wanted me on loan, and in a strange twist of fate, Alex McLeish once tried desperately to get me on loan to Motherwell. I'd have taken both those moves, but I was encouraged by people like John 'Bomber' Brown and John McGregor to stay put at Ibrox. I remember Bomber kept beating the same words into my skull: 'Head up. Be a Rangers man. Work hard. Your chance will come.'

He was right, too. The trouble is, eight years on, I'd screwed it all up, and I was begging for my second chance to come. I also felt my return was a one-off deal: the only time I would have the opportunity to make up for letting so many people down in August 2003. For most of that emotional month, I ate, drank and slept the transfer. One day, I felt it was happening, and I was as high as a kite. The next, it was dead in the water, and I was in my room with my head buried in my pillow in tears. Then I'd come downstairs like a bear with a sore head, snapping the kids' heads off.

I'm the first to admit that I don't cope with that sort of pressure well. Because of the money we earn, I know that people slaughter footballers for whining. They're right, too. There's far too many positive things in my life to dwell on anything bad that has happened to me in my career. The truth is, though, that behind the money and the stuff it brings, you're still a human being with failings like everyone else.

I wanted to try the Premiership. I thought I had to or I'd regret it for the rest of my life. I was wrong, and my position as skipper of Blackburn Rovers became impossible the day I decided to hand in my written transfer request. I was Mark

Hughes's captain; he wanted to mould and construct a team around me. If I was Rangers manager – which I sometimes hope to be one day – and a player behaved the way I did, I would be both angry and disappointed. Yet I looked in Hughes's eyes and saw that, deep down, he understood. He had been in a similar position with Barcelona, desperate to get back to Manchester United. He knew how I felt about Rangers, because he had experienced the same emotions tugging at him to return to Old Trafford. When you have a stand-off like that, there has to be a day when something gives, and that day was 18 January. We had a bitter confrontation, but I could see something inside him. He realised I wouldn't back down; I wanted to go.

It would take 13 more days of tension and tears before the end of the saga that finally brought me home to Rangers, and by the weekend before the transfer window closed, it was becoming unbearable. My mate Phil McTaggart's daughter Kya was being christened that Sunday, and I knew I was coming north anyway. Blackburn were playing Colchester United at home in the FA Cup on the Saturday, and despite all the transfer war-games, I was told to turn up at the match. But I took a chance. I told them that my head was wasted, and I was in no mental state to pull my boots on.

They knew they could probably cope in that game without me, but the gaffer mentioned that I might be needed on the bench. It was 29 January, and I knew the clock was ticking: 48 hours left. They ordered me to come down, and for the first time in my life, I put myself ahead of the club. I took a risk and decided the fine of two weeks' wages would be worth it if the Gers deal fell through.

Rovers were in a rage. I started blanking calls from them. It was out of order, but by then, all I wanted was to come home. I was relieved on the Saturday to see the result flash up – Blackburn had cruised it 3–0. At least there would be no fingers pointed about that.

To be honest, I remember little about being in the church for little Kya's big day on the Sunday – my head was in a swirl. After the christening, we went to a hotel for a few drinks, and I came outside with my agent John to phone Rangers to see if the move was going to happen. I was in the street trying to sort out my future when there was a flash. A photographer was stalking me from across the road – fucking great. I went back inside and stared at my mobile. More calls were coming through from Mark Hughes – he was seething.

When Monday dawned, I was in Uddingston with my agent. At 12 noon, the deal was on. The fee was never the £4.5 million it was reported as – it was £2 million plus the cash Rovers still owed Gers from the original transfer – but they were beating each other to death over it, and at 2 p.m., the deal was off again. At 3 p.m., it was game on once more, and then at 4 p.m., it was a non-starter. Then, finally, at 5 p.m., I got a phone call from the Rangers doctor Ian McGuinness. He said, 'I will pick you up at 6 p.m. The deal is *on*!' It was full speed ahead. We fooled the press by going to Edinburgh to a private clinic as they shivered outside the usual Rangers hospital in Glasgow. For four hours, I went through scans and passed my medical.

The gamble had paid off. I was home, and I was mightily relieved. I knew what I would have been facing if I'd gone

back to Blackburn. I would have been dumped into the
reserves to teach me a lesson, the way Graeme Souness
once jettisoned Graham Roberts at Rangers, the England
international ending up on the bench in Mallaig and all
those places. I'd have taken it, too, because I would have
deserved the four-hour journeys to play for the stiffs. I'd
have taken my punishment without grumbling.

I know football fans because I've been one. I know that the
minute my head came out of the Ewood Park tunnel the boos
would have been deafening. My wife and kids came to watch
the games down there, and it would have been very hard to
tell them not to because Dad was out there taking pelters.

There are regrets about the way that final weekend as
a Blackburn player panned out – of course there are. I
have huge respect for Mark Hughes and his number two
Eddie Niedzwiecki. The training regime they brought in at
Blackburn meant that I came back to Rangers a fitter player
than the one who left. I also woke up to myself in terms of
self-discipline.

However, I have no regrets about my performances in
the Premiership, and there is no way that I came back to
Scotland with my tail between my legs. Anyone who says
that is showing an ignorance of the games I played for
Rovers, because I know I coped well. I'd put my hands
up if I didn't, but I honestly feel I proved I could live in
the company that league throws up. The accusation that I
couldn't hack it will always be there now that I'm home,
because there are those in the media who have always been
out to stick the knife into me in Scotland. That's life, and I
can handle it.

But the truth is, none of that mattered to me. I still wanted to come back – and I wanted to come back to stay. I am at my happiest when I am amongst my family and friends, playing for the club I've supported since I could walk. I grew up with Rangers in my blood, watched my brother Derek be a star there, had Ian Durrant and Ally McCoist always in our house for tea when I was a kid. I'm a Rangers man, and I wanted to come home. If those are the crimes now being levelled against me, then I plead guilty as charged.

I have battles to fight at Ibrox second time around – debts to pay. The biggest will always be to David Murray. He brought me back, and I have to repay him for putting his money where his mouth is. The feud is forgotten now; we have had a long chat about it. I told him I had made a mistake, and that was good enough. Now, the chairman and I have the same relationship we had before I left. It had always eaten away at me that I had lost that bond, because just a few months before my head got messed up he'd given me a long-term deal, and he had always treated me well. But we have put it behind us now, and I admire him for being big enough to do that.

At times during the 2005–06 season, I experienced some of the darkest days I have had at Rangers: the fans outside Ibrox singing 'McLeish must go' after the 2–2 draw with Falkirk, then losing 3–0 at home to Hibs in the cup after which the chairman was being flayed too. I understood those frustrations after ten games without a win and a trophyless season beckoning – so did the gaffer. He knew we had it coming. But I couldn't believe the criticism the man at the helm was taking. He ploughs money out of his own pocket into Rangers. Others might have forgotten what he has done for the club, but I won't.

He also knows and understands the essence of my relationship with this football club. It comes down to this: life is short, and I prefer to live mine with those I love and trust around me. I'm lucky enough to do that playing for the club that means the most to me, and that's what I want to do now until I hang up my boots.

All through that month of January 2005 I had to sit and bite my lip while I was slaughtered in print and on the radio a hundred times. I heard all the crackpot theories being put forward by people who had never met me or my family. Rangers second time around was never about my wife Margaret and the kids not settling in Lytham – because we would have eventually adapted to the changes in our life together – this was about *me*. And it comes down to this: I can't help the way I feel in my heart.

Lack of ambition – they're the three words that keep being thrown at me. 'He's Rangers' answer to Paul McStay.' That one is aimed at me as if it is an insult. Well, I'd be proud to be compared to Paul. He's a Lanarkshire boy who grew up to captain the club he'd always supported. Just like me. He stayed there all his career, he won 76 caps and he can take his kids and show them he's in the Scotland Hall of Fame. Just like I want to one day. He's a legend and the Celtic fans still call him 'Maestro' even now – and I'm supposed to be ashamed to be compared to him? Sorry, but I just don't get that.

The only way I will leave Rangers now will be if they kick

me out. I have my contract until 2010, but if Walter ever chooses to let me go, there will be no hatred from me. I understand managers have decisions to make.

I realise where I am with the Rangers fans now – I am not a stupid man. I am down a couple of rungs in their estimation. They are quicker to jump on me when I make a mistake, leaping in with criticism whereas in the past they would have supported me. I recognise it, and I understand it. I am there to be shot down now, but I won't hide from it.

If I want to know why they feel like that, I only have to think back to what I did to them. It wasn't right. It hurts me badly that even when I finish, whatever I do, I won't be forgiven by some people. I can't sit every one of them down and explain how I feel about what happened. This book is my attempt to do it now.

The worst incident was in the street in Larkhall after I left Rangers. I'd come home from Blackburn for a visit, and I took my boys to their favourite shop where they can get their sticker cards and toys. There were people wanting my autograph, and I stopped outside to sign them all when this Gers fan walked past and sneered, 'You are nothing but a Judas bastard, Ferguson.' I was boiling with rage, but I had my boys with me, so I had to try and hide it from them. I wanted to rip his head off. Then the red mist started to go, and I realised that for some Rangers fans this was always going to be the way they saw me.

Judas or captain? Traitor or hero? It is down to me to try and change some minds in the time I have left in a Rangers jersey.

3

Growing Pains

'Ferguson, just face it: you are *never* going to make it at football. You better learn to stick in at this.'

Barry gets the message from one of
his teachers at Brannock High School.

Night terrors. The term just doesn't do justice to the naked fear of an illness that once left me in a shrink's office with my anxious parents stuck helpless behind a two-way mirror, watching me, scared stiff that I'd be locked up. Night terrors? You just can't write off eight months of suffering in two words.

I want to be open about what happened to me as a kid – to be honest. The truth is, I was once a very scared ten-year-old boy who went through the most hellish of nightmares. What happened to me was never properly diagnosed; I never discovered whether something had just flicked a faulty switch inside my mind. I'll never know if one dark fear kicked it all off. All I do know is that I was terrified and that there were nights when I felt like I was going mad.

Looking back on it now, it makes me sound like a basket case, but the memories still chill me to the bone. I can't put my finger on why or when it started; I just know it did. I became sick with fear of falling asleep, because when I did, I would have the same horrible dream. I was stuck at the top of a hill, and there was a thick forest on one side – no way down that way. On the other side, soldiers, glaring at me with their guns ready, would march relentlessly up the hill, coming to get me. Night after night, that went on. Closer and closer. I dreamed I was trying to shout out for help, but my tongue felt like it was crispy-fried bacon. It had gone rock hard and was almost choking me; I couldn't speak, and I would try to pull it out of my mouth. Every night of my life for those awful eight months I had these horrifying visions.

During the day, I was a normal kid with so much energy to burn. I would kick the ball about the street with my mates and run around daft, and then I'd dread going home to bed at 9 p.m., because I knew that once I was under those covers the nightmares would come again.

When it happened, I would freak out. I'd be lashing out and squirming around in my bed, bathed in sweat, and my dad would have to carry me downstairs to dry me off. He would sit me up on the kitchen unit, holding me tight, trying to calm me down. I'm not talking about a one-off bad dream here: I'm talking about a condition, an illness.

It devastated my mum and dad. They were worried sick about me, and I was really scared. My mum, in particular, was in turmoil; she had convinced herself they would have to treat me by locking me up somewhere secure. But instead, when the night terrors that were plaguing me refused to go away, I was taken to Strathclyde Hospital and assessed by a psychiatrist. My family were beginning to fear that there was something seriously wrong with me.

I can remember being in the psychiatrist's room, playing absent-mindedly with a toy car, as she asked me a series of seemingly pointless questions, and I knew deep down that the mirror on the wall wasn't a normal one. It was a two-way mirror like the ones I'd seen on telly, and my mum and dad were behind the glass staring in at me, willing me to get better. It was like a scene out of a movie, except it wasn't a criminal being interrogated on the business side of that mirror; it was a bemused kid being questioned by a head-doctor. I couldn't understand why I was there during the day struggling for the words to describe what was happening to me; they should have just come to the house at night. Then they'd have seen it all unfolding in glorious technicolor.

As it was, I had to take medication throughout that time. My mum would set it out for me before she went to work and I left for school, and I learned to stick to the regime. At one point, the doctors even thought I had TB, and they reckoned it was somehow messing with my mind, but it wasn't that. They continued to test me until one day the drugs worked – thank God. As quickly as the awful affliction had settled inside my head, it left me, and I could sleep again and rest without being transported to that fearful place I had come to hate. The illness decided that it had haunted me for long enough. Yet those were some of the most frightening days my family has ever had to go through.

When I began this book, I wanted it to be the truth of my life so far, but those are still very hard days for me to talk about. I also know that by being open about this now, I might shock people and risk ridicule from those with narrow minds and empty heads. But I don't care about that – I can handle whatever comes with this. The fact is that I recovered. And I just hope that somewhere there is a scared little kid who reads this and realises that they're not alone in feeling the way they do and that they can get better and go on to be someone in this world. Pills, injections, tests: I went through it all too. I experienced the most gut-wrenching feeling of sheer hopelessness at one point, but it left me, and I grew stronger from it. From being what they'd call these days a 'problem child', I went on to be the captain of Rangers and Scotland.

I still get little flashbacks to whatever it was that happened to me, and I think that the white-hot outbursts of temper I have had at times in my life can be traced back to what I went through. And reflecting on it now, I wonder if that horrific experience shaped the fiery temper that would see me clash time and again with my teachers at high school, throwing chairs in the classroom, losing the plot and flying off the handle when there was no need to.

I can remember my report cards well: daydreamer; talks too much; could achieve more; nice boy, prone to outbursts. Every report card with the name Barry Ferguson at the top of it ticked too many of the boxes that my parents didn't want to see. None of them was good. The teachers had seen thousands of kids come through those battered, paint-chipped school doors with their heads full of the notion that they could make it as a professional footballer – I knew that. 'What are you going to do with your life?' 'Where do you think you are going to end up?' They pounded these questions into me, and I'd just shrug my shoulders and say with a cocky smile, 'I'm going to play for Rangers – I'll be at Ibrox. You can come and watch me play.'

As I worry now about what will become of my sons Connor and Kyle and my daughter Cara, I can fully understand why I infuriated the teachers at Brannock High School and why many of them were glad to see the back of me. One of them hated me. She said to me, 'Ferguson, just face it, you are never going to make it at football. You better learn to stick in at this.' She was in a no-win situation, though, because Mr Moncrieff, my head teacher, took the school football team, and every time I was in trouble, he would find a way to get me out of it so I could play in the next game.

It's true. My report card always did read 'Daydreamer, talks too much, could achieve more, misbehaves'. But daydreams? They were right about them. I had some belters – and in every one of them, I played the starring role. I was Roberto Baggio. As soon as I came in from school and escaped that dreaded place, I would scarper upstairs, change into my strip and boots, grab my ball and then run down to the park.

When you grow up as Derek Ferguson's kid brother, it stands to reason that it wasn't a Rangers player I would pretend to be. Too close to home. Nah, I was Baggio, 'The Divine Ponytail', Italy and Juventus. I don't know what it was about him, but I thought he was everything a superstar should be. He looked like a movie actor who wouldn't struggle with the birds, and he played football like a god.

I had an Italy strip like Baggio's, and at night after the game at the park broke up, I would come home to our garden and throw the ball off the house, making the walls inside shudder, so I could practise my chest control and then smash home shots the way I'd seen him do it. My mam would be inside going mental, because she was trying to watch TV and the photographs were flying off the walls. Then my old man would be out the door shouting, 'You're chewing up that grass, you. Beat it.'

I had come screaming and girning into this world on 2 February 1978, born at Bellshill Maternity Hospital and then brought home to 21 Striven Terrace in Little Earnock in Hamilton. That was home until we moved to Bellshill when I was seven. There is a ten-year gap between my brother and me, but I was a much-wanted baby by then, and that was always the way I felt.

My mum Maureen and dad Archie worked seven days a week at times. My dad was a roof-sheeter and still is, and my mum was a carer for old people. Nowadays, the money Derek and I have earned means they could sit at home and have an easy life, but they don't. He still hikes sheets up onto the roofs in all weathers, and she works part time, visiting old folks, making their meals and ensuring they are safe and feel wanted.

Before I sat down to try and make sense of my life so far in this book, I read all the football autobiographies I could get my hands on: José Mourinho, Roy Keane, Mick Quinn. Their backgrounds fascinated me: how they grew up to become the football men they are. But when it comes to me, I don't need people feeling sorry for me because of my childhood illness, and I refuse to spin a rags-to-riches tale. I'm not going to paint myself as some poor kid with the arse hanging out of his trousers who made it despite all the odds being stacked against him. That's the easy way to write it, but it's not true, because I wasn't that boy. My parents were proud, working-class people who bought their house and put everything into it. Whatever struggles we had, I always had a ball, boots, a strip and a trackie. They were all the worldly possessions I wanted back then.

My life revolved around having a ball at my feet, and my first memory stretches back to being a three-year-old kid at the side of the park with my dad watching Derek play. I couldn't wait for half-time to get onto the pitch for the kickabout. By then, Derek was 13, and the scouts had already spotted what I would come to realise when I grew up: he was special and had a way of rising above the others. He always played with his head up, looking for a pass. I loved that. He also did this thing when the opposing goalkeeper hoofed a ball up the park. He'd scream 'Fergie's!' and fake to go for a header then pull the ball down on his chest and make the pass to put his team back on the attack. Time and again I saw him con his marker like that; he was brilliant at it – way ahead of his time. I vowed that one day I'd be as good as him.

My dad took me to every game Derek played, and I can remember my first Old Firm game as if it was yesterday, standing on the terraces at Hampden as an eight-year-old kid watching the 1986 Skol Cup final. Rangers beat Celtic 2–1, and Derek bossed it. He slung in the late cross, Roy Aitken hauled back Terry Butcher in the box and Davie Cooper sank the penalty. I leapt on my dad the same moment Derek was out on that park jumping on Coop.

He was my big brother, the guy I sat across from at the dinner table, and he was the Man of the Match. After the game, Graeme Souness said, 'He's the best young midfielder in Britain, better than I ever was at that age.' Yet I didn't feel pressure because I was Derek's brother; I was just so proud of him.

I would walk past people in the street after Rangers games, and they would say, 'Your brother was shite today.' I could never let that lie. I always walked back with my fists clenched ready for a ruck, just as they wanted me to. As I grew up, I was a target on the street and on the pitch, but I lived with it – learned to thrive on it. My brother played for the Gers, and I was constantly being compared to him, but I was never going to let that be a negative thing for me.

It was a positive thing that I had him to look up to because he was a good person. The first time he had money and my mum and dad were struggling to get me the latest football boots he went out and bought them for me on the quiet.

When I was an eight-year-old skelf of a boy, running around the streets, commentating inside my head and pretending to be Roberto Baggio, my brother was nineteen and the kid the 'Souness Revolution' at Rangers was being built around. That was hard to come to terms with sometimes. But when dreams were coming true for someone so close to me, maybe it was natural for a kid like me, who had started to notice he could make the ball obey him, to hope that he too could make it at Ibrox. I wasn't pulling up any trees at school, that's for sure. I spent most of my time in trouble, standing outside the classroom. I just couldn't seem to stop myself from talking, and I'd be banished to the corridor.

I had chosen Brannock High for one simple reason: they had a football team and my local school Bellshill Academy didn't. So I got on the bus every morning with my mate Paul McCorquindale and travelled the seven miles to school. At Brannock they had huge windows in the classrooms; the slightest thing would catch my attention, and I would look out and drift away. I'd get punishment exercises and save them up for when my folks weren't in and it was only Derek in the house. He'd be lying resting on the couch after training at Ibrox, or hungover from a night out, and I'd say, 'Can you sign this. It's my project from school.' He'd say, 'No problem, wee man.' And I'd get away with it again – another 'punny' exercise signed off by an adult without my mum ever setting eyes on it!

I should have stuck in at school, but the disinterest started when I was at Neilsland Primary in Hamilton. By the time we moved house and I went to Longmuir Primary in Bellshill, they had started to realise that the boy Ferguson only gave his all in one subject: football. The school team was for those in primary seven, but I made it two years before I should have. The manager was called Jimmy Graham, and he was superb with us.

I went to Longmuir with a kid called David Lilley, who was in the same class as me. He went on to play for Queen of the South before moving to Partick Thistle and Aberdeen. He is now with Kilmarnock in the SPL, and it is great to play against him and look back and think we both came out of that same classroom and made a living out of kicking a ball.

Away from school, it wasn't about being Baggio in the street any more: I had to find a proper team and test myself. I played one game for Hamilton Colts, but, for some reason, that was it with them, and instead I joined Mill United Boys Club, which became my spiritual home. I just felt I fitted in, as though I belonged there. And they had great players, such as John-Paul McBride, who would join Celtic but never quite break through.

Right from the start, I played in my favourite No. 6 jersey. The only time it has ever gone from me since was when I went to Blackburn and Craig Short already had it. I chose twenty-four for two plus four and waited my time.

The team was run by this brilliant guy called Danny Cunning, who just lived and breathed football – he was so wrapped up in it all. Because I lived in Bellshill, he'd come over there to ferry me to the games in Hamilton. Looking back, it was the first real evidence I had of football being a kind of escape from the lives we had. Danny worked in the massive Philips Lighting factory in Hamilton, but he didn't live for his shifts stuck in there, he lived for the weekend and managing his team – for the game. Now? Well, now that same bubbly character is the kit manager at Livingston, and every time we go to play at Almondvale, I see a guy who is the essence of a football man. It's great he has ended up working inside the game and not in some light-bulb factory.

I was so little back then, almost always the smallest in the team at Mill United. But Danny never dwelled on that, not once. He'd point to guys like Ian Durrant at Rangers and say that there wasn't anything of him, but he had made it. Then Durranty won a Player of the Month award when the Premier League was sponsored by Fine Fare, the old supermarket chain. I was the most popular boy at the club because the prize was a set of strips for the boys club of his choice, and he chose to give them to my Mill United side. I was made-up – so proud. He came down to our training with Derek, and we got these glistening new tops in red and black stripes. A photographer also took a picture of me on Ian's shoulders in my favourite white Umbro Rangers away kit. When I grew up and we fleetingly played together for the Gers – before Durranty left for Kilmarnock – that snapper made a bit of money off that one!

As time moved on, though, my lack of stature became a real issue, and I saw so many other good players ignored because of their height. This is a Scottish failing and one the scouts should be ashamed of – it is a load of bollocks. Two occasions stand out when I was personally confronted by this attitude. It sickened me and threatened to drive me away from the game I feel I was born to play. The first happened when I was playing for Rangers Boys Club. We made it to a cup final, which was to be played at Petershill Juniors park. It was a big match for us, and I'd played a key role in getting us there, but when it came to game day, the coaches said, 'You're out, son. We're worried about you because you are too small.' My dad and Derek were in a rage, and I was gutted – it killed me. That whole season seemed to be dominated by a debate about my height and not my footballing skills. It was haunting me, this worry people seemed to have about me.

The second occasion was when I had a Scotland Schoolboys

trial. Out of the 22 kids present, I thought I had shone, to be honest. I came off happy that I had stood out, and I felt I was a cert. I started to think how that dark-blue jersey would look on me when I tugged it over my head. Then I was told I was out – I didn't even make the cut. I knew that when I was out of earshot they would be saying, 'Good player, but he's too wee.'

After I found out that they'd dumped me, I ran home, bolted upstairs and hurled myself on my bed, crying my eyes out. My dad came up, and I said to him, 'I think I am better off wrapping this. It's not going to happen for me.' He wouldn't hear of it.

Looking back, my dad might be a roofer by trade, but he has been like a shrink and a personal trainer to me. Even now, I can walk out of Hampden after a World Cup qualifier with Scotland, and he is still the first man I phone. When I was a kid, he wouldn't scream or bawl at me about football; instead, he would have a quiet word when it was needed, and that hasn't changed. He wasn't the kind of mad dad I now too often see at my sons' games, screaming and shouting on the touchline. My old man would wait until we were in the motor together after a game, and then he'd give me little pointers about where I'd gone wrong.

My old man was always there for me – never missed a game. When I was down about the endless jibes about my height, he waited until after one game up at Lanark Barracks when I was twelve. He knew that only one subject approached football for my affections at that time: cars. I couldn't care less about music when I was a kid, but if there was any pocket money left after I had bought my football magazines, it went on those with Porsches and Ferraris inside. So he waited until all the other kids and parents had gone home after the game, and he let me in behind the wheel of his Nissan Micra to drive it around with him helping me. I still carry the memory of how grown-up I felt to this day.

My arms carry the tattoos of six names etched on them. The names of Archie, Maureen, Margaret, Connor, Kyle and Cara – my parents and my family. Dad's name is there to remind me that I want to be the force in my kids' lives that he was in mine. My old man lost his own dad when he was just 11 years old. How do you cope with that? I know that I couldn't have.

He comes from hard stock, my dad. His mum, my Gran Ferguson, stayed put in a real rough part of Barlanark where my old man was brought up. She was the only old woman I knew who swore every second word! I loved it – she cracked me up. When I stayed over at her place, I would go out onto the veranda, look out over the scheme and watch the local gangs knocking shite out of each other. I was a kid then, and the violence on TV seemed glamorous. God knows there was real-life violence up in that place – it was wild. And it was hard staying there when the only heat she had on was the gas fire in the living room. In the bedroom where I used to sleep, the windows were single-glazed and rotting, and I'd be burying myself under the covers, eating the last of the penny chews my 10p at the ice-cream van had bought me. It was freezing – torture. Then, in the morning, it was back to my vantage point on the veranda to view a world that for some might seem brutal but for me was exciting. Barlanark: you don't grow up easy there. I learned that out there on that veranda and saw what my dad had gone through to carve out a decent life for us.

I was 11 when Gran Ferguson died from cancer, and it was my first real experience of the emptiness and numbing loss that you feel when someone close to you is stolen away. I was four when my mum's old dear, my Gran Buchanan, died, yet I still remember standing around outside the hospital in Aberdeen crying.

My mum's parents lived in Peterhead, and I loved them, even if my Granda Eddie was a huge *Celtic* man. He was a 6 ft 2 in. strapping hard nut, but then cancer got him, and he went from a 14 st. brute to 6 st. It broke my heart. It happened just as my son Kyle was born, and we should have been celebrating a new life coming into the Fergusons' world not mourning one going out of it.

One sadness and regret that I have is that of all my grandparents it was only my papa Eddie who saw me make it. Even then, he died before I captained Rangers and Scotland, and he never saw me lift a trophy as skipper. He would have loved that, Celtic man or not.

I realise that death is a part of life that everyone has to deal with, but I find the loss of those I love so very hard to accept. I'm not scared of dying, but I am terrified of losing my mum and dad. They worked so hard for their boys, and the best thing for me about the money I have made will always be that I can look after them. And they guided me on the journey that eventually took me to Rangers – Mill United was just a stop along the way.

At the time, I was at an age when everything seemed so simple, as if it would go on for ever. I couldn't see myself ever leaving Mill, but then the managers had a massive bust-up and the club split – I was stunned. The adults had fallen out, so the kids had to find somewhere else to go. But I was starting to get a bit of a reputation by then, and I was training with Dundee United, Rangers and Hearts. I also had the pick of local sides at that time, but I chose to play for St Columba's Boys Club in Viewpark next. Looking back, I suppose they were a side with Catholic roots – they played in the shadow of a chapel – but that never even entered my mind. Why should it have been a problem? I just wanted to play football with the best kids around, and Mick Small's team had the best. I loved every minute of that. Even when I turned 15 and Rangers offered me terms, I wanted to stay put, but they insisted I play for their boys club, and I left St Columba's behind with regret.

When I went to Rangers, they had also seen the physique that had prompted one of their own boys club managers to doubt me and a Scotland selector to snub me. They liked my passing ability and vision, and the fact that the family footballing genes had been passed down not just to Derek, but would I fill out? I was only 5 ft 4 in. and 8 st. soaking wet. They were so worried about it that they brought me in early. They took me out of school at the age of 15. I was scheduled to leave at the end of fourth year, but they somehow got me excused and dragged me in before then. My height continued to worry me, but when I was 17, I sprouted 4 in. and all those fears were gone. Now they'd have to judge me on my skills alone. They wouldn't have the excuse of my height any more.

I still boil with fury if I hear about kids written off because of their size; it sums up all that is wrong with the development of the game in Scotland. My own battles to win the right to be judged on football brain not brawn gave me an inner strength and a determination to prove those who doubted me wrong. And I know from talking to my dad that he takes pride in the way I reacted back then, although there were times when he despaired of me off the park.

I was a normal kid who broke windows, got into fights and had his scrapes with the 'polis'. We all did, but there were times when I overstepped the mark. Like every kid at that age, the temptations came: drink and women! I was no different. I'd already pestered Rebecca Stewart – who along with her twin sister Sarah was the pick of the girls on the estate – and won my first kiss. I thought I was the big man at 14 years of age. The next step came when we bought our first carry-out. I can still see it in front of me: two little bottles of Diamond White cider and a can of Tennent's Super Lager. Classy, eh?

We were lying in the fields near my house, down the back hill towards the railway line in the heart of the Lochview Estate, hiding in the long grass. I downed my booze and was absolutely blootered. We then walked up from the long grass to a place we called the Widdy Swingy – the wooden swing park for posh folk. (This is all classic material for Jonathan Watson for the next time he wants to slaughter me and portray me as the 'King of the Neds' on *Only an Excuse*.) I was all over the place. I just sprawled there, out of it, and my mates – Paul, Ecky and the rest of them – were all steaming, climbing about the frames shouting and screaming. It was like a scene out of *Trainspotting*, and I was looking up at the sky thinking, 'Wow, this is mental.'

Then I felt something licking my face. I looked to the side, and it was my dog Toby. Was he out on his own? I got my answer soon enough as my mates all suddenly fell silent. Then I heard someone roaring, 'Is that you?' Oh shit. My ma was out on a walk with Toby. I staggered to my feet, and she glared at me but didn't say a word. She got me by the collar and marched me home.

As we went up our street all the neighbours I had never talked to were there sweeping their drives, and I was shouting, 'You all right, mate?' Mum was mortified, but when I got into the house, the smile was wiped off my face. My dad grabbed me by the back of my hair, stripped me down to my boxers and whirled me through the living room and into the hall. I got dragged up the stairs, one by one, and he hurled me into my bed. I had carpet burns from my neck to the bottom of my back, but I learned a lesson. I didn't touch a drink for another two years. My old man had seen enough would-be players piss their lives away, and he didn't want it to happen to me.

That whole episode is funny when I look back on it now. It is nothing to be proud of, but it was just part of growing up. In Scotland, we live in a booze culture. I realise that from the different way we live our lives compared to some of the foreigners who have become my friends at Rangers.

There are many pitfalls to this way of life, and seeing Derek grow up in the public eye prepared me for what would happen to me. People would shout at me that he was crap, overrated, an alcoholic, whatever hurtful thing they could think of. I also saw how all the stories can escalate, especially when he started clashing with Souness a little bit. People said he was out of control off the pitch. They would say he was a boozebag – something that happened to me too at one stage – yet the guy was rarely out of the house during the week. He drank after games, but he was allowed to then. That was his night to relax, and I never saw that as a crime, just as I don't see it as one for me now when I do it. If Margaret lets me out that is!

That side of life as an Old Firm player is a learning process, finding out how you dodge situations that can hurt you. I had to find my own way through that maze. Having a famous brother helped, but I still had to experience it myself, to be honest.

God knows that for every downer there was an upside. For example, there was one time when I was 11 and Derek turned 21, and Ian Durrant and Ally McCoist were at our house in Strathview Road in Bellshill for his birthday party. They were my heroes, and they were at my house for a party! I was sneaking my mates into the kitchen to meet them. At the end of the night, I went up and sat in my room on my Rangers bed sheets and thought to myself how mad it was. I had posters from *Shoot!* and *Match* on the walls, but there were few Gers ones to be honest. I couldn't have a poster of my favourite Rangers player on the wall, could I? He lived in our house and was downstairs getting blitzed at his 21st.

Even when Derek moved out to his flat just a stone's throw away from us, he only lived there at weekends; he still stayed with us during the week. You can guess what that flat was for. I used to sneak up there on a Sunday morning just to see what teammates and women were there and ask him if he wanted me to go and get his papers.

Away from the fun off the park, Derek had earned the life I wanted. Playing together for Rangers would have been something to treasure, but by the time I made it with the Gers, he was long gone. Souness had offloaded him to Hearts for £750,000, and then he moved south to Sunderland.

I had choices before I plumped for Ibrox – they all had a nibble. Celtic – believe it or not – asked me in to train, and I had a couple of sessions there. Then I'd go south to Manchester United and Spurs, and in Scotland, Hearts, Hibs and Dundee United were there for me if I wanted. The hard and fast offers, though, came from Ipswich Town and Everton – and they were tempting. Ipswich was a great place for raising young players at that time, and they had a long association with Scotland: the likes of John Wark, George Burley and Alan Brazil had played there and become legends. Ipswich valued Scotsmen, and they treated me like a king. They even let me travel on the first-team bus to a match. Rangers, though, were simply in my bloodstream.

When I arrived at Ibrox, I was looked after at first by John Chalmers, who gave so much to the youth side and had recommended that the club should sign me. A few years later, he tragically hanged himself because of problems in his private life, and he was a huge loss to the club. John played such a big role in my life, and his death left me devastated. My parents worked so hard that they were out of the house at 7 a.m. every morning, even in the school holidays. They couldn't get me to Ibrox for training, so I would stay at

John's house, and I was very close to his family. His funeral came just as I broke into the first team, and when John McGregor stood up to give the eulogy, there was a lump in my throat as he read out the names of the players John Chalmers had helped rear for Rangers. He should have been there to see me make it, but life got on top of him. However, I'll never forget what he did for me.

After working with John Chalmers, I was passed on to John McGregor and Billy Kirkwood, and I really began to learn what being a Ranger was all about. John McGregor had played at Liverpool before he came to Gers and carried the nickname 'Mad Dog' about with him as baggage, but it blinded people to how good a coach he was. When he was moved out at Ibrox, it staggered me that it took so long for him to get back into football because he is superb at what he does. Yes, he was hard as nails, but there was knowledge behind that veneer, and he was dedicated to making sure you gave of your best every day. That was why he was booting you up the arse all the time, not because he was trying to show he was the tough guy.

My first wage packet for Rangers was £72.50 a week, and I got taxed on that. I took home £200 a month, and I gave my mum £20 a week. I did a lot of dreaming then, especially on the train from Bellshill to Argyle Street in Glasgow. Then I'd walk to the underground and get the Tube into Ibrox. Ibrox is a proper stadium in my eyes – it has its own subway stop, just like Highbury when you went to see Arsenal in London before they moved to their new stadium. You know you are with a big club when they make the Underground stop there.

I would come up out from underneath the city and stroll to the ground. That was when I could see what you could have if you made it. The first-team cars would be parked outside: Mark Hateley's Ferrari, Trevor Steven's powder-blue Porsche, Durranty's BMW. I would look at them and think that's what I wanted.

I worked from 8.30 a.m. in the morning to 6.30 p.m. at night, and I grew to love any moment of quiet I could get; they were few and far between. I spent a lot time in my little sanctuary in the boot room. Next door was the coaches' room. I'd be working away on the boots and the next thing I'd hear was Archie Knox bellowing down the corridor, 'F-E-R-G-I-E!' He was a pain in the arse. I would stoat in to his office and say, 'Good morning.'

He'd answer, 'Where's my fucking tea and toast?' I would traipse back down the corridor to go and get it and feel like spitting in it. They were tough on me but they were trying to teach me things.

I also had to do the kit for the gaffer Walter Smith and Archie and make sure everything was right when their stuff came out of the laundry. Archie was like some lunatic sergeant-major when it came to his boots; he wanted them gleaming so you could almost see your face in them. One of my big tasks of the day was to clean their showers at about 3.30 p.m., and Archie used to wait until the last minute to go back in and get dirt and soap in between the grout and tiles. Bastard. I'd have to go back in and do them again, then go and make sure their fridge was full of fizzy water. Only then could I drag myself back to the Tube station and go home to get ready to start again the next day.

But it taught me discipline, respect and order – what the club was about and how to knuckle down. There was no time for staring out of windows daydreaming the way I had at Brannock High. So I look at the kids now at Murray Park, and whilst I feel for them sometimes, they don't go through all that – they don't have to do what I did on the way up. And, yes, I do wonder when I am in our £14 million training facility if they are getting it all too easy and whether they have the same hunger and desire I had to make it. Then we produce kids like Alan Hutton, Stevie Smith and Chris Burke, who have gone from the youth ranks to starting against Villarreal in the last 16 of the Champions League, and I know it is still there – some kids still have the dreams I had, and they are driven the way I was.

Yet it was a savage environment: it chewed up kids and spat them out. I had a mate called Ross Matheson who was a right good player, but he ended up at Raith Rovers and Morton before drifting out of football. Then there was Jazz Juttla, the first kid to really make it out of the Asian community to play at Gers. He showed a lot of courage to overcome prejudice on the way, but he too didn't quite make the grade.

There was also a stage for me at 18 when I saw those I had grown up with breaking through and playing for Hibs, Hearts and Dundee United. They had made it, and I hadn't, and I began to beg Rangers to let me out on loan, but John McGregor and John Brown, who'd come in when Kirky left to boss Dundee United, played a key role in encouraging me to stay. They kept me believing.

Bomber is a man who is again underestimated because of

the public perception of him as some sort of raving madman, constantly frothing at the mouth in the dressing-room. Yes, there were times when I looked at him and thought that he was not right in the head, quite frankly. When he played, he would hyperventilate before games with Celtic and be sick. They'd have to produce a brown paper bag that he could breathe into to calm him down. And the players in the nine-in-a-row team called him Hannibal Lecter. But you know what? It was his passion for Rangers that made him like that, and I loved that about him. It didn't scare me back then, it inspired me. I cared as much as he did, and he was a great coach in my eyes. He had blue blood coursing through his veins – Rangers through and through.

He makes me think that I would love a job like the one he did at Ibrox when I finish playing. I can see a real reward in guiding a kid that wants it badly – the way I did – and seeing him make it. Yes, it begins with daydreams and they tell me that sometimes in life it is wise to be careful what you wish for. For some daydreamers, though, their dreams can come true.

4

In the Shadow of Legends

'Is it sore down there? Welcome to the big man's game, son.'

Neil Pointon, Hearts.

'Right lads, today we will go with Dibble, Shields, Björklund, Petrić, Wright, Barry Ferguson, Gascoigne, Durrant, Albertz, McCoist and van Vossen.' Walter Smith's lips were still moving, but I didn't hear any more of the team talk; I was looking out of the window of the Caledonian Hotel in Edinburgh in a state of shock. It was 10 May 1997, three months after my 19th birthday, and I had finally made it. I was a Rangers first-team player.

The enormity of it all left me feeling like I was caught in a video that was moving in slow motion. I sat there in that bland meeting room just like the ones in so many hotels around the world I have been in since, but at that time, it was the centre of my earth, and I had to force myself to try and keep listening after Walter said, 'Young Barry will be there in midfield for his debut. I am going to play you

79

today, son.' I swear that I could feel my pants filling up right at that moment!

All season long I had given every ounce of effort I had in me just to make the squad, but when I did, I would sit there thinking that I didn't belong alongside these guys. These were the nine-in-a-row legends, and when I was around them, I still felt like I wanted to hide in the shadows. I was in awe of them, and if I am honest, I *hated* travelling to away games with them because I just didn't feel comfortable when I was in their company.

My first-team debut was on the Sunday afternoon after one of the biggest parties Ibrox will ever see – the night we clinched nine in a row. Brian Laudrup's header at Dundee United had sealed it and made the final game of the season a time to rest players and savour the history of what had been achieved. I knew I was in the side because players were either knackered or being granted more party time – I couldn't have cared less.

After Walter gave me the nod, everything became a blur, and even now, nine years on, I can remember almost nothing about the day until I got to Tynecastle and we were warming up. Then the game started, and I was rudely awoken. All this time on you may not remember Neil Pointon, but I do. He almost smashed me all the way back to Hamilton! The ball bounced up chest high, and he came right through me, leaving me lying on the turf in a crumpled heap. He just looked down at me with that dodgy mullet and porn-star moustache and growled, 'Is it sore down there? Welcome to the big man's game, son.' He was a hardy bastard.

That gave me a start, and I gave myself a shake. I was 19,

and I should have been able to look after myself and not be bullied. I just muttered under my breath, 'Let's grow up here.'

I did OK in the match, nothing special. We lost 3–1, and it was one of those typical last game of the season affairs. I remember John Robertson played for Hearts that day and that, in truth, we were poor, but the team had won the nine in a row, and they just wanted to put the boots away and get on holiday.

It meant everything to me, though, and it was a very special day for my old man. He'd been driven by a dream of seeing his two boys play for Rangers, and now it had happened. It meant the whole world to me just to see his face. I'll never forget looking up to the stands and seeing him and my mum, and thinking about all the worry that I had put them through – that all the sacrifices they had made had been worth it. You can't buy the look my dad had on his face that day, not with any wad of notes in your pocket. It was priceless. That one moment is stuck in my mind and always will be. I wish I'd had a camera to capture his coupon in that split second. Sheer pride. My heart felt as if it would burst for a moment, because I knew I had made him so happy.

That aside, I was in a dream world that day, and if I have a regret now, it is that apart from the look on my old man's face I remember so little. The truth is I was in bits because of nerves. I have seen players who come in and play just one game for Rangers. Very good players. They get a shift when it doesn't matter, and they never play again. That was a real fear. I'd seen it happen, and that sort of thing was messing with my head amidst all the excitement of finally getting the nod.

I remember the kind of zombie-like state I was in that day, and that's why I try to strike a balance when a new kid comes into the side now, such as Stevie Smith during the 2005–06 season. I go over and simply say, 'Good luck. Get a nice touch early on, and keep it easy and simple.' The words you say beforehand are just paying lip service to good manners in all honesty, because nothing will prepare them for what is about to hit them. What is more important is that when you get out on the pitch you have a word in their ear to encourage them and help them through it.

In my first game, the added pressure was that I was walking into a team of legends – that's the only word for them. They'd made history, and I had been like any Rangers fan on 7 May 1997. I will always remember where I was. That's our JFK moment, a 'Were you there?' night. Well, I was in my club blazer in my seat perched over the players' tunnel at Tannadice, but I felt like I had gatecrashed someone else's party. I had a full-blown insecurity complex, and I had pangs of jealousy as I watched the ease with which my mate Charlie Miller carried himself. He belonged with these guys all right.

Charlie had long since arrived by the time I sat in the crowd cheering him on the night the team won nine in a row. I'd seen him make his way up at Rangers. He was three years older than me, and I kept hearing about this wonder boy who was a cert to be on his way to the first team. He was the name on everyone's lips, and when he eventually came through, he was brilliant. We played in the reserves together with Ian Durrant, and I loved it – pure football.

If I have one big regret about my relationship with Dick Advocaat, it is that I never really carried enough authority to try and influence him a little and impose my views on Charlie on him. I wish I'd sat Dick down and sold him on Chico as a player. It killed me when he left, because I thought we could have played a generation in the Gers midfield together, but he was in and out of the side all the time, and he was fed up with it. He just wanted to play first-team football every week, and, looking back, I can understand that.

Still, I wish we'd had more game time together. I could see what we could be if Dick would just give us a chance, but he never really did. He saw something in Charlie that he didn't like. My suspicion will always be that he felt Chico was just another indisciplined Scottish kid pissing his talent up against the wall. Yet for me, this was another guy who had all the tales and rumours following him around Glasgow. Charlie could have four or five quiet beers one night, and by the time Dick heard about it, he'd been poured out of a nightclub into a taxi after a brawl. He was no angel, but he wasn't the waster he was painted to be either – far from it.

The link we had then remains even now, and I always savour it any time he comes back from his new life with SK Brann and we can have a few beers. Craig Moore's surprise 30th birthday party when his wife Heather did him up like a kipper with a do at the Bothwell Bridge Hotel was one that will always stick with me. Charlie was home from Norway, and he walked in with his glasses on, a 31-year-old sensible person! He looked like a stockbroker from a distance, but you don't get many of them in Castlemilk.

We've shared a lot of laughs together down the years, and

that's why when I think of the nine-in-a-row season one of my lingering images will always be the goal that won it. Laudrup's header lives with everyone with Rangers' blood in their veins, but for me, the key moment was in the build-up. Down the flank he scurried, and then I was on my feet as I watched my mate Chico whip in the cross with his swinger – a ball on his left foot that you couldn't have believed and all it needed was the leap Brian met it with.

On the way home that night, I looked around the team bus and saw how much it meant to them all, and I just ached to have days like that, ones that were mine to enjoy. This time it was their party, not mine. But it was still unforgettable to come back to Ibrox that night at around midnight and see thousands of fans dancing in the streets. The joy was incredible, and I thought, 'I will never see the likes of this again.' But I did when we won the league in 2005 on the last day at Easter Road, and by the time we got back to the Brox at 6.30 p.m., there was somehow 30,000 people there.

But that night? I came in off the bus and helped Jimmy Bell put the kit away as the rest rampaged around the place going mental. I sat and had a couple of beers and just watched these legends having a bevvy and whooping it up. Then I slipped out quietly and got myself home. I vowed that one day it would be me making the fans as happy as they were that night.

I recently watched a great TV programme called *That Was the Team that Was* and it summed me up back then. It showed all the players losing the plot in the Tannadice dressing-room, and you could just about see me there in the background. I was this little self-conscious kid at the back trying to join in the celebrations; I looked about eight years old.

These days, I see the boys grow up at Murray Park and will them to make it into the first team, kids like Alan Hutton, Stevie Smith and Chris Burke. They are living, breathing proof that the £14 million the chairman shelled out on Murray Park wasn't money poured down the stank. Some are quiet and feel their way, whereas others, such as my new room-mate Kris Boyd, a daft Ayrshireman, breenge in like a bull in a china shop. But I know that deep down they'll all have little doubts niggling away at them at first about whether or not they belong here. I recognise that in them.

For me, that nine-in-a-row season was all about making the first-team squad, just to be a part of it. I knew I was never going to get a game when it mattered because the nine in a row meant so much to the club. I was the hamper boy at that time, and I learned so much from the kitman Jimmy Bell, even though I was always trying to skive. I would think up new ways to duck the chores I was meant to do so I could just go out and play. Those days setting out kit and cleaning boots seemed like such a bind to me, but, in retrospect, they gave me a sense of exactly where I stood in the food-chain at Rangers. I saw what I had to do to be a top player, and I believe it grounded me a little having to do my share of menial jobs.

I like to think the coaches could see something in me then, because every single time I stepped out of line I would be slapped down so I didn't get big-headed. One time I gave lip to John McGregor on the training field, and he got sick of my cheek. He sent me with the groundsman to pick rubbish up behind the Govan Stand. I did that for an entire week, and it sickened me. I went back in the following Monday with my bottom lip trembling, and Mad Dog just said, 'That's your fucking reality check. That's what a real guy does for a living.'

I once looked at the list of eighty-six players whom Graeme Souness and Walter Smith used when they were winning nine in a row. There is a group of nine players who either started or were a sub in just *one* game of the nine. I'm in there alongside Neil Caldwell, Jimmy Nicholl, Scott Wilson, Steven Boyack, Darren Fitzgerald, Paul McKnight, Seb Rozental and . . . John McGregor. That's me and the Mad Dog: we'll prop up a bar in Marbella one day and bore all our golf pals silly with tales of the part we played in winning nine in a row!

In May 2006, the most famous names from the nine-in-a-row team all gathered again to play a benefit game for Ted McMinn at Derby County. He'd had his right leg amputated beneath the knee, and when John Brown heard of Ted's plight, he vowed to get the nine-in-a-row boys together to help out. I saw them roll back the years at Pride Park, and it brought it all flooding back to me, the way they'd made me feel. Heroes.

Back in those days, I was in awe of Paul Gascoigne, and I was stunned that we had signed him at Rangers. He would walk into the dressing-room with his boots in a Louis Vuitton holdall, and I would think, 'That bag is worth £500.' Then he'd have all the latest gadgets first: a laptop or a Game Boy or whatever it was. They'd come from sponsors who were falling over themselves to have him associated with their products. He was showbiz. He had these Versace suits, and when I look back now, they were torture. But then? Well, then I wanted to have them.

I was a 12-year-old boy when he broke down in tears at Italia 90 on the brink of the World Cup final with England. I loved him; I thought he was the business. This fat kid with all that skill. I couldn't imagine living in the same country as him back then, never mind playing in the same team or sharing the same dressing-room.

He was like he seemed on TV: larger than life. His wind-ups were legendary. One time, he left a fish in Gordon 'Jukebox' Durie's car hidden under the floor where it couldn't be found for weeks, and Jukey went mental trying to find where the smell was coming from. But they are the tales from another team's lifetime, not mine. They still make me laugh, though, and I did witness some of them, like the times when he would get into the bubble bath with the other boys and chat away for ages, and later when they drained it down to the suds, they'd find that he'd crapped in it while they were talking! He was out of order, but he kept them on their toes. He'd piss in the Gatorade canister or throw his socks and pants into it, and people would come in after training and slurp down their drinks as he creased himself laughing in the corner. He was a lunatic.

I wasn't training the day he was rumoured to have pissed on Erik Bo Andersen – the rest of the team were doing press-ups and Gazza allegedly ran up behind Erik and had a slash on him – but I reckon it's a true story. A joke's a joke, but I have to say if he had done that to me, I would have knocked him out, no matter who he was. That was Gazza, though. As Sir Bobby Robson said, he truly was as daft as a brush.

But on the field, he was a one-off, and Paul Gascoigne should always be remembered as the chubby kid who had Mars bars thrown at him when he was starting out at Newcastle United because he was so devastatingly good. I want to remember him like that or think back to the day when we won eight in a row and he scored a hat-trick against Aberdeen. It's a cliché to say people win games single-handedly, and I never really believed a player could do that in a team game. But you know what? He could.

These days I see the demons Gazza fights, and it upsets me. I don't know whom you blame for the problems he faces, but maybe someone up there throws a dice before you even set out on this life and your path is mapped out for you before you start. I don't know whether that makes sense or not, but it is how I feel sometimes, especially when I look at someone like Paul who has gone through all he has with alcoholism and now drug abuse. Yet always he faces up to his woes with such honesty, and he shows the world when he is hurting. To my mind, he is just a genuine working-class guy with troubles. But no one can know the pressure he faces unless they have lived in his skin.

I think that the years he had at Rangers were the best of his career mainly because Walter Smith treated him like one of his own sons. When Gazza was at his lowest ebb, Walter and his wife Ethel had him round to their house for Christmas dinner. How many managers do you know who would do that?

Yet off the field he had been dropped into a goldfish bowl

and everyone was staring in at him swimming around in it. I have found my own problems coping with being a celebrity in Glasgow – a working-class boy made good – and this is my home. These days, I know where to go to avoid the trouble that can follow you, but Gazza didn't. Even now I can go on holiday to Spain or Portugal and find places where no one has the slightest idea who I am. I like that. But Gazza? With the fame he built for himself, there were times when there was no escape, and he was not equipped to deal with that.

Despite all of the nightmares he has been through recently, I like to think that Rangers gave him a refuge, especially after having suffered so many injuries and problems at Lazio. He found the right manager and had teammates – like Alan McLaren and Coisty – who cared for him as a person and as a player.

Gazza and his teammates will never be forgotten, nor should they be because we will never see another Rangers side like them. And it is incredible to think that Gascoigne and Laudrup were signed for a combined fee of £7 million. Walter Smith should have worn a mask. I think the great thing about Ibrox for Lauders and Paul was that Rangers fixed them in a way. Laudrup and Gascoigne were broken in some respects, and they'd had their bad times in Italy at Fiorentina and Lazio. I remember Lauders telling me how he escaped from training in the boot of a car one day because the fans were trying to attack the players for getting the team relegated! They were at low points in their careers when Gers got them, but they came to our club, and they were different gravy.

Brian kept himself to himself – he was a quiet man for a

genius – but I watched him closely. I thought he was special, one to marvel at. In fact, I was a little in awe of him, to be honest. But I will always be grateful that I had a chance to play a few games with him before he left for Chelsea. The boy was a big unit: 6 ft 1 in. and 13 st. – not your typical skinny winger. It was great that he scored the goal that won the nine in a row, but it tells you more about my roots, I suppose, that my abiding memory of that moment is the ball that Charlie whipped in for it.

Dinners for the club are frequent, and I enjoy them. They are a chance to put on a black tie and meet up with your teammates and the stars of the past. But there are so many now, from testimonials to Player of the Year bashes to the Hall of Fame and all the rest, that they can merge into one. One that always sticks in my mind, though, is the vote for the greatest-ever Rangers team, because I was fascinated to see who would be in it. In the end, the fans plumped for Andy Goram (the 'Flying Pig') in goal; Sandy Jardine, Terry Butcher, Richard Gough and John Greig in defence; Brian Laudrup, Paul Gascoigne, Jim Baxter and Davie Cooper in the middle; and Ally McCoist and Mark Hateley up-front. Six true mainstays of the nine-in-a-row team are in that selection, and I think it is fitting that Lauders will always have that great tie with the club.

That team spawned so many characters, such as Andy Goram, or 'The Goalie' as he was also known. It means the world to me that he makes time for me to talk and have a glass of red wine with him at every Rangers dinner we go to. I think people should know just how much he gave to that run of nine successive championships. I personally look at the contributions of all those legendary players and think that the Flying Pig's was the greatest. He wasn't worth just 15 points a season to Rangers as so many say. For me, it was often more than that – more like 20. He was an unbelievable keeper, yet if you saw him with nothing on, you would see he was the oddest-shaped player ever!

Time and again I would watch the opposition striker running through one-on-one, and there to face him would be this strange figure in tan-coloured knee-pads a Sunday cricketer would have thrown away, lurching out to meet another challenge. He'd stay so big for so long and you just knew – just felt in your bones – that he would save it. He nearly always did.

I have heard that team described as a gang of loose cannons and maniacs. Fair enough. Maybe they were, but I saw the team spirit they had at first hand, and it was so special. As Richard Gough famously said, the team that drank together, won together. I see no harm in that, never have. If I was a manager, my team would have their bevvy sessions together not just with my blessing but under my orders. I'd bloody tell them to go. It bonds people.

I can hear the tut-tutting now and the head-shaking about how I am a narrow-minded Scottish bevvy merchant who won't buy into the modern ways of a true pro. Is that right? Well, I am one of the fittest players at Rangers and always at the front of the queue when we are having our body-fat percentage checked and all the other scientific stuff we have to go through these days. But I have learned more about people and groups of footballers when the pints are being sunk, and I still believe in it as a way to bind teams together.

Do you really think that the nine-in-a-row team would have been allowed to take liberties with Walter and Archie Knox? Not a chance. They went on the lash and then sweated it out. They beasted it in training and then walked down from the West of Scotland Cricket Club ground, where they worked out, to Bellahouston to their favourite café to have a bacon roll together!

Now we live a secluded life behind the electric gates at Murray Park, and I suppose it is a sign of the times, but in those days the best team that ever played for the Gers would walk down the main road together and go for a fry-up. That was the mentality then, and as much as it is nice to have the perks of a state-of-the-art training centre, I loved that common touch.

And it applied to us in the reserves as well. After we'd played for the second string at Linlithgow and places like that, Bomber would stop the bus on the way back to get us a chippy as a reward if we'd won. The foreigners would be stunned as I wolfed into my sausage supper, but it was about a laugh and togetherness, and it never harmed us as athletes.

People always say that nine in a row can't happen again, and whilst I agree that we'll never see the likes of that team again, I don't go along with the theory. We have young boys coming through at Rangers now, such as Hutton, Smith and Burke, and they still have a right to dream about things like that. Never say never. The only certainty is I won't win it; I'll be in a wheelchair before then!

There is a nucleus of excellent young Scots at Rangers at the moment, and if I was ever to become manager at Ibrox, then that would always be the way – the Gers have to keep their identity. Then you find the right kind of foreigners who buy into what Rangers are all about, in the way that Dado Pršo did. At first, many of the foreign imports are stunned by what it means to people and how the celebrations go when we achieve something. I think the passion of this club shocks some people, but not Pršo – this is a crazy club, and he is a mental man. He came to Ibrox teetotal, and went away with a drink problem! We spent a lot of time in the treatment room together, and we spoke about how he had found a place that was tailor-made for him. I like to think that as skipper I played a part in helping him find the Rangers way, just as Richard Gough did with new players back in the day.

I never got close to Goughie when he was Gers skipper – I wasn't on the radar of a guy like that – but I remember watching him as his face collapsed in tears when he lifted the trophy that night at Tannadice. He was also in his blazer, because he was injured. That hurt him badly, because he knew he was leaving for less pressure and a new life in America with Kansas City Wizards.

By the middle of the next season, he was back answering an SOS from Walter to try and win the tenth crown, but that campaign always seemed destined to be one big let-down. It was for me. The failed ten in a row was a season of frustration that left me thinking that I should leave Rangers to get first-team football. For two magical months, I played ten games; I was in the thick of it, and I just loved it. Then, after a 1–1 draw at Kilmarnock in the February, I was volleyed out of the team, and Walter opted for experience in the run-in. When I ponder it now, I realise that he had so many options in midfield: Ian Ferguson, Ian Durrant, Brian Laudrup, Jonas Thern, Jörg Albertz, Stuart McCall, and the rest.

Looking back now, I understand why he showed loyalty to the players who had been over the course with him before. But my problem at the age of 20 was that I'd had a taste of it, and I had no appetite for going back to what I'd had before. I looked at guys I was playing with in the Scotland Under-21 side, and it was sickening me. Craig Easton was a regular at Dundee United, and Hearts wouldn't pick a side without Gary Naysmith in it, so why wouldn't Rangers pick me? I couldn't handle it.

But the pressure on the team was horrendous that season. Every time they tugged on the jersey they were having the prospect of another piece of history thrown at them. A lot of them had lived under the cosh for *nine years*, for Christ's sake. Whole generations of Rangers fans – my old man included – had had Celtic's nine successive titles from 1967 to 1976 rubbed right into them. They'd had to swallow lots of stick, but now this was our moment. It was a great time to be a fan, but it put one helluva strain on the players who had to go out there and do it every week, knowing that one mistake might see them branded for the rest of their lives as the man who blew the nine in a row. So when it came to going for the ten in a row, the pressure intensified. Even so, I wanted to be in there, and my sense of hurt grew. I just wanted to play, and I'd hanker for a loan spell, but John McGregor kept telling me, 'Your chance is going to come – stick with it.' I owe him so much.

By the time the end came for Walter's team in May

1998, I had been out in the cold for three months but still harboured hopes he would turn to me again for the Scottish Cup final with Hearts. In the end, I didn't even make the bench. In all honesty, I knew deep down I wasn't going to be involved in that cup final. I had a tantrum about it at the time, but I realised the old guard would all play. This was farewell for a band of brothers – the end of their era. What could Walter do but pick his boys one last time? They had achieved so much for him. I would have done the same.

I was gutted for them that they lost that final 2–1, and I really felt for them as they walked off. I knew they all wanted to go out on a high so much. It was tragic that that team, of all teams, should go out as losers, because that is the one thing they will never be associated with: losing.

For them too – just like for me in 2005–06 – it was a trophyless season. It was a wretched feeling as a Rangers player. It was the first time I'd gone through it since becoming the Gers skipper. I'd left on the high of a Treble and was at Blackburn by the time they ended up with nothing the following campaign. Every campaign that I'd had with the Gers as captain had brought at least one piece of silverware – until 2005–06. I felt so low; it was such a sickening feeling, and I hated it. If I felt like that then, how must those boys have felt seeing ten slip away? That must have been the hardest summer of their football lives, yet they will always be winners in my eyes.

They say in the Old Firm that you're either a king or a clown. Well, I lived in the shadow of those legends, and they were kings. Every one of them.

5

Captain's Log

'He just called us all arseholes.'

Arthur Numan explains Dick Advocaat's
half-time Dutch rant to Barry as Gers trail 3–0
to Shelbourne in his first European game.

I will be cremated in the jersey I wore the night they first made me captain of Rangers, that's how much it means to me. I've already decided I'll be clothed in that light-blue shirt with my skipper's armband on when they send me to the dressing-room in the sky. Morbid? Maybe so, but the arrangements for what I will wear in my coffin have been made. The last will and testament of Barry Ferguson.

I know Dick Advocaat's decision to give me one of the biggest jobs in football is always going to be shrouded in controversy. For every ounce of pride and honour there was for me, there was a ton of pain and humiliation for Lorenzo Amoruso, who was being stripped of the captaincy. Amo had been toiling with his form, and he was becoming the focus for all the criticism that was raining down upon us during a hellish period for the club. Looking back, I reckon Dick just felt that being the skipper was making the world crowd in on top of Lorenzo. Pressure was mounting inside the camp, and we had a vital Champions League game against Galatasaray looming. Dick felt that he had to act; he wanted to get a reaction out of us, to spark something.

His solution would have been hard for anyone to take. I now know how Lorenzo felt: sick to the pit of his stomach. When Paul Le Guen stripped me of the captaincy, I felt like he'd ripped my arm off. So I know what Amo went through. He'd reached the pinnacle of his career winning that armband, and I knew that he was desolate to have it taken away. Yet it had nothing to do with me. The hardest thing about my appointment to the job I now feel I was born to do was that people tried to paint it as some sort of war between Lorenzo and me. He was such a big figure at the club, and they tried to make out that we hated each other, which just wasn't true. We were never bosom buddies, but he congratulated me on the captaincy, and we got on with life. We also went on to be good pals together at Blackburn.

It angered me that there were people trying to make it look as if I had stabbed him in the back – it's simply not my style. If I am going to criticise you as a footballer, then it will be done straight to your face. Amo knew the truth and how highly I thought of him as a player. I didn't like his shaved legs, but I rated him as a player!

I love to see him when he comes up to a game now, and he remains a hero to the fans at Ibrox, as he should be. He has that great Italian way about him: when he talks to you, he shouts and waves his arms all over the place, but he has a big heart and it is in the right place as far as I am concerned. It was sad that people attempted to create animosity and drive wedges between us, but our disagreements were only ever football arguments between two proud competitors. That was it.

These days, I watch those Jonathan Watson *Only An Excuse* sketches that paint me as saying things like, 'Beat it, Amo, ya fud,' or 'Shut it, fannybaws,' and I laugh myself silly, because I did call him a fud once when he tried to steal a free-kick off me! But when the show first started to poke fun at me, it hurt. It made me angry because it depicted me as a brainless street-corner ned, and I felt I was better than that. I would cringe at every sketch. Now I couldn't care less, because I have grown up to be a whole lot more comfortable in my own skin. I can manage my own property portfolio and make my own business decisions, and I don't panic so much about the criticism I take.

There was bitterness surrounding the decision about the armband, though; I can't hide from that fact. It existed, but it was between Lorenzo and Dick. By the end, Amo didn't like him one bit, and he felt he should have been treated far better. But so much hung on that one decision. And when he reflects on his career, Amo will realise that it had taken balls for Dick Advocaat to give him the job in the first place. Lorenzo was a high-profile Italian Catholic being made captain of Rangers, and it would have been far easier for Advocaat to appoint Arthur Numan, a fellow Dutchman and World Cup hero, but this was *his* team now; he would do it his way. I don't think the fact that Lorenzo was a

Catholic even entered Dick's mind – religion never did. He just saw a big presence who knew the club and had already been there a season under Walter Smith. And in Dick's first year, Lorenzo did a great job as captain. It was such a brave call. Mo Johnston had battered down one barrier at the club when he'd U-turned on Celtic and signed for Rangers in 1989 – this was another.

When I took over as captain, we were in the middle of what became known as 'Black October'. It was an awful time for the club. The second phase of the Champions League had been within touching distance, but game by game we contrived to let it slip through our fingers. As a team, we were in the midst of real trouble, yet it didn't ever strike me that I was being thrown into a crisis as the new captain. I just couldn't believe I had the job; I felt as if I had been swept off my feet.

However, that month was nightmarish, although I've been through others like it since. It is very hard to describe what happens at a major football club when all these guys with big egos and so much self-belief start to lose confidence. All of a sudden, the togetherness goes, and some players care only about themselves and how they look to the fans. It's as if you are stuck in a trench, and no matter how hard you scrabble at the walls you can't get a grip and you just keep sinking deeper and deeper.

When we draw at Rangers, it's portrayed as a tragedy – that's when you know you are at a big club. During the 2005–06 season, we went ten games without a win, and it felt like ten years to me. I'd come home from games and not want to take Margaret to dinner; I'd just sit and switch my mobile phone off and brood some more.

I was just a few games into my captaincy when we lost 2–1 at St Johnstone, and Dick must have felt that even the change of leader on the pitch wasn't going to work. He lost the plot in the press after the match and roared, 'There are too many bigheads. They spend too much time writing diaries on their websites or worrying about their golf swings.' He had publicly slaughtered us, and I was shocked. Then I remembered I didn't have a website and didn't play golf, and I didn't feel so bad – Ronald de Boer was gutted, though!

Even so, I was captain of Rangers, succeeding the likes of John Greig, Terry Butcher and Richard Gough – I still have to pinch myself now to realise that it is true. It was that part of the move to Blackburn Rovers that I find hardest to explain: I had a job that meant everything to me, and I gave it up of my own free will.

I did a question-and-answer session during the 2005–06 season at a dinner for Alex Rae's drug rehab charity, and a fan stood up and cut the boozy atmosphere stone-dead. My co-author and I had been working hard on this book, and I was having a rare time that night, watching him try to empty the European wine lake! He was like a piece of cardboard in a black suit, and I remember smiling down on him from the stage, laughing inside because I knew he was buckled and had taken our blow-out day one bottle of Pinot Grigio too far. So, I was firing off one-liners with Alex, Neil Lennon and Alan Thompson beside me, and one Gers fan sobered me up in an instant with a cutting question. He said, 'Listen, if you're such a Rangers man, as you keep telling us, then how could you walk away from being captain?' I completely understood why he asked that question. All I could say to him was that I wanted to erase the 17 months in which I was gone and pretend that they had never happened.

I still can't believe what I did. I am the luckiest man in the world that I got to come back to Rangers, and I will always owe two debts I can never truly repay. The first is to Sir David Murray for sanctioning and bankrolling my return, because he could have turned his back on me. The second is to Alex McLeish for giving me my armband back at the start of the 2005–06 season, although he did the right thing by keeping Fernando Ricksen in the job when I first returned to allow me to play my way back in. The moment Alex made me captain again, my mind went whizzing back five years to the first time Dick Advocaat had taken me into the office and said, 'I am making you Rangers captain, OK?'

I said, 'Aye right, good yin.' I thought he was joking before Arthur Numan, who was with me, dug me in the ribs – it wasn't a wind-up after all. I had the cheesiest grin you have ever seen on my face, and I walked out in a daze. My dad and mates were the same when I hurriedly phoned them. I was stunned; my mind was almost a blank when Dick confirmed it to me, and the team meeting after that is simply a blur. I just remember the wee man standing up and saying, 'We have a new captain, and it is Barry Ferguson.' I was looking at the floor, feeling extremely self-conscious and riddled with nerves. I knew it was one thing landing the job, but I still had to win the respect of the players or I was finished as Rangers captain before I had even begun.

It was the fulfilment of a dream for me, but, at the same time, I knew that Lorenzo was cut up about it. Before I had gone in to see Dick, Amo had taken me into the shower room to tell me he knew what was happening and to say he backed the decision and wanted me to take the job. His face was ashen, but he was brave enough to give me his support.

Following the team meeting, I remember tucking into my pre-match meal and thinking about Galatasaray. Then, I looked at the tablecloth and noticed my napkin had a big 'C' for captain drawn on it in jam! Arthur was at the wind-up again, but it helped break the ice because the atmosphere was electric, every player glancing over furtively to see how I would behave and how Lorenzo would react. It may sound brutal, but I decided there and then that the decision had been made, and that I could only think about myself now and how to cope with the job. I was 22 years old.

We drew that Galatasaray game 0–0, and even though they had Gheorghe Hagi, Jardel and the rest, we should have won. The hairs stood up on the back of my neck when the Champions League theme tune started, and there was one little moment when I took a deep breath before it all started and thought, 'Jesus Christ, some bastard wake me up, I'm dreaming. I'm the captain of Rangers.'

But those were tough days, and when we lost 2–0 at Sturm Graz in the Champions League – having beaten the Austrians 5–0 at Ibrox – the knives were out even inside our own camp. Reserve keeper Jesper Christiansen stuck the blade into Amo for his part in the defeat, and I hated that. I've always tried to avoid what he did that night. Unless the crime is out of order, like spitting or an over-the-top, leg-breaking tackle, you keep your mouth shut about the deeds of your own teammates and stand behind them. People can make their opinions known, but my job is to see that whatever is said is kept inside the four walls of the dressing-room. If you want to kick someone up the arse, you can, but Christiansen was stirring up an atmosphere that was already tinged with desperation.

In time, I would learn to shout at Arthur Numan, Ronald de Boer, Claudio Caniggia and the rest without a second thought, although I was daunted by the prospect at first. The transition was easier than you might think. The experienced players, such as Stefan Klos and the rest, knew I moaned my heart out anyway, and ever since I'd first broken into the team, they'd constantly be saying to me, 'Shut up you little shit!' But being captain wouldn't change me. My desperation for Rangers to succeed meant my mouth just couldn't stay shut, and they grew used to that.

I owe those players, because they accepted me as their skipper even if there were days when my temper exploded – like the day I punched Sergio Porrini in an argument over a bad ball at training. Sergio could look fierce, what with his Mafia hitman's stubble and mad Italian eyes. We were doing a passing drill, and he didn't go for a ball I'd played to him. I said, 'Your turn, in the middle.'

He quickly fired back, 'Fuck off. Who are you talking to? Your fault.' I lost it and smacked him one. All of a sudden we are grappling round the ground, and we were sent home from Stepps where we used to train – a week's wages gone on an Advocaat fine as the red mist descended in one flash of temper.

Two years before Dick made me captain, his arrival at Rangers left me feeling the way so many Gers players felt when Paul Le Guen swept into power for the 2006–07 season. I was living in fear. So many thoughts flashed through my head: he had cash to spend; he might think I was a no-mark; he wasn't going to want me. He killed all my worries with just one phone call. The ten-in-a-row bid was on its last legs at that time, and I had a year to run on my contract, but the chairman wanted to speak to me. He said, 'Come to my office, but don't bring your agent. Bring your mum and dad instead.'

I was intrigued, and we went through to what was then his HQ in an industrial park in South Gyle in Edinburgh. These days, he's moved up in the world: he now controls the Murray empire from a grand office on the corner of Charlotte Square, not too far from Edinburgh Castle. It's all oak panelling and expensive art, and it's more in keeping with someone as minted as he is! Still, back then, we could have been in the boot room at Ibrox for all I cared.

I was nervous as hell when I walked in, but after the small talk, the phone rang and the chairman said, 'It's Dick Advocaat on the line for you.' A clipped Dutch voice came on the line and said, 'Under me you will play. Under me we will build it around you. I want you to stay, and I want to give you a five-year contract.'

I was stunned. I'd seen this bald and fiery guy on television prowling the touchline. I knew his reputation, and now he was manager of Rangers telling this twenty-year-old boy with ten games behind him he was going to be the main man. It was a huge surprise, an even bigger shock than it was on day one when he turned up with a full head of hair!

Looking back, the whole meeting was stage-managed by the chairman, the plan woven together as cleverly as Dick's new barnet. And it worked. I thought it was brilliant and wanted to sign there and then. I felt special that they wanted me so badly, and all my fears and uncertainties just seeped away.

Remember, by that point, with the pressure on Walter Smith to win the ten in a row, I had been out of the first team for three months. But Advocaat's methodical ways and thorough nature meant he'd had a cardboard box of videos shipped out to the Netherlands – it was full of tapes of the reserve games I'd been playing in.

Right from the start, I knew Advocaat was going to be good for me. He was straight talking, he had a dry sense of humour and he knew the game. He became a constant (and pudgy) presence in his Rangers tracksuit, bustling about with a whistle and stopwatch around his neck. He never missed a training session.

In previous pre-seasons, I had run until I had dropped, sometimes until I threw up, but now it was more controlled with game situations and shorter, sharper work. I felt the work was easier, and yet I got fitter; he was opening up my mind to a different way of football, and I felt so fresh. This guy believed in me so much, and the confidence was rising inside of me because of that.

When you live on the road, as football teams do at times, one of the key decisions a manager can make is deciding on who will be room-mates. I wanted a Scot, someone with the same sense of humour who would put up with my moods and keep me sane. Instead, I got Arthur Numan.

He'd just arrived from PSV Eindhoven for £5.5 million after having starred for the Netherlands at the 1998 World Cup in France – Dick had just given me a father figure. There would be times when we were stuck in hotels and I was bored out of my skull desperate to slink away for a fly beer, and an arm would come out of the door and drag me back in by my collar. I think the wee man used his head there; he saw what I had inside me, and he knew Arthur would be a calming influence.

Still the fines came, and Dick never hesitated to dish them out no matter who you were. That's the penalty I have always found the toughest – when they hit you in the pocket. Mobile phones were banned, and all of a sudden we were together a lot more. We all ate at the same time every day, and you couldn't leave the table until Dick had finished every last scrap. You couldn't even start until he had – it was like boot camp. There were times when he would mop up his gravy with his bread or have a final Kit-Kat just to wind you up. I'd be sitting there thinking, 'Hurry up, you little Dutch bastard, I want to go home,' and he'd have a mischievous glint in his eye as he savoured his meal.

However, when I look back, I realise that he did all of this for a reason: he'd had to pull together a team in no time at all, and he needed to create togetherness. Nowadays, I hate to see people dash in for shower and leave five minutes after training. Some people don't appreciate how lucky they are to have a job like this.

In the future, people will look back at Murray Park and

realise that whilst he might not have slapped the cement on the bricks himself, Dick Advocaat built that place – at least in my mind. He wanted that sort of home to improve his players, and he wouldn't have come to Rangers if it hadn't been agreed, but the chairman backed him up.

David Murray had a great relationship with Dick. After all the turmoil he has gone through with managers during his 18 years of being at the helm, I think it demonstrates his decency that there have only been five Gers bosses. And every one of them before Paul Le Guen – Souness, Smith, Advocaat and McLeish – was there to sit together at David's son's wedding.

Dick had around £30 million to build his first side, and he found players of the quality of Arthur Numan, Giovanni van Bronckhorst (Gio), Rod Wallace and the maverick that was Gabby Amato. They had one thing in common: a true winning mentality. Sure, there was a few bob wasted, but every manager makes signings that don't work out.

We started out under Advocaat against Shelbourne in the UEFA Cup at Tranmere Rovers' Prenton Park; it was 22 July 1998 and half the Gers fans were still on the Costa del Sol watching it in beach bars. I remember being distracted before the game, because it was all kicking off outside. There were scraps between rival supporters and the police in the street beside the ground, and I could even hear it in the dressing-room. There was an ugly atmosphere when we ran out, and we were only seven minutes in when Porrini deflected one into his own net. By half-time, we were 2–0 down to a team from the Irish League. I thought to myself, 'Christ, they'll feed my contract through the shredder.'

The Gers fans must have been wondering about Dick at half-time, but he was calm after a bout of swearing in Dutch. I was staring at the floor whispering to Arthur, 'What is he saying?' He wouldn't tell me until after the game.

Even after the break, things didn't improve straight away, and we lost another to some guy called Pat Morley to go three down. But then Albertz nicked a penalty, and it sparked us at last: we got two goals from Amato, one from Gio and another spot-kick from the Hammer, and we escaped. After we'd won 5–3 and it had all calmed down, I begged Arthur to tell me what the gaffer had been ranting on about. He said, with a shrug, 'He called us all arseholes.'

Advocaat was so driven and passionate. And he was decisive, something I loved. If it wasn't working after even 20 minutes, he would change things and make a substitution. Jesus, how that kept you on your toes.

Dick knew the midfield position and, like Graeme Souness later in my career, he was great at telling me how to find angles for my passes. He would teach me little things the fans might not notice, such as opening your body up to receive a pass to give yourself one more split second to play the next ball and kill a defence. And one day he said to me, 'I just wish I'd had you in my team as a kid.' I was puzzled because I still felt like a kid, but I think he saw something in me and wished he could have been there to mould me from the start. I think I have grown into the captain he wanted me to be; I've grown up to be better at handling it all in my eyes.

It was an education playing for Dick, and that first season gave me a taste for European football that has stayed with me. After the near disaster against Shelbourne, we drew

PAOK of Greece, and Salonika turned out to be one of the scariest places I have ever been – it was dark and threatening as we guarded our 2–0 win from the first leg. Before the game, there was a hulking monster on the pitch dressed like Conan the Barbarian. He would thump a drum and all their fans would scream – it was terrifying. We got out of the place with a 0–0 draw, and I looked around me and thought we now had players with real courage.

After then beating Israel's Beitar Jerusalem, we landed Bayer Leverkusen. We won 2–1 in Germany thanks to Jonatan Johansson's winner. JJ was a great example of the ability Advocaat had for getting the most out of players. Jonatan had previously looked like a winger with pace but a clumsy touch, but Dick adapted him and used him through the middle. The kid Walter Smith got for £500,000 from Estonian football would become a guy we got £3.75 million from Charlton for, and that's a side of Advocaat too often overlooked.

Dick was also able to help me so much because his video analysis was perfect. He'd show me how much time someone liked on the ball and get me fired up to close him down and hound him. And he knew how to do that because he'd been like that as a player himself. He could pick out an opposition player's weakness, and it is unfair to look back and say he achieved what he did at Gers simply because of the money he had.

After we beat Leverkusen, I began to realise I could cope against teams at that level. I was not overawed to be facing the likes of Emerson and Ze Roberto, despite the fact I was just a baby in their world. I just had a determination and feeling that I would show them what Barry Ferguson had. I'd make sure they remembered my name, respect me. I didn't want to learn from them. I thought, 'They can learn from me. Fuck them.' I know how this sounds, but I want my book to be different from the nice words and platitudes so many players dish out.

That European run ended against Parma with Porrini's red card, and it was a crying shame, especially as it meant I finished the match with my tongue hanging out at right-back in the Italian sunshine as we lost 3–1. It was over, but I would be better for the experience. And I'll never forget my last image of that first campaign in the sort of arena I love the most. I walked into the stadium after the match, gutted, and there was Gianluigi Buffon – the world's greatest goalkeeper who would later cost Juventus £32 million – lounging against the doorpost of their dressing-room. He'd taken his goalie top off, revealing a Superman T-shirt underneath it, and he was having a *cigarette*. He just looked at me, dragged on his Marlboro Light, shrugged and said, '*Come sta?*' I nodded and thought, 'Now that is cool.'

I tried to take in every detail on days like that, desperate to make sure I didn't let it all pass me by. After all, I'd yearned to be a Rangers regular. But it would have been difficult to forget that first season as it seemed to throw up one dramatic landmark after another. It was proving to be some journey. For example, my first league goal came when I was playing against my brother Derek who was with Dunfermline at that time. I gave him a couple of digs, he gave me the message back and I scored my opener in the league for the club, but the whole day was almost surreal.

People ask me whether it was a dream for my family to see us play together at Rangers, but it was enough that we'd both played for the club, especially for my dad. That day almost sent him over the edge; he had no idea who to support.

Advocaat opened the door to give me a life in football, and he will always mean the world to me. But I am intrigued as to how he will be remembered by the Gers support. Will it be as the man who inherited a team that was broken up and then won five trophies out of six? Will they always point to the money he spent? I like to think that if Dick came back to Glasgow for a Rangers function, then the place would be on its feet. I think it should be.

I don't need to leap to his defence over his departure, because if you had £70 million given to you to spend on players then you would do it too. Yes, there were mistakes, but John Hartson's failed medical at Ibrox was not Advocaat's fault, let's be clear on that, and neither was the £12 million price tag for Tore André Flo. Those were the prices then – they'd gone mental. And in football there is hype: was it really £12 million, or was it nearer £8 million? My transfer to Blackburn goes down in the books and on the websites as £7.5 million, but it was less, and my coming back is quoted as £4.5 million when it was nearer £2 million. It is a media game of sums. Dick would admit to you himself that he made bad buys at times, but if I was the boss with £70 million in my pocket, then I know that five out of my twenty signings would not work. Some players don't settle or they are swallowed up by the intensity of the football here – this is one of the hardest leagues to play in whatever the knockers say. The away games, in particular, can be a nightmare for foreigners. Early in the 2005–06 season, I looked around at Aberdeen when we lost 3–2, and I could see genuine shock on the faces of people like Julien Rodriguez – seasoned pros. He couldn't believe the passion and the pace, and he had played in a Champions League final for Monaco against Porto. Scotland is a unique place to play; it is a small league, perhaps, but one with two monsters in it. Dick came to realise that and famously said that four years in the Gers hotseat was like eight anywhere else.

I think Advocaat saw Martin O'Neill catching a wave of popularity, the way he had when he had first come in. The signings O'Neill made back then were either British or with a British mentality, and I looked at what he did and thought that was the way I would go if I was a boss. Yes, you might find better technique with a foreigner but not the desire in some cases, and that is what you need in the SPL.

The following season, O'Neill began haunting him all over again, and I was dismayed when some Gers fans screamed 'coward' when Dick decided to take the offer of the move upstairs to make way for Alex McLeish. Not me. I liked it that Advocaat realised it was his time to go; he could have hung on, but he knew the dressing-room needed a change, and he made way.

I went from being an insecure kid, who'd first heard Dick's voice crackle on the end of a telephone line, telling me I was important all of a sudden, to becoming a man. And Eck inherited a better footballer. I now believed in myself and knew I could go to Bayer Leverkusen or Parma and have them worry about what I was going to do on the ball. That was my focus then, and it still is. I don't think I am the king of the world, but I could be playing against Diego Maradona, and I wouldn't bother my arse. That's not disregard for my rivals, it's just the way I was bred to think by Advocaat. And that is also why any special opponent's jersey I swap in a European game goes to my missus Margaret's dad. It means little to me to collect strips like some anorak of European football; the jerseys I treasure are the Rangers ones. My first game, my first as captain, the ones I have worn every time we have won a trophy, those are the jerseys I have had framed for my grandchildren to inherit and look at – the ones that belong to Rangers and Scotland. They are the mementos I want to have when I am 60 – not some Parma away strip.

6

The Battle of Bothwell Bridge

'You either grow up now or you go the wrong way, the easy way. It's up to you.'

Dick Advocaat lays it on the line, then fines a scarred Barry the maximum two weeks' wages.

Smash! A bottle clattered into the left-hand side of my face. Someone spat venom and was mouthing off hatred at me, and my head was swimming for a couple of seconds. Unsteady on my feet, I dodged away from more blows, cleared my vision and waded back in. What would become known in every newspaper as The Battle of Bothwell Bridge was unfolding in a nightmare of street violence around me, and I refused to end up a defenceless casualty left lying on the pavement.

I could feel the blood trickling down my face, and when I saw the wound over my left eye in the bathroom mirror the next morning I felt an icy shiver run down my spine. If that bottle had hit home another inch inwards from where it struck me, then it could have taken my eye, and my career would have been over.

Eight hours earlier, I had trudged off the Parkhead turf, sent off in disgrace with nine minutes left in a whirlwind Old Firm game that we had lost 6–2. The Celtic fans were in their glory, baiting me, taunting me, just loving it. I snapped and flicked a V-sign at them on my way off. Idiot. I thought life couldn't get any worse than that. I was wrong.

I made a fateful decision after the game that had seen Martin O'Neill's derby debut and one of the most soul-destroying houndings we had ever suffered in an Old Firm match. I decided that having a few pints to drown my sorrows was the answer. Before we took that hiding at Parkhead, I had arranged to go for a drink after the game at the Bothwell Bridge Hotel with Derek and some friends. When the game turned sour on me with that shock result and a sickening red card, I was going to cancel our plans and stay in – we'd been humped after all. But I was 22 and stupid, and I thought I would be safe in the Bothwell Bridge Hotel. I knew the place, and I wanted to have some dinner and blow the froth off a couple – escape from what I'd done on the park.

Going out that night was one of the worst calls of my life, and thousands of urban myths have grown up from what happened. Now, at the age of 29, I simply wouldn't go out after a game like that, but it was a bad day at the office, and I wanted to forget about it for a while with a few drinks. I wanted to talk to my brother who had been through it all before – have him tell me where I had gone wrong, put an arm around my shoulder and console me.

Derek talked me round, and the atmosphere in the place was fine – there was no trouble in the hotel. Not a cross word passed between my group and the Celtic fans who were in the bar, just the usual slagging and banter. Then we decided to call it a night and walked out. We couldn't get a taxi outside reception because there was a wedding on, and it was busy. So we phoned one instead and told them to pick us up at the library, which is just down Bothwell Main Street, around 400 yards from the hotel. I walked out with a mate of mine called John, who had done the odd job in my garden. I turned to walk past the church and heard a couple of shouts of abuse, then BANG! It was all kicking off.

I wasn't drunk, far from it. Every guy near the scene that night had another story to sell to the papers afterwards, and so much of it was bollocks. The truth is those shouts came, then I looked back at my gardener who was getting a doing from two guys. If you are any kind of friend, you run back and help. What was I supposed to do? Think I was too famous to go back, and run away? Not a chance. I couldn't stand there and watch my friend being attacked. It is for others to judge me, but I think that would have been wrong. You jump in and ask questions later. If it ever happens to me again, God forbid, I will expect any pal with me to bail in and help me out. If they don't? Fuck them, I won't speak to them again – I will disown them.

It makes no odds if you're a footballer or a gardener; it's not about that. It's about looking after your pals. That's the way I was brought up, and there was no debate in my mind what course of action I had to take. I had to wade in, and I did, both fists flying, trying to get them off him.

I can still remember the scene vividly. The initial shock had worn off by that point, but as I glanced around, I couldn't believe what I was seeing. Other folk had rushed out of pubs, sniffing trouble and spoiling for a fight after a day on the sauce. There were people coming from all directions – it was a full-blown street battle.

I then had a moment of clarity. There were guys with their belts off, swinging their buckles as weapons and swishing them through the air to batter each other on the head. 'Jesus Christ,' I thought, 'I shouldn't be here,' but there was no escape. I was in the thick of it. And that was when the bottle did its damage with a sickening crunch on my temple that sent me staggering sideways. But I didn't have time to go down and worry about it; God knows what might have happened then.

I tried to shake the blow off, forget the blood and keep swinging, because there were people trying to do me in. After that, I admit I lost it: I was punching out for fun. It wasn't like any of the Mike Tyson videos I'd pored over, indulging my love of boxing. No one was ducking and diving or bobbing and weaving, picking their punches. This was street fighting for survival, and I refused to let myself be dragged away, instead running into the scuffles to try and help my mates and brother.

In the aftermath, the best story they peddled was that I had wandered into the Bothwell Bridge with my Rangers tracksuit on, but that was complete and utter nonsense. We were sponsored by Nike at that point, and I had one of their tracksuits on, but I read some reports that said I'd gone home to change into my Rangers stuff especially to taunt people. Jesus, give me a break. Was I wearing a Gers tracksuit and falling about pissed? Lies, total lies. The one bit that rang true? That I was running back like a maniac, trying to get involved again, and being dragged away. That was true. The anger did run away with me, and I had careered out of control. Gone. Why? Because I could see the bastards who had started it all sneering at me, and I wanted to shut them up. I was that angry.

I have no pride about what happened that night – not a shred. I am thoroughly ashamed of it, and I was wrong to go out. I should never have gone beyond the front door. I was a fool, and I let down myself, my family and Rangers, but I learned my lesson. I realise now that after one of those games, when you've lost the way we did, you can't go out to places like that, which is sad in some respects. Still, it was an awful piece of judgement to go out after I had been sent off, and it was my own stupid mistake.

But I don't care what anyone says. People moan that a man in my position shouldn't have got involved. Listen, that's the part of the trouble I will *never* regret. I protected my friend, and that's what mates do. I didn't cause that fight, but I wasn't going to run away from it. I have learned not to go out at a time like that, but if a similar situation ever happened again, I would jump in again. Sorry, I wouldn't walk away and let my friend take a pasting just to protect the name of Barry Ferguson. We were outnumbered. What kind of a man would I have been if I had jumped a wall and run away to avoid a front-page headline that might have damaged my precious reputation? The answer is I would have been no sort of a man.

But I will never be able to escape the fact that I shouldn't have put myself in that situation in the first place. After we took a beating like that, tensions were always going to be running high. I could have stayed behind closed doors and had a quiet drink – that's what I'd do now.

The game had started at 1 p.m. in an attempt to cut down on trouble, but there were still 62 arrests after the game. It kicked off across the west of Scotland that night: there was an attempted murder linked to the match, and some poor guy was badly beaten with sticks and golf clubs after being chased by a posse of men in Maryhill. I put myself into the mix of that sort of night, and that was indefensible, but I have never been allowed to forget it.

The incident even became a cheap-shot gag for Labour MSP Michael McMahon, who represented Hamilton North and Bellshill. In a debate about conservation in the Scottish Parliament, he pointed out the area's value and said, 'The Battle of Bothwell Bridge was of great significance in respect of the involvement of the Covenanters. That battle is not to be confused with the battle of the Bothwell Bridge Hotel, which involved Barry Ferguson, some Celtic supporters and a kebab.'

I was fair game, and when I look back to that day, I try to see myself through other people's eyes. I can focus on how I looked as the sun scorched down on Parkhead and we walked into that arena. I remember that I'd had a No.1 with the clippers at the barbers, which was shorter than usual – I got it shaved right into my skull. Walking out looking like a skinhead seems to attract referees towards you.

Parkhead is always a cauldron, but it just seemed to be cranked up beyond belief that day. There were so many factors: a roasting hot day; O'Neill's first Old Firm game with all the hype and hope the Irishman had brought with him; and we were right at the start of the season with everyone still champing at the bit.

Celtic came out of the gates snarling and tore at our throats. Within *11 minutes*, we were 3–0 down. My head was spinning. Chris Sutton, Stiliyan Petrov, Paul Lambert: they'd all scored, and I just thought, 'What the fuck is going on here?'

It was a nightmarish game. Usually when you go to their place, you try to settle in and take the sting out of the match for the first 20 minutes to silence their fans, but they'd just battered us, and we were all over the place. Bobby Petta was terrorising Fernando Ricksen, and Dick dragged him off after just 22 minutes, hurling Tugay on to try and stem the flow, but every single one of us was having an absolute howler, me included. It was gut-wrenching, just awful.

Claudio Reyna gave us a glimmer of hope before half-time, but Henrik Larsson put them 4–1 shortly after the break, and Billy Dodds scored a penalty as we scrambled for some sense of respect. Then Larsson chipped a classic finish over Stefan Klos, and I knew 27 August 2000 was going to be a day the Celtic fans remembered for the rest of their lives. I could see their club video already.

I got booked for a late tackle on Petrov, and with about ten minutes remaining, I thought Alan Stubbs had fouled me on the edge of the box, so I fell and grabbed the ball. I don't know if the referee Stuart Dougal was going to give the decision or not, but the next thing I knew, Jonathan Gould careered out of his goal waving imaginary cards in the air and saying I should be booked again.

That is one gesture I hate from a fellow pro; it makes my blood boil. I detest seeing it when I watch foreign games and there's a foul. If the victim isn't doing three forward rolls and yelping in imagined pain, then he is pleading with the ref to get the cards out again. It's low behaviour. It has been imported into our game with the influx of foreign players, and I can't stand it. The players get fouled, and they are whining to the official, 'Book him, book him.' I hate that – leave it to the ref.

Now I had my own Scotland teammate doing it, and we were about to join up for World Cup duty in Latvia. I was seething at him, and I thought, 'You prick, Gouldy.' I was sickened, and I had a shove at him. It was handbags really, but for the first time in my Rangers career, the red card came out of the ref's pocket – I was right in the shit. Perhaps Dougal was reaching for the red anyway for deliberate handball, but Gouldy made sure of it, and that's what disappoints me even now. The place erupted, and the cheers were deafening. I'd given them what they were desperate to see, and I just wanted the ground to swallow me up so they didn't have the satisfaction of seeing me disappear down the tunnel.

The walk from where I was sent off on the edge of the box to the sanctuary of the mouth of the tunnel was about 100 yards, but it felt like 100 miles to me that day. Celtic's entire support was laughing at me, at our club and decking themselves at the 5–2 scoreline when I got my marching orders. They were having a day they would never forget – I just couldn't stomach it. Was I thinking rationally at that point? Hell, no. I was seething at myself and how the match had gone, and I flicked a V-sign at the fans taunting me on the way off. Another bad move. Jimmy Bell put his arm around me to get me out of there and hustled me down the tunnel. When I got inside, I booted the dressing-room door open, took one of my boots off and launched it at the wall. Then I just sat with a towel over my head and wished that I could somehow magic myself out of that place.

I have had that empty feeling after being thrown out of a game five times in my Rangers career now, and there is always a feeling of uselessness. I want someone to blame, but deep down I know that I usually only have myself to thank. I have no idea what I am like to referee as a player – a headache I would imagine. But not dirty: the times I have gone it has been because of frustration or mistimed tackles rather than a naked attempt to go out and do someone.

I have respect for the top referees, such as Hugh Dallas. I felt he was simply in a league of his own because I could talk to him during a game and have a relationship. Too often now they are ignorant, arrogant or programmed like robots to just ignore you and talk down to you. They could learn from Dallas or Mike McCurry, who both have a way with players that helps the game flow and keeps a measure of regard between you and the guy with the whistle.

When you've been given an early bath at Parkhead, you are divorced from reality in the away dressing-room as the game rages on without you; you can't hear as much as you would think. It felt like a prison cell to me that day. I heard one more muffled roar bang on full-time – Sutton making it six – but by then I was in the deepest pits of depression. I wished that I had cemented someone and been sent off for that rather than trying to grab the ball off Jonathan Gould and shoving him. It was all just so shabby and pointless.

I went to the Scotland camp after that, and Craig Brown kept us away from the media, but behind the scenes, Gould and I had to sort it out. His defence was that he had lost it in the heat of the moment, and I had to accept that. There was no point causing a riot when we had an important game in Riga coming up. I would hope, though, that when Gouldy looks back he is disappointed in himself at having behaved like that – I would be.

After the game, Dick tried to give us all some home truths, but I didn't absorb a single word of it. I had my head in my hands thinking, 'What the fuck have I done?' I'd given all those who I felt had an agenda against me at times the bullets they were looking for. They were going to have a field day, and it was all my fault.

If the game was bad, what followed was worse. By the next morning, I was plastered over every newspaper in the land, tagged a thug and a ned. In so many ways, that reputation still sticks to me even now.

The police came to question me when I got home after the 'Wild West' street brawl, and within an hour of getting back, I was sitting on my stairs with my eye cut speaking to CID. Then the press arrived, and I had it all; I was living in the middle of a circus. There hadn't been a policeman there when the fight had kicked off, but before I knew it, I'd been grassed on. And mine was the first door they knocked on after the fight had broken up and everyone had scampered. In the end, the charges were dropped, but I told the police to do their worst because by that point I was in a world of trouble anyway, and I felt like I was past caring.

After a sleepless night sitting up with Margaret and worrying about the consequences, I had to think what to do next. Should I stay holed up in my house like a criminal? I thought that would be pointless. I had to get to Ibrox and tell the club what had happened. I cuddled little Kyle on the way out of the door to give me strength, and then I walked out. Another mistake. They accused me of using him as a human shield, and I had my house and kid on the front page of the papers. I hated it.

Day after day, the stories grew arms and legs: I was kicking in car windows; I'd drunk 15 pints; I was battering people with my belt despite the fact I had been wearing a tracksuit. It was spiralling out of control. Slowly but surely, a picture was being painted: Barry Ferguson, spoiled footballer, thick ned, bevvy merchant and thug.

I went into Ibrox and asked the medical staff to look at the wound beside my eye, but it turned out that it had been open for too long to be stitched. I then went to Dick's office and said to him, 'I've been involved in a fight. I could go into details and try to justify myself, but I shouldn't have been there. I admit I was wrong, and I apologise. I have let you and Rangers down. I'm sorry. Fine me, but fine me for being out, not for defending my pal.'

I knew the maximum fine of two weeks' wages was coming, and sure enough he doled it out, and I took it on the chin. Dick's lecture was straight and to the point. He simply said, 'This is now about how you react to what has happened. You either grow up or you go the wrong way, the easy way. It's up to you. I am disappointed in you, not angry with you. You have simply disappointed me to go out after we lost like that.'

Even as I was holding my hands up to being bang out of order for going out, I still told Dick that if something like that happened again on a night out I would jump in. I pray I never have to lift my fists to defend anyone again, but if I need to do it to stand beside my mates, then I will.

My reputation as both a player and a person was battered from pillar to post in the weeks that followed what happened at Bothwell Bridge. It was the worst 24 hours of my life, and when it is brought up even now, I realise that it has labelled me for life in some people's eyes. I am a ned to them – a wild boy from Hamilton with no idea of how to behave.

It crossed my mind in the time after the fight that Rangers might kick me out the door. It had happened to bigger and better players than me – it could happen again. I'd seen Derek, Durranty, Coisty and Ted McMinn go through the same thing, and now I was facing it. I worried myself sick about what people were thinking about me, and I knew people were staring at me everywhere I went. But all that matters now is that those who are close to me know who I really am.

The wound is still there because I didn't get it stitched, and I can feel it on my eyebrow. I sometimes give it a rub and think back to what happened if I want to remember the lessons. But overall, I just want to forget it. I felt like a piece of shit after that night – like I had become worthless, even if the papers kept calling me the £10 million-rated thug. I'd been put up on the pedestal as a rising star, and it was being booted away. I was being knocked down, and people now said that I was an out-of-control lunatic.

I have talked about The Battle of Bothwell Bridge very little since it happened, because the whole episode makes me angry and sad. It is depressing that in some people's eyes that night now represents the essence of what I am about. I hope that people realise that I'm a good husband, father and mate to those I trust and value – not some senseless ned.

I had to react the right way after that with Advocaat watching my every move. I had to show him that I wasn't some sort of mindless thug. Two months later, he made me the captain of Rangers at the age of 22. That meant the world to me as I must have shown him something to confirm that I was made of better stuff than what the papers wrote about me after that terrible night.

NB The real Battle of Bothwell Bridge happened in 1679 when a force of 10,000 government forces, led by the Duke of Monmouth and Graham of Claverhouse, dispersed 6,000 Covenanters who had gathered at Hamilton. There was no Old Firm game that day.

7

Hell on the Hill – Heaven at Hampden

'Let's get into these bastards.'

Berti Vogts, Scotland manager, before
facing his native Germany at Hampden.

'This is fucking unacceptable!' Paul Lambert booted in the dressing-room door, foaming at the mouth. A quiet, thoughtful man transformed into some sort of raving, bulging-eyed lunatic, screaming at people to try and drag some sort of response out of them. Welcome to life inside a football nightmare: the Faroe Islands 2, Scotland 0. And it was only half-time.

I still shudder when I think back to that day as we set out on the long road to try to make Euro 2004. I was in a daze, just walking around that pokey little dressing-room – the place looked like a village Sunday league ground, which was pretty fitting: we were playing like a pub team. No, sorry, that's a slur on pub teams.

I kicked the wall in a fury, the arguments started, angry voices all merged into one and I looked to Berti Vogts. He was in a state of shock, staring at us in sheer disbelief; he didn't say a word. This was supposed to be a new era, but it wasn't. It was a fucking shambles.

Everyone of that Scotland team was a full-time professional, and here we were against fishermen, a hi-fi salesman, some guy that flogged fridges and a primary school teacher called John Petersen who had scored two goals in the first-half of the game of his life. Embarrassment, hurt, humiliation: Christ, I felt the lot. We were playing boys who trained twice a week after working a ten-hour shift at their day jobs, and they could have been beating us by even more.

It was live on TV with the nation watching back at home on a Saturday afternoon. I kept seeing the scoreline in my head and imagining a Scotland fan like my old man, a roofer who had worked all week, sitting at home with his hard-earned carry-out watching such a terrible performance.

The Faroe Islands is an outpost; we'd flown in – on landing, the plane had almost tumbled over a cliff at the end of a tiny runway – then taken the ferry from Torshavn and stumbled onto the bus to get to Toftir. I was trying to be professional, but a little part of me was thinking, 'What the hell am I doing in a place like this?'

Then the game started on a forbidding mountainside with the rain slanting in, and we played like that; it was just horrible. I'd spoken to some of the fans and heard all the tales of the bizarre journeys they'd made on fishing trawlers and all the rest to get there. In return, we'd given them 45 minutes they'd never forget, all right – I was ashamed of myself.

Berti had my respect. He was a World Cup winner as a player, and he won Euro 96 as a manager for Germany – he deserved my respect. But that day was when the language barrier and all the problems that it created came crashing down on us. We needed a manager to grab us by the front of those stupid pinstriped Scotland jerseys we were wearing and kick some arses to try and boot some life into us.

I knew the enormity of what we were looking at as players; it could end international careers, wreck reputations, harm people. I looked at players like Stephen Crainey at left-back and feared for him; big Kevin Kyle up front was missing chances and having a torrid time. They weren't ready for the slaying in the media that I knew was coming to us. We ended up in a total mess. Paul Dickov came on at right wing-back, the smallest guy I had ever seen play there. He was out of position, out where he shouldn't have been. After the game, he was out of the Scotland team for two years. So much went wrong that day.

Half-time was harrowing for me, to be honest. Berti needed to get messages across, sit the team down and give us both barrels, but he didn't have the command of the language to do it. In a one-to-one situation, he could tell me what he wanted, but in the frenzy of the dressing-room he was just lost. Deep down, I had feared for the experiment of a foreign manager and always worried that it wouldn't work for Scotland. Berti needed to get torn into us, but Tommy Burns was trying to put the message across instead. I wondered what he wanted from us: was TB getting what the manager really wanted to say to us across? Tommy found that hard. I found it difficult to cope with, too, and despite the respect I will always have for Berti Vogts, it made my mind up – we should *always* have a Scottish manager to lead the national side. That has been reaffirmed under both Walter Smith and now Alex McLeish as we got to as high as 14th in the FIFA rankings when we were down at 88th at one point under Berti.

I watched Sven-Göran Eriksson and the record England built under him. It seemed to work for them for a while, but he had a crop of exceptional players, and as a nation they are different from us.

We scrambled a point after Lambo fired one in off someone's heels, and I lofted in a late equaliser. I couldn't even feel happy about it – we had been a sick joke. It was the first competitive game for me under the Vogts regime, and even though we'd lurch on and have some highs under Berti it was in many ways the beginning of the end for him.

It is on days like we had on that hellish hillside that the shit really hits the fan. It is at those moments that your togetherness as a group of players is tested, and as the recriminations started after that result I knew there was going to be trouble. The press were filleting Berti, pounding him for explanations, and he blurted out that Christian Dailly and David Weir had played as if they had just been introduced. Was it down to a lack of command of the language? I don't know. I just know the end result was that Berti slaughtered big Davie after the match, and that ended it for the big man with Scotland. He thought about it and then he wrote a letter I know would have pained him, telling the SFA he wasn't prepared to put up with what had been said – he wouldn't be back.

For all the loyalty and sympathy I felt for Berti, I have to say here and now that I think David was correct to do what he did. He certainly had no argument from me. He had every right to think, 'Was it only me out there?' There were 11 of us who failed the nation that day. Now he has returned to play for Scotland, and I think that bringing him back was one of the cleverest moves Walter made during his time in charge, because the big man has been a rock for Scotland, even if he is old enough to be my dad!

Like David, my pride in being Scottish is that we are

unique – in truth just a little bit mental. Berti couldn't get his head around that. But if there is a part of being Scottish that I would change, it would be our love of a hard-luck story. In my eyes, a loser is neither glorious nor brave – he's just a loser. That's why defeat hurts me so much and why at the end of that Euro 2004 campaign I was ready to deck the man who made me at Ibrox and first appointed me captain of the club.

The play-offs to make Portugal had started so well: James McFadden's goal at Hampden put us one up against the Netherlands and somehow we clung on to win. But losing the second leg 6–0 in Amsterdam left me feeling hollow inside. I had this growing sense of sadness, and I was becoming haunted by the belief that these tournaments were always going to pass me by. So I didn't need Dick Advocaat coming into the Scotland dressing-room, which was like a morgue, and patting me on the head. He ruffled my hair and tried to console me. I felt like punching him. It was arrogant and condescending, in my eyes, and I thought, 'Fuck off. Where were you on Saturday when we won 1–0 at Hampden?'

He has done everything for me in my career – everything. I have so much time for him, but he disappointed me that night. I know it sounds churlish, but we had been pummelled, and I didn't want someone messing with my hair and saying, 'Unlucky, son.' I was spewing, sick to the stomach at that result, and Dick knew it. He was maybe trying to be genuine, but I just wanted to volley him. My teammates were looking at me; I could feel them glancing over and being embarrassed for me. Then a few just muttered, 'Bastard.' I looked at the floor; another major tournament had gone from us.

That 6–0 loss is what motivates me as a Scotland player

now. I couldn't bear to experience that feeling again. I have to believe we can be better than that and give the country a team to be proud of once more. I am determined that whatever happens we won't crumble like that again.

I think I once lost 6–0 when I was a kid at Mill United Boys Club but never as a professional. We'd gone out there with the aim of keeping it tight for twenty minutes, but ten minutes from half-time we were 3–0 down, and we just couldn't recover. The scary thing is it could have been *more* than six. It was shameful; the margin of the defeat hurt every one of us in that dressing-room so badly.

There was criticism after that game – heavy criticism – but I expected it. We deserved it. Yet I remember reading words to the effect of, 'Where was our supposed captain? You wonder why he has the armband at all.' That kind of stuff lives in the back of my mind and drives me on, even if it deeply upsets my family and friends. It hurts, but I can live with it. Shit will get heaped on me as skipper, and I am big enough to take it.

We got thrashed, I expected heat, but there are those in the media who make it personal. I was 90 minutes away from Euro 2004 – just think of that – and 1–0 up after beating the Netherlands at Hampden. Say it like that, and it sounds close, but the truth is we went to Amsterdam and were torn to shreds. They battered us, and even now I find the memory of that night bitterly disappointing.

I didn't even watch one minute of the European Championships that summer. I know how that sounds from a footballer, and there will be others, good pals of mine, who studied every game. But I went on holiday with Margaret and the kids to Spain, and I binned it – I wasn't interested. I wanted to be there myself, not watching it in a pub. I don't like sitting there like some bar-room genius thinking, 'So near and yet so far.'

Berti's brief had been to get us to the finals or, more realistically, to reach the play-offs and take our chances in the shoot-out that follows – we did. We got a bad draw and got murdered. After that, his aim was to get us to the World Cup in Germany. When the qualifiers started, a 0–0 draw at home with Slovenia wasn't the worst result, but then we lost a scruffy game 1–0 to Norway. Moldova loomed, and the dread was settling in your bones.

After a wretched 1–1 draw in Chisinau, I could sense that Berti was done for. The results were piling up on us. We'd draw with Germany and beat Holland and then play some superb football before the lights went out one night in Valencia when we were drawing 1–1 with Spain in a friendly. Then we'd come up with a performance like Moldova.

For all that the Republican Stadium was a hellhole – it was freezing, the place was a dive and the pitch was appalling – you just can't live on excuses as a player. That is all they are: a way for weak players to explain why they have failed. I try to stop those sort of quotes from dropping out of my mouth; it's bollocks. The truth is, Scotland should beat teams like Moldova. Always.

I have enough pride and belief in the team to still think like that, even though we only drew with Moldova. We'd gone behind before Stevie Thompson scrambled an equaliser. We had been a sad imitation of what we can be, and I will never forget the look on the manager's face when we walked in. Some of the Tartan Army were hanging over the tunnel screaming at us, and Berti even had to sit amongst those baying fans, because he'd been banned from the touchline after our defeat by Norway the Saturday before. There were supporters at the end of their tether that night – it was ugly.

As skipper, I had to stop and do a TV interview for Chick Young, and I swore at one of the punters hurling abuse. I instantly regretted it. I only wanted to show I was hurting just as much as they were – more even. I hadn't helped myself, though, and I trudged in feeling lower than a snake's belly.

Losing kills me. Training, playing pool when I am out with my mates, it sends me into moods – I kick things. But if I felt bad . . . I glanced over at Berti in that cold, dank dressing-room and knew it then: he was finished. What followed was soul destroying, and it jarred my memory back to something I'd seen on TV when I was a kid. It was before Italia 90 – the first World Cup I really sat glued to – and they did a preview showing those famous pictures of Ally McLeod with his head in his hands and the fans, with their faces all twisted with hatred, showering the manager with abuse after we'd drawn with Iran in Argentina in 1978. That was what it was like when we walked out that night in the back of beyond with our manager on his way out. I never thought I'd see those faces again from Scotland fans, but I found myself in the middle of an action replay. I felt hollow and a very long way from home. I wanted to get out of there, shut the door on that night and just be with Margaret and the kids.

At the airport, one nutter burst away from his mates and spat on our video man, then Berti arrived and told us he'd been gobbed on at the stadium, too. That is low-life behaviour. I respect the Tartan Army and all they give to follow us, but for someone to spit on you is a sick joke.

The politics would play themselves out for too long after that – the haggling over pay-offs and all the crap that goes with people losing a job – but, in my eyes, Berti had been finished from the moment I looked at him in the dressing-room at the end of the match in Moldova. He was broken.

I felt guilty as I sat in my living room watching the TV as the breaking news flashed across the bottom of the screen on Sky Sports: 'Berti Vogts sacked as Scotland manager'. I knew in my heart of hearts that it was partly down to me. I had let Berti down, simple as that. I was his skipper, we didn't get the results he needed and he lost his job. That man made me captain, and whatever those who snipe against me think that was a childhood dream. I tried to give him everything I could, and I gave every shred of effort I had. But it wasn't enough. We didn't play well enough, and that's the bottom line.

Berti released a statement talking of his pride that I had stood shoulder to shoulder with him – I was never going to do anything else. I had seen the side of him that others hadn't from all the times when we sat in hotels around the world and just talked football. I saw a decent man, a man who was hurt badly when it didn't happen for us. Then the game face had to go on, and he had to be brave in front of the media. Berti gave Scotland everything he had; the guy could not have given more effort to our cause than he did.

In my career, I have seen other managers go: watched Dick Advocaat go upstairs at Rangers and Graeme Souness quit Blackburn for Newcastle. But this was different. They were going to other jobs; Berti was on the dole. He had been a part of my education, too; he has a vast knowledge of the game, and I absorbed that when we chatted about it.

It infuriated me when we played the 4–1–4–1 system in Valencia against Spain and people suggested he was a weak man letting Jackie McNamara and me pick the team. That was sheer garbage. Instead, he sat us down as adults, told us his ideas and asked us how we thought they could be used for Scotland. We had our input, but Berti and TB put it into operation, and it worked against Spain before the torrential rain and lightning saw the game abandoned.

If Berti was guilty of anything, it was perhaps underestimating the passion Scots feel for their nation and the depth of emotion that hits us when it goes wrong. I had a great relationship with him, however, and that will remain even though he is gone. A good football man gave everything he had for Scotland, and he genuinely worked his heart out for this country.

One of Berti's last acts as Scotland manager was to congratulate me in his speech in our hotel in Moldova after the SFA president John McBeth gave me a silver medal to commemorate my 25th cap. He must have been in turmoil, but he still had enough class to say nice words about me in front of the boys when he knew the end was near for him. That was the sort of touch that sums him up. It was never about the money for Berti. I heard all about the £500,000 bonus he was on if we made a major finals, but he had enough cash. It meant something to him, something demonstrated by the team talk he gave when we played Germany at Hampden on the way to those Euro 2004 play-offs. It was his own homeland we were playing, but before we got the 1–1 draw he was prowling about the place, screaming, 'Let's get into these bastards.' I was shocked at first; I couldn't believe it, because I'd never heard him speak like that before, but I *loved* it! I'll always remember that and the way we played against Germany, Holland and Spain.

Then we'd slide into depths that I just couldn't get my head around: the 3–0 loss to Hungary in a friendly at Hampden was one of the worst. Those sort of nights weren't just pushing Berti to the edge, they were shattering players. I felt I could cope with the flak, but we were asking so much of James McFadden and Darren Fletcher, and they were only 21. They were getting hammered and branded duds when Scotland lost, and it damaged them. James is a special player and a genuine guy, and I tried so hard to get him to Rangers; I pleaded with the manager and the chairman because I thought he would have been some signing for the club, but, for a variety of reasons, it never happened. Fletch also has what it takes: he is playing for what I consider to be the biggest club in the world, Manchester United, and he copes with it all so well. At the end of the 2006–07 season, we at last played together at the heart of the midfield when we won in Austria, and I loved it. On that form, he's a natural footballer, and I bounced off him.

James and Fletch both survived the sometimes brutal flak of Berti's era, and I think it should be remembered when they walk into the Hall of Fame – because they both will – that they were Vogts' idea. He had the bravery to pick them.

I think there were those in the media with agendas against Berti from the start. They know who they are, and some of the things they did to that man should leave them tossing and turning at night. But I admit there were times when he had a desire to fire us up into the sort of frenzy he'd seen in Mel Gibson's *Braveheart*, and I couldn't work out what he was up to. Before a Euro 2004 qualifying game against Iceland, we were at our base in Cameron House, and Berti split us all up into groups – goalkeepers, defence, midfield, attack – so we could have separate meetings. It was thorough and meticulous. Afterwards, I walked in with Lambo and the rest to find a massive flag spread out on the floor with Berti standing next to it. He said, 'We will walk out, pick this up, shake the flag and rouse the crowd.' I couldn't believe what I was hearing. I burst out laughing for about 90 seconds solid; it was schoolboy stuff. I just couldn't stop. Lambo and I were decking ourselves, and Berti's face was getting redder and redder. He was raging.

I had to hang about until everyone had left so that I could apologise. I said, 'I'm sorry, Berti, it's just not me. I'm passionate, but I can't do that in front of 53,000 people.'

He glowered at me and said, 'We're doing it.' We did, and I felt like a fool; it was half-hearted, and I just couldn't see the point.

All the *Braveheart* speeches, the 'call me "McBerti"', etc., were designed to try and get the fans on his side, but it smacked of desperation. He was trying so hard, but that was the point – he had to force it.

There was an article I read after Walter Smith took over, and the headline was brilliant: 'The Quiet Patriot'. I loved that. People watch me in the team line-up before a game as the camera flicks over our faces and wonder why I don't sing. Simple, I can't! No, I am at work, and I am focused and concentrated. Do people seriously think that captaining Scotland doesn't matter to me? It is one of the biggest things in my life: what I dreamed of as a kid kicking the ball around the streets. For me, you don't have to wave flags or scream 'Freedom!' or paint your face to prove yourself a Scotsman. I know it is there in me.

From the first get-together with Walter, I knew he was the right man to restore the pride we had lost and repair all the wounds. At the end with Berti, there had been a siege mentality with the media – Them v. Us. It helped no one, but Walter knew how to keep the majority of the press on his side. For me, he stood out a mile as the best candidate because he has an aura. He walks into a room and commands instant respect from footballers. He comes in when we are all sitting and you think, 'Let's be quiet and listen.'

It is a stupid little thing, but when he walks in for a meeting – even now that he is back as my club boss at Rangers and I work with him every day – I sit bolt upright, like I am back at school again. He commands that sort of respect.

Our first meeting with the new gaffer was a relaxed camp in Manchester: no game, just some light training and a social one night so he could ease himself in and look at what sort of characters he had. It was a masterstroke. Some of us had a few glasses of red, others cracked open the Budweisers, people loosened off. He told us what he wanted, and Coisty was there firing off the one-liners. But Ally was also keen to show the guy he has always called 'Gaffer' that he'd been right to bring him in as a coach. When I first broke into the Rangers team, Ian Durrant and McCoist used to tell me that Walter was a legend, and I just wouldn't listen – now I was hanging on his every word.

It broke my heart that I couldn't get into the nine-in-a row team, but I have since worked out there was a simple reason – Walter knew I didn't belong in it. He was right. Then when Gers were going for the tenth crown, he gave me my break, but I was left out of the team towards the end of the season, which ended trophyless, and Walter quit. I was raging when he dropped me. I was 20 years old, and I thought I was ready. One of the happiest turnarounds of my career is that I have had the chance to work under him as a man – with Scotland and now again with Rangers – and not as a stupid wee boy who spat the dummy.

Walter is simply a good coach and a great manager who knows how to treat players. That nine-in-a-row team loves him, every one of them. He made them into legends and became one himself. All I wanted was a chance to see if they were right, and now I know they were. They have the same sort of relationship with Walter as I have had with Alex McLeish; they trusted him, and they could speak to him about anything.

Walter went through a lot with that nine-in-a-row team, and now I know why they achieved what they did. I realise what they had; I know why they made history. He has nothing to prove at Gers the second time around; he knows his job and you look and listen. He has the respect of all of us.

I started out walking in fear of the man; there are times when I still do. It began at Gers when I had to make his toast in the morning, and I was scared stiff of burning it. When I started at Ibrox, I think he saw something in me but wanted to keep my feet on the ground and stop me from becoming a smartarse. The answer? He made me the coaching-staff skivvy. It was my job to make Walter and the rest their tea and toast, and they called me 'The Boy'. That was done to keep me in place. I'd try and skive, but I'd get hollered at and told to get their kit ready and get their breakfasts. I don't even make tea and toast for Margaret, but I made it for Walter.

When he took over as Scotland manager, many observers thought the fact that I had a big mouth when I was a kid meant that there would be a problem between us. They forgot he was the man who gave me my debut for Rangers on the day we celebrated winning nine in a row at Hearts. We lost 3–1, but it was the biggest day of my life, and Walter let me know early on that I would be a part of it all. I got to play for the club I supported in a season when they made history, and I'm proud I will always have that to look back on.

He was a magnificent man-manager, and he created such an incredible atmosphere with all the mad men who were in that team. But he had to put up with so much pressure in what would become that failed ten-in-a-row season, and all I could think about was getting a game. Looking back, there was stress etched on his face every day, and he didn't need this kid moaning at him to be allowed to play more. He was 100 per cent correct in the way he handled me – bang on. I got my ten games, and then the job was left to the men; he was correct to bump me back into the reserves.

Back then, though, I couldn't take it. I thought he was wrong and out of order. I watched that Scottish Cup final against Hearts in 1998 with my old man, and when Stephane Adam's shot crept in and we went 2–0 down I just couldn't take it any more. I felt like putting my foot through the TV screen, and I walked out. I roamed the streets and didn't see the end of the match. I felt like a joke. I was just a stupid young boy who was desperate to play for Rangers, and, in my eyes, he was denying me the opportunity.

Now, I see it differently and understand that you must have something in you to cope with playing for this monster of a club. I see the kids at Murray Park, moaning about the gaffer in the corners, venting all their frustrations, and I feel for them. That was me once.

I sometimes think that I would like to be a coach when I finish playing, and I study Walter. I have learned so much from his methods. For example, I think that you can overdo the information – Berti did. There are times when players just shut off; in my opinion, you really only have 20 minutes to get the message over. Walter knows what players want, and it was different in his Scotland camp, I won't lie to you. The foreign mentality is to have things regimented: a meeting then another one with videos. There were times when a meeting would last up to an hour, and the players' concentration would be lost – that's just footballers for you.

I think that Walter knew what players wanted and enjoyed in the build-up to a big international. Two days before a match, he'd crank things up and the business heads would go on. It was like a slow burn to make sure we were ready to explode on match day against a team like Italy when we drew 1–1 in the last World Cup qualifiers.

This game has become my business now. I know I am guilty of seldom playing with a smile on my face; I walk over that line scowling, in a bad mood and obsessed by winning. Yet there are times when I have played in a football theatre like the San Siro and part of me is back there kicking a ball about the back garden and dreaming of playing in games like Italy v. Scotland.

In Milan, there were *three* of my boyhood mates in the team – and no jumpers for goalposts! The occasion was even more special for me because those boys I've known since I was 12 were there too. Zico – Paul Hartley to those who don't know him – was the year above me at Mill United, and I knew he was quality even then growing up in Hamilton. He'd been on the brink of a move to Celtic when we were boys, and he would finally end up there, as he had always wanted. But back in 2005, the deal was wrecked in a row over the price. He could have hidden in his shell, but instead he just got better at Hearts and earned his place against Italy that night.

Then there was Stevie Thompson, whom I trained with

HEART OF THE FAMILY
My parents Archie and Maureen mean the world to me; their names are tattooed on my arm. Here we are on holiday together.

PRIZE GUY
Learning to lift a trophy for the first time with Mill United. Check out the shorts: I was always No. 6, even back then.

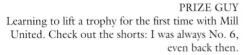

EARLY BATH
Having a laugh in the suds with my big brother before getting packed off to bed.

LIFE AND SOUL OF
THE PARTY
Here I am in my Scotland strip, right in the middle of Derek's 21st birthday party. Ally McCoist cuddles my dad, while Mark Walters and Ian Durrant help my brother celebrate. I was sneaking my mates in to the kitchen to meet them.

UPSETTING A LEGEND
Lothar Matthäus couldn't take my attentions in the 1–1 Champions League
draw with Bayern Munich in 1999 – so he poked me in the eye.
(© The Scottish *Sun*.)

NATIONAL SERVICE
Scoring my first goal for Scotland against the Republic of Ireland in a
2–1 friendly win in Dublin in May 2000. Their fans loved me!
(© The Scottish *Sun*.)

GONE
Stuart Dougal flashes the cards and sends me off in misery in the 6–2
Old Firm defeat at Celtic in August 2000. Worse was to come.
(© The Scottish *Sun*.)

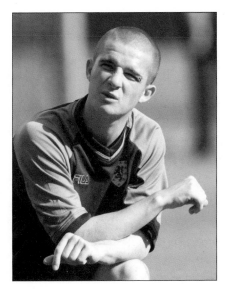

SCARFACE
Marked up after the 'Battle of Bothwell Bridge'. You can see the scar
over my left eye during a Scotland training session.
(© The Scottish *Sun*.)

DREAM TIME
My first goal against Celtic in a 5–1 Ibrox win in November 2000.
I'd always wondered how it felt. (© The Scottish *Sun*.)

DUTCH MASTER
Dick Advocaat takes stick from some of the fans, but he moulded my career.
Here we are after a UEFA Cup penalty shoot-out win over
Paris Saint-Germain in 2001. (© The Scottish *Sun*.)

BEST EVER
I have never peaked emotionally on the pitch the way I did scoring this goal in the 2002 Scottish Cup-final win over Celtic.
(© The Scottish *Sun*.)

TICKER-TAPE
Lifting the title as skipper in 2003 after the 6–1 win over Dunfermline – they did *not* lie down.
(© The Scottish *Sun*.)

KIDS STUFF
Craig Moore celebrates with his son Dylan as I party with Kyle and kiss Connor after winning the title in 2003. This is one of my favourite pictures.
(© The Scottish *Sun*.)

SECOND SALVER
With the Scottish Football Writers' Association Player of the Year award, won for the second time in 2003. I want to make history by taking a third before I quit.
(© The Scottish *Sun*.)

X-RAY VISION
Showing the extent of my knee damage. Look at those wires!
(© The Scottish *Sun*.)

KEEP BELIEVING
Helping Marvin Andrews lift the gaffer after the final-day title win on 22 May 2005.
(© The Scottish *Sun*.)

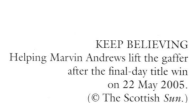

AT HOME WITH THE FERGUSONS
With Margaret and the kids for a winter portrait at our house.

MY SECRET MATES
These are the friends I tell all my problems too, and they have never breathed a word to anyone. At home with my Great Danes Homer and Holly; taking them for a walk is a great way to relax.

THE MISSUS
I first started going out with Margaret when I was 16, and she has put up with me a long time now. This is us dressed up in the good togs at Steven Thompson's wedding on the Isle of Arran.

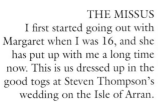

PLG? NOT FOR ME
With the manager who ended up stripping me of the Rangers captaincy, a job I love, as he attempts to put his message across. I tried to make it work with him, but his 200 days in charge became a dark time for me.
(© The Scottish *Sun*.)

KRIS AND MAKE UP
Celebrating my goal with Boydy, the man who'd set it up, in the 5–0 thrashing of Dundee United that signalled Walter Smith's return as Rangers boss. I was captain again that day and felt reborn.
(© The Scottish *Sun*.)

at Dundee United when we were kids. Thommo was my room-mate at Rangers and the life and soul of the place. A little part of me went with the big man when he left for Cardiff City. He'd been banged up with me in hotel rooms all over the world for three years and had put up with all my black moods. The Christmas night out before he left was especially sad. It was a spree, as every office do is, I suppose. We stayed up through the night and were still going when the other guests were coming down for breakfast. We ended up in the foyer of our Liverpool hotel, handing the night porter a soggy bundle of crumpled tenners to go and buy us a guitar from the music shop. He arrived back, earned his £100 tip from our band of maniacs, and Thommo strummed a few chords and launched into Oasis's 'Wonderwall'. He was brilliant – a better singer than a targetman! I sang myself hoarse, we flew back up the road later that day to head for a curer and big Bob Malcolm ceremonially smashed the guitar against a bus stop. End of Thommo. Football's like that. But it was great that he played against Italy.

The same goes for big Lee McCulloch, who was with me at Rangers Boys Club. Four boys who grew up together, all playing in the San Siro. I look back on it and have a wee laugh when I think how far we've all come. We lost 2–0 that night, Andrea Pirlo swirling home the sort of free-kicks only hours of training can provide, but I felt we played the ball around so well. I remember thinking, 'Now we're getting somewhere. Now we're looking like a team.'

I've learned that football at that level is about respect. It is not given to you, it is earned. Well, we earned Marcello Lippi's respect. I knew we had it the moment he took off Francesco Totti and brought on a more defensive player in Daniele De Rossi – that meant we had his respect. Gary

Caldwell stuck to his job, squeezing them in the defensive midfield position, and they took their main man off. It was the sort of performance that would eventually win him his move to Celtic from Hibs. It was also a great team performance and the best I had felt as a Scotland player since we beat England at Wembley.

Looking back seven years to my Scotland debut, a 0–0 draw on a cowfield in Lithuania, one thing sticks out for me: Craig Brown had real guts to pick me for Scotland, especially as I was just a kid and they still had the likes of Ian Durrant in the squad. All I remember of that trip to Vilnius is an overpowering feeling of shyness – I was shitting myself in all honesty. I used to go down for meals, bolt my food and rush back up to the room so I didn't get in the way, although Durranty's presence did help settle to me.

I survived that trip, despite Ian coming up out of the darkness and tickling my feet at three in the morning, and then, slowly but surely, I felt I belonged – I was a Scotland player. By my fifth cap, we were winning at Wembley in the Euro 2000 play-offs, and that topped everything I had ever felt in a dark-blue jersey until our 2006 win over France. Up against Paul Ince, Paul Scholes and the rest. Growling in their faces.

I'd seen Jim Baxter's keepy-uppy at Wembley against England and Kenny Dalglish's famous goal. I always wanted to experience what that felt like – it felt magic. We murdered them that night, and the only disappointment was the place itself: we were too far away from the Tartan Army. I had to go on a sponsored run to celebrate when Don Hutchinson scored. It was still the place of legends, though, and we pulled a flanker and stole the home dressing-room – anything to try and cancel out the 2–0 defeat at Hampden on the previous Saturday. I played with John Collins that night; he was pushing and prodding passes, and we outclassed them. The victory was there for us, but Christian Dailly's header smashed off David Seaman at the death, and it wasn't to be.

Craig had faith in me, but half the time I was a day-dreaming kid, flicking things at people's heads when he was talking! I couldn't take it all in – the enormity of what it means to people. Now when we have young players who are rookies in the squad, I tell them to pay attention to every second, because I know that when I was a kid I was looking out the window and waiting for the game.

And that is the way I have always felt with Scotland when the big finals come around: like some kid at the school disco asking for the last dance and getting a knockback. I can see what I want, but I can't have it. Maybe that's why when we meet up at Cameron House for international duty they all mutter, 'Here he comes: the ultimate moaning-faced git.'

All week bouncing off the walls around a hotel away from my family never helps either. Come game time, the snarl is there from minute one; I just want to get out and play. I've had enough waiting.

I have read some comments from Rangers fans saying that they worry that I am becoming too crabbit on the park. They reckon I am in a permanent bad mood when I play. They're right. I am that way because I want to win every game, make the most of every minute, and maybe that spills over. But I can't change, and I won't change.

My teammates react to it, I think. I will always be seen as the grumpiest player they ever worked with, but I will live with that if we're winning. It's the same with Rangers now. Those standards have to be what we aspire to – because I don't want to stray onto the manager's wrong side too often.

I know the perception of Walter Smith is that he's supposed to be the friendly uncle, and people say to me what a nice guy he is. They're right in some ways, but I also know that he is one hard bastard. Half-time against Belarus? 0–1? Friendly uncle? Don't think so. He ripped into us, but it was done with honesty – frighteningly brutal punch-you-in-the-face honesty. He told us not to bother coming back in after the match if we went out and played like that again, then he laid into people. Not physically – the verbal assault was enough. That's how it should be. My dad has always said to me, 'Don't have two faces. Don't hide behind other men. Tell it straight.' That's a chapter in Walter's book, and he missed no one that day. It was the only time he'd had to slaughter us since he took over.

It killed me to lose to Belarus like that and see the chance to put pressure on the Norwegians for second place slip away from us. And it was typical that with me banned the boys sparkled to win 3–0 in Slovenia in the next match, the final one of the qualifying stages; we'd crafted yet another bloody story of glorious failure. But Walter had kicked life back into a World Cup campaign that was all but dead after the first three games, and people should remember that.

He carried that momentum into the Euro 2008 qualifiers, even if we sat with our heads in our hands when we watched the draw in Montreux. Italy, the World Cup holders, France, the team they'd beaten in the final in Berlin, and Ukraine, who were a bit of a dark horse and made the last eight in Germany, were all in our group. I looked at the England section and thought, 'Jammy bastards.'

But if you're Scottish, a defiant part of you can't help but fancy yourself against Luca Toni, Thierry Henry, Andriy Shevchenko and the rest. And we caught a flyer, humping the

Faroes 6–0 at Parkhead then winning 2–1 with something to spare in Lithuania.

Next up was a day that will live in the minds of those who played for ever: 7 October 2006, Hampden – Scotland 1, France 0. My win at Wembley remains so special, but that day against France was a victory for togetherness, the collective will of 11 guys and the tactical nous of a wise manager beating the superior technique of a team who I rate up there with the world's best. Yes, they have better skills than us, and I am not hiding from that. It is down to us to develop and try to reach the levels they have. But in the wake of that game, there were times when I wondered just what it is that some people want from us. Writing in the *News of the World*, Gerry McNee slaughtered us, criticising us for celebrating when we should have been ashamed of the performance because we had been lucky. Give me a break. We were playing against the very best on the planet in the likes of Patrick Vieira and Claude Makélélé, and Walter Smith called it bang on the button. He told us to give them the ball in the first half and let them lord possession. We were to sit with two rock-solid banks of four with one of the strikers dropping back in to help if need be. We wanted to frustrate the hell out of them by letting them play across and in front of us – and it worked. They only cut us open twice, and we survived. Then, in the second-half, after we'd kept it to 0–0 in the first, there were stages before and after Gary Caldwell's goal when *we* dominated.

From the moment Walter came in, he transformed Scotland. He got the camp buzzing, and bringing David Weir back out of international retirement was a masterstroke. Walter turned Scotland around, and when he quit to come home to Rangers his international legacy was best demonstrated by the fact that Alex McLeish had very little to change. Alex has kept things ticking over, and now I can't wait to meet up every time we have a game. It's a good place to be.

It was summed up for me at the end of the 2006–07 season when we went to the Faroes and got the monkey off our backs. All the publicity beforehand had been about the draws in 1999 and 2002, but we didn't dwell on that, and we got the job done with a 2–0 win. We were mentally strong, and that's what Walter did for us.

I admit that before he took over negative thoughts might sneak into my mind – a fear that if we lost, I'd be caned in the media. Now I don't care who we are playing. I am up for it, and I believe we will get a result, because I am surrounded by characters like Stephen McManus. At the time of writing, I don't know if he is Celtic's next captain, but he should be. He is an old-fashioned, in-your-face centre-half, and he loves his club the way I love Rangers. We get on well together, and I spoke to him about the rivalry between our teams. I just said, 'I like you, Mick, and I respect you, but for four games a season I have to hate you. That's life.'

He just shrugged and said, 'I'll hate you, too.' We had a laugh, and I think the same respect will be there as I hope it was with Paul Lambert and Neil Lennon. He'll be my enemy with Celtic, but I sense Mick is going to become a man I'll be proud to stand beside in a dark-blue jersey and someone the Tartan Army can really relate to.

I grew up wearing the red Scotland away strip with the big badge. Now that was a strip. I always remember that Kenny Dalglish scored with it on just after he'd been knocked out in a match in Israel.

You measure time by your Scotland strips, don't you?

These days I measure bedtimes by them, and I would love to have some of those people who say I don't care about the national side round to my house when my little daughter goes up to bed with her old light-blue away top on – the one that says 'Cara 6' on the back. That's what she sleeps in. Don't care? Don't think so.

I read headlines and listen to radio phone-ins. Don't pay any attention to players who say they don't – they're at it. I have heard all the things I have been called at various times by Scotland fans: traitor, con man, coward, king of the call-offs. It makes me sick, but those in the camp know that I have *never* faked an injury for Scotland. Any time I have had a problem, I have made sure that I have gone to Cameron House to have my scans which show that I am truly not fit. It cracks me up – so much muck has been thrown at me about this that it has started to stick. It guts me because I have always played with knocks in qualifiers, gulped down the Voltarol painkillers, kept going. I don't want the sympathy vote for that, but Rangers pay my wages. I have played through an injury in qualifiers, but in friendlies you have to think deeper than that.

Scotland matters to me all right. Whatever money I earn, I will always live here, because I am a home boy. I could have earned more cash at Blackburn and signed for two more years added on to the three years left on my deal; I could have gone to Everton or Newcastle United. I didn't because I wanted to come home; I wanted to sit in the corner of my local and take pelters from my mates watching the fitba. I'm home because I love this country, and I play for Scotland for nothing. That's the deal we negotiated for the last World Cup campaign, and it is still in place now under Alex McLeish. Jackie McNamara, Christian Dailly,

Steven Pressley and I – four of the most senior players – walked in and told the then SFA chief executive David Taylor not to pay us. In my opinion, that is how it should be. Rewards should come if we qualify; if we don't, then keep the appearance money and the bonuses. We don't want it. It's not about a couple more quid in your hip-pocket for us, and people should know that.

I want to take my kids and show them that I am in the Hall of Fame – that matters to me. As I get older, I think more about legacies and the impression you leave behind when you hang up your boots. If I don't make a major tournament with Scotland, then I can't hide from the fact that there will be a gaping hole in my career. Some footballers are guilty of counting the dough – it's a cynical, cruel game at times – but the World Cup and the Euros? Craig Moore, one of my closest pals, was running in a swimming pool in Newcastle, recovering from a hamstring injury, when Australia made it through to the 2006 World Cup in Germany. I phoned to congratulate him, and all I could hear was him leaping around in the water with the physios, losing the plot. It was priceless – sheer joy. I felt so happy for him, yet jealous too. I have two chances left: Euro 2008 (although with France, Italy and Ukraine in our group, it is going to be some challenge to qualify for that tournament, despite that superb start we've had, amassing 15 points from the opening 21); and the World Cup in South Africa in 2010, which, realistically, will be my last opportunity. I'd be the proudest man alive if I could lead Scotland out in one of those tournaments – I might even sing.

8

From Treble to Trouble

'When they doubt me, I remind myself that I
am special. I am *the* man.'

Shy and retiring Ronald de Boer tells Barry
his philosophy during the Treble year.

I felt like I was floating four feet in the air; I could hear
ghostly voices, and the air was swirling all around me. I was
dreaming that we had won the Treble, and my head was in
the clouds. Then I woke up in my crumpled club suit with
my tie all over the place, sprawled on a sofa. I'd been shaken
by the shoulders and given an alarm call by two grumpy
removal men. We *had* won the Treble, but I'd forgotten we
were moving house.

The four-day bender to celebrate had taken its toll, and I
was unconscious that morning. Margaret was fed up trying
to rouse me, and she left me to get packed with the rest of
our belongings. It was not one of my 'Husband of the Year'
moments. She just couldn't move me, and all I remember
is someone shouting at me, 'Barry, for God's sake, wake

up.' I was up there floating about, looking at the sky and thinking that Greigy had been right all these years: winning the Treble as Rangers captain really did feel special!

Those celebrations were over the top, but they were the release of a season's worth of pent-up tension, and when I look back on my Treble year as skipper, I remember that Rangers players have been going for clean sweeps for one hundred and thirty three years, but we've only done it seven times. When you do achieve it, you have a right to think that it might never happen again, so I celebrated as if the world was ending.

But I partied so hard mainly out of a sense of relief, because on 4 May 2003 at Dens Park I had been convinced they'd remember me only one way – as the man who blew the Treble. We'd drawn 2–2 with Dundee, throwing away two priceless points in the run-in, and I had missed *two* penalties in the one match. Yep, two.

I'd been flying that season, playing at my peak, yet on one afternoon the split-second decisions I made could have cost us so much – perhaps even the title and the Treble. We'd just lost a vital Old Firm game 2–1, and we needed to show we had what champions were made of at Dens. I remember coming out of the tunnel bristling with aggression, and within *37 seconds*, we were ahead, big Lee Wilkie sticking out a leg and sending Arthur Numan's cross past his own keeper.

It had the feel of one of those pivotal days that would decide a season, but then we somehow lost our way. Fabian Caballero scored twice, and I felt hollow. I could see us throwing away all our good work and handing Celtic the championship. Then Mikey Mols tortured Wilkie again, and he was decked right on the stroke of half-time. Penalty! I was confident I'd fire us back into the match, but I got too much height on the kick, and I smashed the ball off the underside of the bar and away.

Still, we had 45 minutes to save the game. But after throwing everything at them, we were toiling until big Lee coughed up another penalty late on, and my boots somehow dragged me forward to the spot. Again. This time, to my utter horror, Julian Speroni dived to save my kick, and even though Mikel Arteta rescued a point from the *third* spot-kick that ref John Rowbotham had the courage to give us, in a run-in rife with all the usual conspiracy theories, I just couldn't believe what I had done. Was I brave or stupid to take the second penalty? Would the fans ever forgive me?

I got my answer to the second question when I was walking off the pitch. I was looking down at the ground, wanting the turf to open up and swallow me whole, when the fans rose as one and chanted, 'Oh, Barry, Barry. Barry, Barry, Barry, Barry Ferguson!' I couldn't fathom their response after the mistakes I had made that day. There were tears welling up in my eyes – I was choked. I just didn't expect that sort of reception, and I couldn't believe they were cheering my name after missing two penalties in a game that meant so much. I vowed then that I would repay those fans by bringing the title back to Rangers. That's all I wanted to do. As I was walking off and the fans were singing my name, I just wanted the game to start all over again. Sadly, it never does.

At times like that, I admit that I lose all sense of perspective.

This game means so much to me that failures such as that feel like a death in the family, and I just can't lift myself out of the doldrums. But I'll always remember slumping through the doors of the house that night. My son Kyle came bouncing out and almost knocked me over with a welcome-back hug and a blurted-out question. 'Daddy, Daddy,' he hollered. 'Did you score today?' Those were the wee man's first words – he hadn't seen the game. I was carrying the weight of the world on my shoulders, and I didn't know whether to cuddle him or send him up to bed with no supper! In the end, I just cuddled him. It helped put it into a different light somehow. Not much could have made me smile, but when I thought about him asking me if I'd scored when I had missed two penalties, it made me laugh.

I'd been inconsolable in the Dens dressing-room as the dust settled that day, turning over what I had done in my mind time and again – torturing myself. I'd actually felt good throughout the match – apart from those penalties – and we began the game really buzzing. But we just couldn't get a second goal. Sometimes that season I just wished we could score one that flew in off someone's backside instead of always trying to construct the perfect goal.

The funny thing is that I had watched Speroni before and noticed he usually went low at penalties, so I decided to give the first one some height – sadly too much height. The second time Speroni was moving around and jumping up and down, and it became a guessing game.

I knew there would be countless debates over why I went up there again. I just felt I had to show that I had the bottle to take it – I am the captain of Rangers, and there is a responsibility that goes with that job. I knew that some people were going to say I was stupid to take the second penalty, and I would have to live with that. I made the choice, but I was cursed on the day, simple as that.

I stuck my shirt over my head when Mikel ran up for the third one, because I just couldn't bear to look. It had crossed my mind to try and take it, but I thought better of it – and big Eck might have taken a hidden revolver from the medical bag and shot me if I had tried. I was just glad Arteta scored it and that the title was all still in the balance.

What followed was a journey to redeem myself, to earn a chance to try and somehow make up for Dens. The support of the fans got me through a dark day, but I knew I couldn't make them forget what I had done. I just hoped I'd be able to have them forgive me. We took it to the wire, of course, and then the title was clinched on the first of two amazing final days under Eck. We beat Dunfermline 6–1 at Ibrox, and Celtic defeated Kilmarnock 4–0 at Rugby Park, but we still edged it by a single goal.

Chris Sutton said he always knew the Pars would lie down to us, and even now that pisses me off greatly. I knew Sutty, because we shared the same agent, and liked him, but that was out of order. What he said was not needed, and, more importantly, it was miles off the mark.

At one stage that day, it seemed as though we had lost it. Jason Dair scored a belter for Dunfermline, and if that was him not trying, then he's some actor. I mean the boy is 'Slim' Jim Baxter's nephew: he'd probably get his head kicked in if he ever went back to Hill o' Beath in Fife where

Slim was born having not given it his all. The bottom line is, whoever is on top of the league at the end of the season deserves to win it, whether it is by a goal, a point or 20 points. Deep down, as good a pro as he is, Sutton knows that.

But the night after we beat Dunfermline, I couldn't give a toss what Chris Sutton thought of how we won it. We walked down Paisley Road West to the District Bar in our club suits and joined the fans – it was a night to treasure. The celebrations kicked off at that point, and if I am honest, they carried on too long as we still had to face Dundee in the Scottish Cup final. We'd won the league in what we then thought was the sort of dramatic fashion that could never be topped, and the final became flat by comparison.

We didn't go back to work until the Thursday, and the training-run pictures from that day are a riot. All you can see is alcohol flowing out of bodies. Yet we put the business heads back on and recovered, and Lorenzo Amoruso's header got us over the line against Dundee and kicked off another party to remember.

We had made history, and I knew it. I thought that it might never happen again for me, and, yes, I savoured it. We had faced up to a manager who I believe will always be seen as a true Celtic legend and won five trophies on the spin. When I hang up my boots and Rangers tell me I'm not wanted any more, I will always be glad that I won my first Treble as skipper under Big Red.

When Dick Advocaat decided enough was enough, I heard that the new manager was going to be Alex McLeish from Hibs, and part of me rejoiced, to be honest. I wanted a Scot;

I wanted a younger man who understood what Rangers was all about. He did – he was born and bred in Barrhead, and he'd been raised with the Old Firm all around him.

I'd worked with him with the Scotland Under-21s, and what struck me then was his freshness and his enthusiasm on the training ground. He was a football anorak in the nicest sense – he knew every player. He could quote who was leading the leagues in South America, who the up-and-coming stars were there. Now this bright, clever guy was the Rangers manager, and I sensed right away he couldn't care about the timing of his appointment as the 11th manager in the club's history. He knew there were financial problems at Rangers, and deep down he probably recognised that if there weren't, he might not have been given the job. But he couldn't care less. He had the job he wanted, and I warmed to him after I got over the fact that when I had watched him play for Aberdeen he always looked like he enjoyed beating Rangers too much!

No, seriously, I had always known he rated me as a player, because when he was manager at Motherwell he tried to get me on loan. I thought about that one seriously, but there were problems when I look back on it now – after all, I'm a Hamilton Accies boy. They were always my team after the Gers, and I saw as many games at Douglas Park as a kid as I did at Ibrox. If I have a spare weekend even now, I still go back to see the Accies. In February 2006, I watched the Scottish Cup tie with Dundee from a hospitality box, and I loved my day out. They have this guy in midfield called Alex Neil, and he's very good to watch – a proper player who always looks for the right pass. He was top-drawer. It was

0–0 and baltic, and the players struggled on their new plastic pitch, but watching him was worth the admission money.

Back in the day, I always had my favourite Accies players, and I would jump over the turnstiles to see them when I first went to the matches. They had Rikki Ferguson in goal, big John McNaughton, who the fans called 'Wurzel', a great winger called Paul McDonald and John Brogan, who was superb up-front. They were heroes to me as much as the Gers players were. I went there with my mates when my dad was working and we couldn't go to Ibrox. Back then, Douglas Park wasn't like the new stadium is now. The inside of the old stand was like a broom cupboard, and any time I made it in there looking for autographs, I could never work out where the teams actually changed – it was tiny. They also had another little stand that looked like it was imported from Subbuteo. The Accies Supporters' Club was situated there, and it became one of the places at the heart of my life. Mill United Boys Club would have their Player of the Year dances there each year, and Paul Hartley and I would go with our good gear on once a season praying we'd win the awards for our different age groups. So, when I think about it now, if Alex had taken it any further at Motherwell, I'd probably have told him that because I was an Accies boy I couldn't jump the dyke.

When Alex had first come to Rangers in 2001, Celtic had the league in their grasp, even though it was only December. The following season, they surrendered a 12-point lead, but before that happened, I was running on blind hope at times, just praying that they would crack and we could catch them. Deep down, though, I feared we would need a miracle. I remember all the talk at that time was of another Treble for Celtic, that O'Neill had Rangers in his pocket and we were a spent force. As captain, I hated to hear things like that, and I vowed we would return to winning ways and get the better of them again.

There are moments that change a manager's career, and there are times when those moments come from the most unexpected of sources – from Bert Konterman, for example. When we came to play Celtic in the CIS Cup semi-final in Alex's first season, I think there were large sections of the Rangers support who needed to be convinced about the manager. I didn't – I could see how hard he was working to turn the season around. But there are times when you need one slice of magic from someone; I just didn't expect it to be big Bert who produced it with one of the best hits from distance you'll ever see. We won 2–1, and we had First Division Ayr United in the final. I could sense my first trophy as skipper was there to be grabbed.

I scored against Ayr in a 4–0 win, and I will never forget that day. The feeling wasn't any less sweet because it was a game we were expected to win. I loved every second of it.

Two months later we were back at Hampden for the Scottish Cup final against Celtic, and five months into his reign, Alex had two trophies. But Konterman sparked it all. His goal that night in the semi-final of the CIS changed Eck's career and was the foundation for the Treble in 2003.

We used to call him 'Bambi On Ice'. He hated that nickname, but I thought it summed him up. And I used to love his press conferences as much as the media boys. If he was chosen to go in, I'd text the writer I trust afterwards just to find out what he had said. We were in Warsaw once for a UEFA Cup tie against the Russian side Anzhi when the big man produced another 30-yarder that smacked off someone and went in to give us a scruffy 1–0 win on a neutral ground. It had been a dismal game, and I was happy to let big Bambi go and face the press boys. He summed up the match by saying, 'Lads, the sun didn't shine in Football Land today.' I was pissing myself laughing. Where did he get this stuff? If Neil Lennon or I said that, the papers would have us sent for analysis on a psychiatrist's couch.

Konterman was a character – a Christian who was a connoisseur of red wine and came on every night out. In fact, the Dutch boys are all wine snobs. When we went on nights out, the red wine would come out and Ronald Waterreus would sniff it and say, 'I don't think so. Too bland.' Then he'd send it back. I'd be like, 'Bollocks, give it to me!'

It is strange how a season that sees you win everything can be built on the despair I felt when we lost in the UEFA Cup to Viktoria Žižkov. We'd been flying at the start of the season and were unbeaten when we got to the Czech Republic for that game, but we just froze. It was a disgraceful performance, and I walked off booting water bottles in the air and giving the snappers a field day. We'd lost 2–0. They were a poor side, too – bang ordinary.

In the return leg, we won 3–1 at Ibrox in extra time, but the away goal put them through, and you could have heard a pin drop in the stadium when they scored. We were out of Europe without a parachute – it was an absolute nightmare.

If you'd told me that night we were going to win a Treble,

I would have recommended you for treatment from a head-doctor. But we did – we pulled ourselves together and won the lot, and I'm sorry, but I am not having the excuse that is always trotted out that Celtic were tired because they were heading for the UEFA Cup final in Seville. It's a factor, but that's all it is. Three games in a week if you prepare in the right way is always possible. You might be a little tired in spells during some matches, but it is an excuse. Simple as that. Tiredness from a heavy schedule is a factor, and travelling can drain footballers, but you don't win a Treble because your rivals have been hopping on and off a few flights to Europe. I'm not having that.

My own preparations have changed and evolved over the years. At Blackburn, Graeme Souness would tell me how he could literally sleep standing up, and I'd envy him, because you need to be able to recharge your body at this level. I'm too restless for that, and these days I will sometimes have a glass of red wine the night before a match to put me to sleep. There's no harm in that. In fact, I learned it from the foreign players who are some of the best and most disciplined pros I have ever worked with. And I always make sure the cork goes back in the bottle after one. The first time I saw them doing it was at a hotel the night before a match. Some of the foreign players had a glass of wine, and I asked for a lager-tops, but Advocaat battered me across the back of the head! Foiled again.

I think it was throughout that Treble season that I could feel the trust building between me and Alex. It has always been like that with me – a slow process. I find it difficult to trust people straight away, but I like to think that once I get to know someone that is worth knowing they'll find me a loyal friend. In my private life, I think I can appear ignorant before getting to know someone, and I worry about it because it's not the case at all – it is just a basic shyness.

It was the same with Alex at work, because I was worried he wouldn't rate me as a player or like me as a person. And he could have taken the captaincy away from me, too. But he kept me as his skipper, and our relationship developed from there. He would take me into his confidence at times but only about the systems and what he was thinking about. And I was only ever consulted and asked for an opinion, despite all the crazy rumours I heard at various times that I was picking the team. I have never heard so much bullshit in all my life. That was an insult to Alex McLeish and hurtful to me. I never once had a player named to me before the rest of the team. I had formations sketched out and broad outlines given to me, and then I was asked for my input. That was it.

I think speaking to senior players is a sign of strength not weakness. I know Sven-Göran Eriksson did that with the England squad, and I see nothing wrong in it. You have a common purpose and the same goal – what harm is there in canvassing some people to find out what they think? McLeish is a forward-thinking, modern-day manager, and he did ask for input, but he was never once a weak man in my eyes.

In that Treble season, he was up against the best Celtic manager since Jock Stein, and he got his measure. That has to be remembered. But if some sections of the Gers support are honest with themselves, they'll admit that they were waiting for him to trip up because they thought he was Aberdeen's property and not a true Rangers man. Nonsense. The club mattered to him every bit as much as it does to me.

I don't like reserved managers when you have won things. I want to see their emotions, and Alex was like a kid in a sweetie shop whenever we won a trophy. I think sport is about feelings of triumph when you achieve something, and if you can't savour the moment after all the practice and the training sessions, then what is the point? For example, I was glued to the 2006 World Snooker Championship final because Graeme Dott is a Lanarkshire boy and a big Rangers fan. I was watching the last session, willing him on, but he wasn't playing well, and he knew it. Peter Ebdon got right back into the match, but then Graeme cleared up. He was losing it, punching the air in delight, and I loved his response – it reminded me of McLeish when he won things.

Sport is about emotion in my eyes, about seeing the mask that the players carry until the moment they've won come off. Snooker fascinates me in that way. Stephen Hendry was so intriguing to watch. I sometimes get calls during the World Championship to go here, there or wherever, but they get blanked, because I'm glued to the snooker. The way they can plot their way round the table is something to admire. The next move is always on their mind, like the way the best midfield playmakers will play two nothing balls then murder you with a killer one inside the full-back. I love the cold, calculating strategy of that. Hendry had it at his best, and he looked like the 'Iceman' while he was playing, but when he won, the emotion was always there.

My other escape has always been boxing and watching, in particular, Mike Tyson. When he was at his peak, he was just so destructive. He was wrong in the head at the end of his career, but at the height of his powers, he was a force of nature. At his best, he demonstrated a sort of controlled fury, and you saw his emotion when he won. This was what he had trained all those years for under old Cus d'Amato in the Catskills. I read lots of stories about him – I couldn't get enough of them. Stories about how d'Amato had taken in this broken-up, troubled kid and honed him to respect boxing and his own body. My love of boxing started way back in the days of 'Iron' Mike Tyson, who was the first fighter I really idolised. Sometimes I'll finish up a training session with five minutes battering the punching bag with my gloves on. It's a release.

Snooker players and boxers are men I admire. Both are very different sportsmen, but they are still driven in their own ways by the emotion of what they do. And that's what drives me. Every time we win a trophy, I am in that dressing-room trying to *eat* bottles of champagne, and I will see a foreigner in the corner thinking that their captain is not right in the head. But you can't beat that feeling – you work all season for it, and you are making memories to last for the rest of your days. I felt I had met a kindred spirit in Alex when we won things together. He'd be hoarse and losing his voice, and I loved that about him. It mattered to him.

There were some big-hearted men in the team that won the Treble: Amo and big Oz at the heart of defence; Ronald de Boer, Shota Arveladze, Mikel Arteta and Mikey Mols. I scored 19 goals that season. A clutch of them were penalties, but the rest were made by Ronald and Mikey. I just loved going to work with those guys. I have never met anyone who believed in himself quite as much as Ronald did. He just bred confidence in everyone – he was some player. But some weeks he was appalling in training because of his knee. Forty-eight hours after a game, he could barely walk. There were mornings at Murray Park when I was ready to call the medical staff to get a wheelchair to bring him to the dressing-room. Then, on a Saturday, when he heard the roar of the Ibrox crowd, you could see his chest puff out, and he was ready to perform again – and he would be magical. But throughout that time, he couldn't straighten his leg, even in training.

The word great is bestowed on people too easily now, but he was a true great. He is up there with the best I have ever played with. Whenever I got the ball, I could actually see de Boer in my mind's eye – I swear I could. It was like telepathy, and I always knew he would be making an angle for me to bump the ball off to him. We had this incredible understanding, and playing with the likes of him, Shota and Mikey at the top level was the best education I could ever have had. They were so intelligent.

Ronald once said to me, 'When they doubt me, I remind myself that I am special. I am *the* man.' I was pissing myself laughing at that, but do you know what? He was right! I could find him with a pass without having to look, and he became a close friend off the park as well. For all his supposed arrogance from his days at Ajax and Barcelona, he was at every team night out in his immaculate clobber, putting us all to shame.

Mols, Numan, de Boer and Arveladze all knew the value of bonding together, and they were the glue in that team. I loved that side – playing in it was one of the most enjoyable times I have ever had in a Rangers jersey. I would go to away games with them on the bus *knowing* we were going to win. I'd be itching to get there, dying to get on the pitch, always thinking, 'We're going to pump this lot. How many are we going to take off them?'

That team had a determination, but Eck still had to manage it, massage the egos and keep it all flowing. He had a group of men he believed in, and often all he needed to do was give his team of accomplished players a reality check and get them back to the level they should be at. We were training at a tempo, and I loved getting the trackie on every morning to get out there.

Alex very rarely had to lose his temper with that team, but in the Scottish Cup semi-final against Motherwell at Hampden in 2003, he did. We were down at half-time and getting battered, and he exploded into the dressing-room and roared, 'You lot are a fucking disgrace. You've gone out there and thought all you have to do is step across that white line and the game is won. Well, it is not fucking won. You are a joke. Now get fucking back out there and prove me wrong.' We won 4–3 in the end. We trounced them in the second half – the shock treatment had worked. He kicked all the arrogance and cockiness out of us.

It is hard to explain how I went from enjoying the high of the Treble win in May 2003 to leaving three short months later, but much of it was down to losing some quality players. Arthur was on his way, Neil McCann was being sold off to Southampton for £1.75 million and Amo was also out of the door when Blackburn Rovers came in. I saw these men as all but irreplaceable, and I felt that something very special was slipping through my fingers. I couldn't bear it, and it started to mess with my brain. I started to hear whispers in my head telling me that I'd gone as far as I could and that it couldn't get any better than a Treble. My head became scrambled, and it was all a reaction to the prospect of having to go into the trenches without those special guys beside me.

The finances meant we just couldn't hope to bring in players of the same quality, and I began to feel cornered and isolated. I should have conquered those feelings and stayed put as Rangers captain, but instead I let them fester and then find a place to breed. I was a lost cause at that point, not open to reason. I should have stayed to gut it out – I know that now – but it just felt as though we were heading in the wrong direction.

For someone so often ruled by his heart in football matters, I tried to turn myself into a cold-eyed businessman and chase the best contract – forget my emotional ties to Alex McLeish. It was a period of turmoil, and all I remember was that I felt like I had stepped on the train to England and it wasn't making any stops to let passengers off. My mind was in a whirl. By the time I came to my senses and properly cleared my head, I was gone from the club I called home. I was Barry Ferguson of Blackburn Rovers – and I only had myself to blame.

9

Souness, Sparky and Life at the Rovers

'I believe in you, son. I always will. You're my captain now.'

Graeme Souness, while manager of Blackburn Rovers.

The jagged hole I had punched in my front door seemed to be a symbol of what I'd done. I felt like I was breaking my family apart. Upstairs, my son Connor was a kid being torn to shreds, homesick and lonely. Paying the price for the biggest mistake of his dad's life: moving to Blackburn Rovers in the first place. I felt fury and frustration but most of all a sense of burning shame that wouldn't go away. It was all boiling up inside me.

Margaret had been fine about the move when I sat her down and told her I felt that I had to leave Rangers and try the English Premiership. She realised when we got together that this would be her life. But I was putting my kids through sheer torture. They were up in their rooms crying their eyes out because they hadn't wanted to leave their pals back home in Scotland.

Connor had been cut adrift from everything he knew and was terrified of his new life. We had bought him a mobile phone so he could keep in touch with his pals in an attempt to get him through it. Then Margaret's mum told us that he had been phoning his aunt in Cupar Angus, whom he holidays with each summer, breaking his heart down the line to her. The wee man was being so brave. He would phone his aunt to unload his troubles then get her to swear not to breathe a word to his mum and dad because he thought we'd be disappointed in him. Then he'd come downstairs and have his dinner and not show us that he couldn't handle it. We thought everything was rosy.

Eventually, it all came tumbling out, and I was horrified. We confronted him, and he was in tears again telling us the truth about his new life in England and how he felt about it – the new life that I had forced him into. I couldn't cope with it. I walked downstairs and out of the house, punching a hole in the front door on my way out. Jesus Christ, what had I done to my family? I hadn't thought this through. I knew by then that the move was one huge blunder, and later I looked at Margaret and said, 'I have done this to us. I am some sort of father, eh?'

That was seven months into my new life in England, and it is a part of transfers that the fans never see. But how did I arrive there? Why did a boy who was born to play for Rangers grow up to captain the club and somehow think he could hand back that armband and only ever be fulfilled as a footballer if he left? And why Blackburn Rovers? So many people have asked me those questions, and when I sit down and analyse it all now, the answer can be summed up in one word: Souness.

It was a crazy time in my life, and I was in utter turmoil when I decided I had to quit Gers. My mind was all messed up, and when I heard Graeme's voice on the phone, I knew my destination would be Ewood Park. I had five enquiries at the time and knew that Liverpool were lurking in the background, but the concrete offers came from Blackburn Rovers and Everton. Others wanted to be kept informed, and I knew Gérard Houllier was waiting to be brought into the mix and take me to Anfield if I wanted to push it, but he wasn't Souness, was he? He didn't hold the aura Graeme does for a Rangers man like me.

But almost immediately after all the emotion and adrenalin of a big-money transfer had died down and I had thrashed out the most lucrative contract of my life, the reality of my situation became clear, and I thought, 'What the fuck have I done?'

I had listened to the media back home and had heard all the criticism: I was going to become Rangers' answer to Celtic's Paul McStay; I'd played in Scotland all my life and would forever be an underachiever with no ambition – a player without the bottle to test himself against the best; the Premiership was the greatest league in the world, and if I didn't grasp the opportunity to play there, then I was a coward. They drummed their arguments home, time and again, until I couldn't bear to hear or read them any more.

I took notice of all that was said and written, and I'm not scared to admit it: I was goaded into joining Blackburn Rovers. Even now, I am raging that I was not strong enough to resist the opinions of the press. I was so vulnerable then, and, to be honest, I wish I could say that I slept for 17 months and woke up to find that I'd never left Rangers – that choosing to go to Blackburn was a bad dream. But it did happen. I regretted the decision to leave the minute I walked out the door, but the big plus is I got to redeem myself and get back to Rangers. I was lucky.

Glasgow's own special brand of bigotry would have you believe that my agent John Viola forced me away from Gers because he is a Catholic and a Celtic man. Am I that weak in spirit? Of course not. I make the decisions about my career, and I go into negotiations and thrash out my own terms. Every decision I have made in my football life has been down to me, whether they are ones I have celebrated or those that I have lived to regret.

Yes, I knew within days of signing for Souness that I had made a mistake, but I didn't want to admit it to myself. That does not excuse the behaviour that followed, but it maybe goes some way towards explaining it. My wife and kids did not move south for five months after I joined Blackburn. Instead, I drove up and down the road to see them almost every day for the first three months of my new life at Rovers – until a seething Souness caught me at it. He was watching me lurch into training at Brock Hall every morning with my eyes like pissholes in the snow, complaining to the physios about a sore back because of the time I was spending in the driver's seat. Then one morning, he was doing a workout on an exercise bike after training when I walked into the gym. He shouted me over and said, 'Are you fucking daft? I know you are driving up and down that road every day. I'm warning you that if you want to make a go of this, you have to move your family down.'

I liked that bluntness about him. You knew where you stood with Souness; there was no two-faced stuff. If he liked you and rated you, then you were one of his men. If he didn't rate you, then you could beat it to pitch five and train with the reserves! He was straight like that.

At Rangers, Souness had his clashes with my brother, but there was never a suggestion of him ever holding a grudge against me or allowing that to colour our relationship. All he told me was that he was desperate to get me to his football club, and I was happy with that. He's a straight-talking man who takes no shit – that suited me. If someone steps out of line, they will be punished; if they play badly, they will be dropped. There is no messing about, just honesty and simplicity. No discussion. You get others in this game who are scared of making hard decisions, but not Graeme Souness.

I was only eight years old when he arrived from Sampdoria to check in at Rangers as the new player–manager, and I used to watch videos of him playing for Liverpool and Scotland. I loved to see Souness swagger around with an arrogance in midfield. I'd seen the player he was, and that did pull me towards Blackburn – I wanted that to rub off on me. And he did help me: he taught me how to dictate play from deep and then how to spring forward and be an attacking influence; and he showed me the passing angles and how to bring my wide players into the game. He certainly knew how to pull the strings from central midfield. He had widened his footballing experience in *Serie A* – it was like going back to school in a football sense – and I respected his knowledge of my position. He knew it inside out.

In the end, Souness had one conflict after another with my brother, but that all came from him wanting to see Derek make the best of himself. Graeme despaired of Derek and the scrapes he got into off the field. He always felt Derek could have gone further than he did, and he didn't want to see me end up with similar regrets when I hung up my boots.

There are figures who become legends to Rangers and Celtic fans, no matter how much they are hated wherever else they go in football. I guess Martin O'Neill will always be a god at Parkhead for picking them up when they were in danger of becoming a laughing stock under John Barnes and crafting a team to get to the UEFA Cup final, which they lost to FC Porto in Seville. Well, for a Gers supporter, Souness should have that kind of status. He took a dying club and breathed it back to life. So, when he told me he wanted to sign me, I went.

At first, I was filled with all the wonder of a kid with a new toy. When the deal was signed on the Friday afternoon before the transfer window closed, my registration couldn't be hurried through in time, and it became clear that I would have to be a spectator for Blackburn's trip to Chelsea the next day. I flew down anyway, had a meal with some pals in the Chelsea Village next to Stamford Bridge and strolled through the crowds towards the game almost unnoticed. I quite liked that – it wasn't Glasgow.

Graeme was nice enough to include me in his team talk, but then I was left to my own devices. I stole some Jaffa Cakes out of a hamper and stood at the mouth of the tunnel watching the team Roman Abramovich had given Claudio

Ranieri over £100 million to construct. José Mourinho – 'The Special One' – hadn't arrived yet, so Abramovich was just giving 'The Tinkerman' the loose change.

It was a release to be there that day. Back home, I was being slaughtered for leaving Gers, and my reputation was being kicked from pillar to post. The critics said I had joined a team of middle-of-the-road nobodies, but Blackburn didn't look like duds or a nowhere side that day. They looked like a coming team who deserved to win the game. It fascinated me watching it. I was standing there wishing I had my boots on when 20 seconds into the game Marcel Desailly lost the ball out on the touchline, and Matt Jansen crossed for Andy Cole. *Goal!* I was standing there thinking, 'I've joined the right team.' Then the ball sizzled from Juan Sebastián Verón to Jimmy Floyd Hasselbaink to Frank Lampard. His pass caught Lorenzo Amoruso sleepwalking and Adrian Mutu, who'd cost Chelsea almost £16 million, was in and around Brad Friedel to score the equaliser. After the break, Carlo Cudicini flapped at a David Thompson cross, and Coley scored again. The boys should have won that day, but Geremi's cross thumped off Lucas Neill's arm from point-blank range and Hasselbaink buried the penalty. Cruel.

In Scotland, I was also being called a coward and a traitor who had turned his back on Rangers, and it hurt badly. But the football pitch has always been a place for me to escape from any criticism, even if I am only watching. I got lost in that game at Stamford Bridge, and for 90 minutes, I could forget about leaving Ibrox. Looking back to that day now, I was genuinely excited by it all. I was as sick as anyone when referee Mike Dean gave that penalty. I just couldn't believe it, and I'd have been giving him pelters if I had been on the park.

I moved because I thought I could only improve coming to the Premiership, and going to Stamford Bridge confirmed that to me. Tugay and Garry Flitcroft demonstrated what good players they were, and, at that time, I felt that I would be kicking lumps out of myself all my life if I missed out on the chance to play in England. Within 17 months, I would have my face buried in my bedroom pillow, crying tears of rage because my Gers return seemed to be collapsing and I thought they were ripping up my ticket home. But at the start, I came back from Scotland's 2–1 Euro 2004 qualifying defeat by Germany in Dortmund keyed up for my Blackburn debut. (Maurice Ross had been sent off that night, and Germany had dived, play-acted and cheated in the mud – they did our heads in. Christian Dailly stormed off at the end and bellowed, 'Cheats, fucking cheats!' in the middle of Berti Vogts' live TV interview!)

I felt drained after that trip but ready to start life as a Rovers player, and my first game flashed past. With 13 minutes gone – and the scoreline already 1–1 – Lucas Neill waded in studs-up on Liverpool's Jamie Carragher – red card. For the second time in a week, it felt like I was fighting the best with one arm tied behind my back. At the end of the match, my legs felt as though they weighed 40 st. with lead boots on the end of them. I was raging because I thought we could have taken them, and I was sad that I didn't get a chance to even try to dictate anything because I was chasing my tail with the side down to ten men.

We lost 3–1, and the media was telling me that it must have been hard living in this daunting new world. The truth was I didn't notice any major differences from the SPL. It wasn't as physical as I had first feared it might be. The only bad thing that happened to me was when I got sacked on the halfway line by Vladimír Šmicer, and they pinged it wide to Harry Kewell, but Vratislav Greško rescued me from his cross. That was the only time when I looked at my debut and thought I had really let myself down. Sure, Liverpool were clever when they had the spare man. They got wide and stretched us really well. But deep down, I was already having doubts if this league, for all its stars and hype, was all it was cracked up to be. Obviously, there are world-class names in every Premiership side, but I genuinely feel that many of them would struggle in the SPL.

My temper is quick to the boil, and I would genuinely go off my nut in that Blackburn dressing-room when they wound me up about the supposed 'Mickey Mouse football' I had come from. These were my mates they were laughing at when they called the SPL the 'Walt Disney League'. I got sick of their sneering. It's not a wind-up designed to get your back up – they genuinely mean it. Michael Gray – who had been on loan at Celtic and knew the demands of football in Scotland – would back me up. He knew how hard it was and that I was being honest when I said there were times when life was easier in the Premiership than in the SPL.

I will never disrespect Blackburn; I made friends there, and there was a little inner circle of people behind the scenes who knew just how homesick I would become and had the kindness in their hearts to help me. But the truth is that once you play for a club the size of Rangers, few clubs can ever come near it. And even on my debut against Liverpool – supposedly one of the biggest clubs in Europe – the atmosphere was nowhere near to what I was used to at Ibrox.

It all hit home on the bus coming home from a derby win over Bolton Wanderers just before the transfer window opened. It was like a zoo: the players were all so delighted, sinking beers and partying, but I just couldn't feel the same buzz. They'd told me at Rovers that this was it – this was the game that meant *everything*. Bolton Wanderers at the Reebok Stadium on 28 December 2004: this derby was the match Blackburn wanted to win more than any other.

We did win it, too. Paul Dickov scored early, and we protected our goal in an ugly scuffle of a game. There were 27,038 fans there that day, and I have to be brutally honest and say that when I looked around that's when home and Rangers really started tugging at me. I respected what the game meant to Rovers and the fans, but I looked around and knew I was in the wrong place. I thought of *my* derby, the one that means everything to me. And I knew then that Bolton v. Blackburn just wasn't my place. I was brought up dreaming of representing Rangers against Celtic. And I'd just had 18 months of being a Rangers *fan* at Old Firm games. It was good for me in some ways – a nightmare in others. It reminded me what people who are committed to either side go through when they are watching these matches.

On the bus back from that game, I needed to talk to a

mate about how I felt. I hit speed dial and said, 'This is it for Blackburn – the big one. There were less than 30,000 there, and I can't feel the way they all do. This is not the Old Firm.' Simple as that. I had been born to play in the biggest derby of the lot, been lucky enough to play my part in it, but I had walked away of my own free will. It was stupidity.

But Souness rated me and that mattered. There are plenty of people in football whose opinions mean nothing to me – his did. And it meant so much to me when he made me his captain because I had only been at the club nine months – and I had been injured for a huge chunk of that. But I was also wary of that armband, because my first season had to all intents and purposes been a write-off. I'd only played 16 games for the club, scored a couple of goals and started winning some Man of the Match awards. I had been getting used to the tempo of the game in England and was beginning to look like a player when *smash!* I broke my kneecap at Newcastle on 28 December 2003 and ended my season.

Now here I was walking in for the new season, and Graeme was making me his skipper – I was a little stunned. I was just enjoying being out there on the training field again when he called me into his office and said, 'I believe in you, son. You know that. You're the captain for this season.' I kind of nodded, thanked him, walked out to my car in a daze and thought, 'I haven't even played for six months.'

I started the new season playing well. I was gutted when big Amo was sent off at home to Manchester United, and Alan Smith equalised for them when the ref had the whistle at his lips to blow for full-time. Then we lost 3–2 at Southampton, and I managed to get a *referee* suspended for the first time in my life. Something to be proud of!

The referee in question at St Mary's was Andy d'Urso, and he just lost the plot. I had already been booked when he gave them a penalty, and I kicked the ball into the crowd. He booked me again, and I should have been off, but he didn't show me the red card, so I stayed on. There were Southampton players saying, 'Get off. That's two bookings, you Scottish twat.'

I just shrugged and said, 'He hasn't shown me a red card, mate, and until he does, you can all get to fuck!' He never did show me that red card, but I bet he wishes he had – he got bumped out of the Premiership because of me.

We were still laughing about that at the Scotland camp in Troon as we gathered for the first World Cup qualifier with Slovenia at Hampden, a game we'd draw 0–0 to put Berti Vogts even further under the cosh. I was sitting in my room at the Marine Highland Hotel on the seafront when my mobile rang. I checked the screen, and it read 'Gaffer'. He was quick and to the point: 'Barry, I'm leaving the club. Newcastle United have come in for me, and it is too big – I can't turn it down. You've been buzzing. Just keep playing the way you are, and I will come back for you in January when the transfer window opens.'

He would be as good as his word, and come the turn of the year, he came back in for me. But at that point, I had to get my head around his departure just 13 months after I'd signed for him. Souness was on his way to Newcastle as Sir Bobby Robson's replacement. I think his job was always safe at Blackburn, but you couldn't blame him for taking the move. I was shocked and gutted, but I couldn't feel truly angry. It was an offer he couldn't refuse.

So many managers have failed at Newcastle: Kenny Dalglish, Ruud Gullit, even Sir Bobby, who was a local hero. But Graeme's nature meant that he thought he would be the one to win the Geordies their first trophy since the Fairs Cup in 1969. Sadly, 17 months later, he was sacked, done in by Michael Owen's broken foot. You pay £17 million for a player and then that happens. You can't legislate for horrible luck like that.

Newcastle is one of those jobs that seems to be cursed. They are probably the biggest club in Britain apart from Manchester United, they have a massive fan base and a great stadium. If you built a home for 150,000 fans, they'd still fill it, and every second person you see there has a Newcastle top on – even the grannies. It's a fantastic footballing place, and the passion is just the same as Souness would have felt when he was manager of Rangers all those years ago. In my opinion, that's a major reason why he went there. We just didn't have that at Blackburn – neither of us.

I know that some of Souness's ex-players line up to have a pop at him, but not me. Graeme bought me and made me his captain, and he helped me through my first major injury. I was on a downer, and he saw it. He told me to beat it out of the treatment room and take off to Dubai, a place I have come to love. I chilled out and cleared my mind of all the pressures. It got my head straight and helped me to get over the injury.

With Souness gone, it was time for the fifth boss of my

club career: Sparky. Mark Hughes the player was one I marvelled at. Every goal he scored seemed to be a killer volley – brilliant. As a manager, he'd bossed Wales, but I knew little of what to expect – he turned out to be top-drawer. His backroom team of Mark Bowen and Eddie Niedzwiecki were superb, and their training sessions were so well thought out and punishing. Every day, you came off dripping in sweat, and I loved that.

I was enjoying working for Hughes, but my homesickness was nagging away at me, even when he called me into his office and said, 'You are staying the captain because I want to build this team around you.' That's why I found it so hard to tell him I wanted out, but it wasn't about him, and I told him that. It was about coming home to Rangers. The bust-ups and the bitterness of that January transfer window will always linger, I suppose, but I hope that when we are finished in this game Mark will reflect on that time and see how highly I rated him.

I hope and pray that this chapter does not sound like a downing of Blackburn Rovers. I hope I have found the right words to express that is not how I feel about the place. I made a mistake trying to put my heart and soul into Rovers, because they were the property of another football club – they weren't mine to give. But if any of my Scotland teammates told me that Blackburn were in for him, I'd say, 'Go.' The people there and the facilities where they train in the Lancashire countryside at Brock Hall make it a place where any footballer would love his life. Any footballer perhaps but me. Jack Walker's legacy will always mean there is money at that club, and under Mark Hughes they can be a top-six club again – I know they can. There are dreams to chase there, they're just not my dreams. I was kidding myself to think that they were.

But the English adventure gave me days to cherish. I played against Patrick Vieira at Highbury, and Arsène Wenger told our backroom staff that I had impressed him. I liked that. I got to play at Highbury, Anfield, Old Trafford, Stamford Bridge and the rest, which I loved. But it is not the best league in the world in my eyes. I think that tag belongs to Spain. If I want to see the finest technique, I tune in to *La Liga* and watch Ronaldinho at Barça and Riquelme at Villarreal – marvel at them.

I can't help the way I feel, but I am a home-loving boy. Now I can live in my skin, and be happy with what I've got. I'll never be pushed into a transfer again. I think you could see it in my eyes when I came home. I had blanked out the other clubs, and if the Rangers deal didn't happen, then I would have stayed at Blackburn. Forget Newcastle and Everton. I only wanted one move.

The best way to understand it is to try and remember the way Robbie Fowler looked the day he joined Liverpool again. He didn't need to leave Anfield; I didn't need to leave Ibrox. At least I didn't lose four years of my life languishing away from the place where I belong – unlike Robbie. I saw his face the day he returned to Anfield from Manchester City and smiled. I thought he looked just like I did the night I made it back to Rangers. That red shirt he wears means as much to him as my light-blue one does to me. Maybe we've both now learned that staying at home doesn't make you a failure.

10

Wounded

'Playing again could be a major problem for you. We will have to see – it's in the lap of the gods. It is 50–50.'

Paul Rae, surgeon.

I sat there shivering on Lytham seafront with my crutches balanced on the wooden bench, staring out bleakly at the water and into the darkness and talking to myself. I had a skinful of drink swilling around inside of me – I was a gibbering wreck. Was I just another pissed-up, washed-up footballer with a hard-luck story? I couldn't be, could I? Even with my mind in a fog after another session drowning my sorrows and feeling sorry for myself, I knew that it was starting to look helluva lot like it. In my eyes, I'd become someone to pity, sitting there babbling to myself like the down-and-outs you pass mumbling to themselves in Glasgow. Christ, how had I ended up like this?

My left kneecap was shattered: there were three horrible cracks in it, and my heart felt like it was broken as well. My life was in pieces. The move to Blackburn Rovers had been a terrible mistake from the start, and in my heart of hearts I knew it. But I'd tried to bury all my misgivings and make it work. Now I was badly damaged goods, and the only way I could think of to forget that fact was to get drunk.

In the days and weeks after the injury that changed my life, my mobile rang and the texts flew in from my pals back home in Scotland, but my childish answer to their concern was to ignore everyone. How could they help? How could they know what I was going through? I am ashamed of my behaviour when I think back, because all they wanted was to be there for me, and I blanked them. Those were some of the lowest times for me.

My solution was the oldest one in the book for a working-class Lanarkshire boy. I drank – and I kept on drinking. I was giving up on myself. I would hobble down to the Ship and Royal in Lytham on my crutches and drink my quota – back in the old routine.

Last summer after my ankle operation, I was still bang on my playing weight – 12 st. dead – when the plaster came off. That was down to the positive attitude I had and the knowledge that my ankle would be stronger and I'd at last be playing pain free again. It was in stark contrast to the way I behaved after my knee operation. The weight piled on – a stone in no time – but I couldn't have cared less. I didn't even want to go near the club, and when I did go in, I behaved like a horrible little bastard. People were trying to help me, and I didn't care – just wouldn't listen. What did they know? I had found my way out. I'd even drink in the house, which is something I never do. And I started to sink them when I was sitting in on my own, another thing I never do.

We had a masseur at the club, an old guy called Bomber who was about 65, and he became my drinking mate because he lived near me in Blackpool and could drive us to the boozer. I'd give him a bell and get ready to hit the bevvy again at the Ship and Royal.

I'd read books about players with serious injury and how they had got through them, and I had heard all the tales from those in the game. But when the 'Bad One' hits you, it's finger on the release button time. All those Friday nights of sober sacrifice when you were stuck in as your mates went out and got blitzed are forgotten, and now it's your turn to get smashed with no game the next day and no consequences. That's the answer. It's not, though. I know, because for a month I lived that life and cheated myself.

I had a moment of clarity one morning when I woke up with another looming hangover – this shite had to stop. I went back into the club and took the bollocking that was coming my way from Graeme Souness. I knew that I deserved it.

But I felt so sorry for myself back then. I'd look at my mess of a knee and wonder why it was swelling up. Now that I think about it, it was probably because there was ten pints of lager inside it. Drink and footballers, eh? It's a bad mix.

I do think about it – you can't fail to when a teammate like Fernando Ricksen goes through the problems he has. But I will always defend the value of bonding sessions and a few drinks together. When we win and we have worked hard to achieve it, I like to unwind and still enjoy being with those I trust, having the time to loosen up, enjoying a laugh and a few beers.

But back then all I could do was sit there with a pack of ice on a knee that was in tatters. I was bored out of my head. I lost the plot, I really did. I was constantly thinking, 'Will I ever kick a ball again?' And I was in agony, taking all sorts of painkillers with the bevvy on top. I was a real living health advert. For the one time in my life, I threatened to become one of those boys I'd seen sitting in the corner of the pub when I was growing up. You know the ones. The guys who are on the fringe of the crowd not even watching the fitba on the telly; they are there to drink – that's their sport. That was me but only until I woke up and came to my senses.

The blackest time of my career was born on 28 December 2003 at St James' Park, Newcastle United v. Blackburn Rovers. We won the game 1–0 thanks to Paul Gallagher's goal. But by the end of the first Saturday after Christmas, a win bonus was the last thing on my mind.

Newcastle's Olivier Bernard – who would later be a teammate at Ibrox – played the ball into Gary Speed, and it went under his foot; his one moment of miscontrol almost ended my career. I went in to try and nip the ball away, and the next thing I knew, I was lying on the ground staring up at the sky over Tyneside. There was nothing, no pain at all, then 30 seconds later, *bang*! It felt like I had been cast in a scene from *Goodfellas*; I felt as if Joe Pesci was standing over me, smashing my knee with a baseball bat. Repeatedly. I looked down in horror, and my knee had just *gone*; it was flat, and there was a massive hole where it should have been.

I looked at the faces around me, a swirling sea of them, all etched with concern, all staring down at me – the ref Mark Halsey, our physio, my teammates. The one that got me, though, was Souness.

I've always thought of him as a never-to-be-messed-with character, ever since he made his Rangers debut against Hibs in 1986. They pushed him too far, with fly elbows and liberty taking, and then *smack*! The boot went in on George McCluskey, blood was dripping down his knee from a stud hole and Souness walked before he'd even been shown the red card. You can't condone that – he let his team down and they lost 2–1 – but it demonstrates that he could be one nasty bastard.

When he walked onto the park at Newcastle, he took one look at me and turned away, putting his head in his hands. I thought to myself, 'He's a hard man. If he is reacting like that, then I am fucked.'

I was carted into the dressing-room, and the Blackburn doc Phil Batty was hanging over me saying I had to take a jab for the pain. It sent me into the land where students must go when there are having one of *those* parties: I was stoned. They'd clamped an oxygen mask over my face on the pitch, but I later found out that he was so worried about my struggle to breathe that he felt the only thing that would make the pain stop was the same sort of jab given to wounded British squaddies on Iraq's battlefields.

I was in a panic before the drugs kicked in. Then I looked to the side and saw a guy trying to feed me a drink of Lucozade to calm me down. It was Newcastle's Craig Bellamy, who wasn't playing that day, and when our paths crossed again in Old Firm matches, I couldn't ever hate him the way some Gers fans did. When he came to Celtic on loan, he scored a belter at Ibrox, and they beat us 2–1, so the punters just detested him. He wound them up the wrong way from the minute he pulled on the Hoops. But my mind would flash back to the time when I had been at my lowest ebb, and he thought enough of me to come to the dressing-room to try and help. Peter Beardsley made his way down there, too, as did my Scotland teammate Steven Caldwell – they knew it was bad. It is at times like that the footballing fraternity bonds, because other players know the depths of despair you are in.

When the drugs wore off a little, I screamed at the doc, 'What's wrong with me? Don't hide it from me. Tell me.' I was told I was going to hospital in Newcastle. Every bump the ambulance hit on the way sent waves of pain shooting through my knee, and every corner we took was agony. I began to scream once more, and the needle with its blessed relief drove home again.

The X-rays came, and by that point I was lucid. I knew what was happening, and I knew I was in trouble. The doctor went round to the side of the lightbox, where they look over the pictures, and he thought he was out of my view. He was shaking his head sadly. I bit down on my lip and insisted, 'You have to tell me what is wrong with me. I have to know.'

He looked at me gravely and said matter-of-factly, 'Fractured patella and other damage. There are cartilage problems in there, too.' Patella? Before my injury, I'd have told you he was the full-back for Roma. I was about to learn all about the workings of my knee.

These days, I have the X-rays in my medical file at Murray Park, and I don't try to forget what happened any more because I can't. I know that. There's no sense trying to bury it. I will be a different player now, older and wiser, always carrying the scar with me.

After the hospital, I remember that they somehow got me back onto the Blackburn team bus, and I lay there, throwing up all the way home from Newcastle. Rovers were so concerned that a people carrier was waiting at a service station when we were nearly home to rush me to the surgeon's house. Paul Rae was waiting for me there at 9 p.m. on a Saturday night. I'll never forget his dedication. He abandoned his time with his family, because he knew my career was on the line.

Mr Rae was brutally honest with me – just what I needed. He said, 'Listen, this is a very serious injury. I've never seen it in a footballer before. The only time I have seen it was when a ball smashed into a cricketer's knee. Playing again could be a major problem for you. We will have to see – it's in the lap of the gods. It is 50–50.'

Just like that, all those balls I had kicked around the streets in Hamilton, all the dreams I'd had pretending to be Roberto Baggio, all the games I had played to get to that point in my life, meant nothing. He was telling me I could be finished at the age of 25.

The operation was a blur, the aftermath a haze. I had a mask next to my bed that gave me morphine for the pain; that mask became my best friend. Souness came to see me, and the Blackburn boys came to comfort me – or so they tell me now. I don't remember a bit of it, because I was out of my face! Eventually, the nurse came in and said, 'Mr Ferguson, this machine is going.' They thought I was going to get addicted to the morphine. I was raging as it was wheeled out – my hand was clawing in the air, trying to drag it back.

I looked at the X-ray pictures of my knee after I came out of the surgery, and I despaired. There were two wires down the side and then another figure of eight. All that metal was holding my knee together. Slowly but surely, I tried to move and flex the knee, but I just couldn't straighten it without excruciating pain. I was at my wit's end, and I began to believe Paul's dark fears were right – it was over for me; the wires hadn't worked. The straight wires in particular were niggling me. Then, one day, the club doc jabbed me with local anaesthetic at both ends of the straight wires, and my knee was moving fluidly all of a sudden. I realised then that I understood my own body and needed those wires out.

Mr Rae had the experience of working on Roy Keane's knee, and he'd operated on Wes Brown, too. He knew footballers through nursing Manchester United's best back to health. I knew United would only invest in the best medical care, and they trusted him implicitly. That gave me faith. But he was so reluctant to go back in – not happy about putting me through another operation. Still he stuck with me and told me if that's what I wanted then he would go back in and clip the wires. He did and it worked.

However, there were still bad days when the knee would balloon up again, and I was worried sick at all the setbacks. Blackburn rescued me: they sent me once again to my bolthole in Dubai on holiday with Margaret to try and get my head straight, but when I came back at the start of March 2004, there were still problems. I pleaded with the surgeon to take *all* the wires out. I felt that they were the root cause of the problem, but Paul didn't want to do it. I was adamant, but he'd say that wasn't the way it worked, and I'd go back to work knowing deep down it wasn't happening. I kept expecting to be all right, but I had a foreign body in me – a lump of metal. He relented a little in the end, and all that remains now is the straight wire bracing the kneecap – it's there to stay.

I felt like an outsider at Blackburn, and I'd be lucky if I watched six games during all the time I was out with my injury. I'd slink away and leave at half-time. It's the same now when I miss games with Rangers, and it's why throughout my career I have taken so many injections and swallowed so many Voltarol painkillers. I can't watch because I want to play. It hurts too much to miss out.

After that awful day, Gary Speed faxed and phoned me at Blackburn time and again to check on me – I won't forget that. And I had a ball at my feet after nine weeks, which lifted my spirits. However, I had lost so much muscle in my thigh it had wasted away – it was like a pencil. Rebuilding that was a slow process, and I didn't have the patience for it. Coming back from my injury was a fresh kind of hell. I used to love the swimming pool, but the rehabilitation process has now turned me into a man who walks past the water on holiday unless the kids insist I go in. Running in water stops you pounding on a hard surface and putting stress on the knee – I understand the process. But I ran lengths of the pool for 90 minutes a day with the Blackburn physio Dave Fevre – who had been at Manchester United – willing me on. At first, it was just me running, then I'd be dragging a sledge with weights on it behind me. It was torture, and I'd be shouting at him, 'You are nothing but an English wanker.' I terrorised that man, but he saved me in the end – saved me from myself at times. I was my own worst enemy.

When David Thompson and Jay McEveley were in rehab with me, it was easier. Thommo had two years of hell with ligament damage, and Jay had dislocated his kneecap. They both helped me. Then they'd break down, and I would be on my own again.

But I eventually got there. I dragged myself through it all for seven months – the drink, the depression, making everyone around me miserable – all for the moment when I got back on that pitch in a pre-season friendly in the middle of nowhere and . . . I saw him lunging in, two feet over the ball. His studs thudded into my left knee, and blood gushed down my leg.

It was the height of summer in some place called the Donaustadion in Ulm in Germany, and this charged-up Bohemians Prague player had just done me. Over the top: the worst sort of tackle. For ten seconds, the end of my career flashed through my mind. I thought, 'Shite, that's me this time.' Then I stood up, looked at the wound and the blood that was dripping down. I was *delighted*. Why? I knew I would need stitches, that the scar had opened up again, but I also knew that inside my knee was solid, and it had stood up to the impact – I was overjoyed.

I walked off wounded and gave the little band of diehard

Rovers fans the thumbs-up, clapping them. They looked on, totally bewildered, at this bloodied maniac. The next morning, I was running in training, six stitches or not.

What happened to me in that friendly is a process I had to go through. I needed a smack on my left knee to clear my mind. I had to survive something like that to know I was really back.

I will always have the legacy of that awful day up in Newcastle. I knew that the minute I came out of the operating theatre. My knee is thicker now, and it always will be because of the scar tissue. I asked them to keep my wires; I had this thing about seeing what was inside me. I thought about making a coat hanger out of them! But I was out for the count, and they were a gory mess when they came out, so the surgeon binned them.

Football is my life. From a young age, this was all I wanted to do. I chucked it at school and didn't even try in my lessons, something that I still regret. What would I have done if I didn't have the game, though? I couldn't be done at 25 could I? Looking back, that's when I started to think more about every part of my life. I began to put money away and learn that I couldn't walk around without a care in the world any more. I'd been living in a bubble, pocketing money for something I had always dreamed of doing. That injury was my wake-up call. I realised that this life can be taken away from me in the blink of an eye, and for all the money, the house, the cars in the driveway and the other trappings, it is the game that counts.

I go into Murray Park some mornings, and they say we are running. I start moaning, 'Jesus Christ, get the ball out.

What are we doing this for?' Then I think about it and shut my mouth. I run for an hour, I feel good, I have a shower and I have worked myself hard, but that's me done.

At that minute my old man Archie will be up on a roof somewhere, working away in all weathers, doing his shift. He will never quit doing that despite every second guy on the site that says to him, 'Does your boy not look after you?' Well, I do, and I hope I have, but he is a working man. When I was a kid, I sat with my mum Maureen and said, 'One day I will play for Rangers. I will have kids and care for them, and I will look after you and my dad and buy you a nice place to live.' Those were my three aims in life. Well, now they have their bungalow with the conservatory and a nice car, and I am proud of them.

My parents helped me through my injury, but it will be with me for the rest of my life. I'm not going to lie and say there is not a legacy. It feels different, but there is no pain any more – that's what matters most. Yes, I get stiffness when I get a knock on it, but Paul Rae did a great job.

I have never spoken publicly about the toll playing through injuries has taken on my body, but I know that I am now damaged. I have gone to the limit. I have a bad ankle, a reconstructed kneecap and a weakness in my groin. That is the price I have paid for playing when I was not 100 per cent, and it is one I have always been willing to shell out. I hate to see players use this as an excuse, and I refuse to do so; I have made my own decisions. No one has forced me into taking a pain-killing injection. I know what is going into my body, and I won't do it if it is going to harm me in the long term.

Voltarol is my drug of choice to get me through a game. It got to a stage when I needed a hernia operation but kept playing for Rangers, and I was taking the tablets like Smarties. I gobbled down so many of them I ended up damaging the lining of my stomach, and I couldn't keep my food down. That side of football is far from glamorous. Now, I get a jab in my arse cheek instead! That's the doc's job at Rangers – no wonder we're close.

I must have a high pain threshold when I think about it, because in Alex McLeish's first season at Gers I played for three and a half months with *three* broken ribs. A specialist from Ross Hall Hospital secretly came to every game with us. I was given a block under my arm with a tube in it, and the injection flowed in to freeze where the ribs were broken. Then I'd go out and play.

I hid that injury from the first leg of the UEFA Cup last-16 match against Feyenoord when their wily midfielder Paul Bosvelt did me. I was tripped running through, and when I was falling, he saw his chance – a pro's foul. Blooter: he smashed his knee into my ribcage and followed through. He got away with it, too.

That injury was murder to go through because the treatment basically froze my ribcage, and I was running about thinking, 'No pain, no pain!' Then it wore off! And those injections scared me because they can puncture your lung if they go wrong. It was worth it to play, but when I look back on these things when I finish, I will think I was really stupid.

At the beginning of 2006, as my 28th birthday loomed, my right ankle was troubling me again. The cure? More needles. I went to Edinburgh and took *four* thumping steroid injections in my ankle. Once again, I found myself looking up at a lightbox as a rod poked around inside me to find the right spot to inject. The legacy will be arthritis, but I can live with that. My main worry is how long I can keep going.

I want to finish my career with Rangers; I don't think I could bring myself to play against them. I'm lucky enough to have an apartment in Dubai now, and I could finish out there, but I want to go at the top. I don't ever want to be seen as a man who cheated Rangers – I will know when I am done.

What I have gone through is nothing compared to Ian Durrant, who had seven operations and 1,000 stitches in his knee after Neil Simpson's tackle at Aberdeen the day he smashed his cruciate. He still came back to play for Rangers, though. Even now, I can remember 8 October 1988. Gers were away, and I was in the car with my old man when the news crackled over the radio. Simpson had committed a horrible challenge, and they'd carried Durranty off. My dad winced; it was too close to home, Ian being Derek's best mate.

I was just ten years old at the time, so I didn't realise the enormity of what had happened. Then the next day it was on TV, and I'll never forget what I saw. I just stared at the screen. Ian was on physio Phil Boersma's back, being taken off the park, and had his hand covering his face. I thought he was being strong, not letting the Dons fans see him cry. But his leg didn't look natural. It was just hanging there, and I shuddered. This guy was larger than life. Not long after that, he was in my house on his crutches slaughtering everyone at Derek's 21st birthday party. He was the life and soul of the party.

When you look at what he came through, it was just unbelievable that he was able to come back and play at the level he did. We talked about it at Blackburn once, Souness and I. He said he looked at Durrant and saw a player who would walk into a Serie A side and sparkle. Graeme knew how special he was and that his edge as a footballer could never be replaced after that one awful tackle, no matter how much courage he showed in his comeback. That will always be the hard thing to accept, but I don't think Ian is the type to live a life in mourning, full of regret. Durranty is not about what might have been.

I see him every morning now because we have him back at Murray Park as a coach, back where he should be. For me, people such as Ian Durrant should always be there at the heart of Rangers – people who know what the club means. The club has tried other supposedly more sophisticated routes under Dick Advocaat and then Paul Le Guen, but we will always need those who live and breathe Rangers.

Durranty's knee has been completely rebuilt now, but you could still roll a marble down his scar, and there are times when his knee looks like an alien is trying to break out from inside. I have got off lightly compared to that. And towards Christmas 2005, I picked up *The Sun* one day and read about Ted McMinn. He had had his right leg amputated below the knee, but he was talking about how he would fight back. I couldn't get my head round his courage. He was another who had played with my brother Derek at

Rangers, and those guys were my heroes – I thought they were invincible. So, I look down at my own knee now, and although it's not great and it's not pretty, I know I'll live.

During my hard times, Ian McGuinness, the former Rangers doctor who is now at Newcastle, became more than just the guy who looked after us. He was a friend and someone I could turn to when the pressures were mounting. If I was ever in his room talking about an injury or a fitness worry, I would look at the X-ray in my medical file and wince. The chilling thing is that if the injury had happened in 1998, it would have finished me. I was just lucky surgery had advanced enough to keep me playing. There are other players who have had similar injuries and have had to quit.

When I went back to St James' at the start of the following season, I felt strangely drawn to the spot where it happened to me, like going to a tombstone in a family plot in a graveyard. The pre-match stroll on the pitch is generally for small talk, taking the mickey out of whoever has been featured in the programme, deciding what boots you will wear and all the rest. When I returned to play there, my teammates couldn't wait to wind me up. I went for my stroll on the pitch, and the boys rushed over, making ghostly noises, and said, 'Look, there's the spot, Fergie.' Footballers have a dark sense of humour. But I couldn't let them see they were spooking me, so I went and stood in the exact place where I'd lain after the injury with an oxygen mask clamped to my face, and it was a weird feeling that shot through me. I looked down at the ground and thought, 'I could have been finished right there.'

The journey from that moment had taken me to a lot of dark places, until I sat on Lytham seafront that night with a skinful inside me and began to realise I had to get a grip of myself. I had learned all about surgeons and morphine, wires in your knee and depression – and I knew that while I never wanted to make that trip again, it had made me a better person.

11

The Firm

'There are big questions to be answered in these games. Have they got the heart for it? Can they take a slap or not?'

Craig Moore, former Rangers defender.

Your heart stops for just a fleeting moment; it skips a beat, then you focus, look at the keeper, give him the eyes and sweep it into the far corner. Then it seems like your head is going to explode – that's what it feels like to score against Celtic.

I'd dreamed of that moment time and again, watched all the videos of games gone by, asked players who'd experienced it how a born-and-bred Rangers fan would feel right at that second. Nothing they said did it justice; it's the ultimate high.

I listen to all the arguments about the evils of the Old Firm game – about the sectarian baggage, the religious bigotry, the stabbings, the human cost you can see in the aftermath of the matches in the accident and emergency rooms of Glasgow's hospitals – and I do take them in. I hear them, and I understand them. Sure, there are some wretched and ugly parts of this rivalry that I would want to wipe out, but I won't change my mind on one thing: it is still the greatest game in the world.

It can be brutal and cruel; it can wreck players' careers. It once made me the most vilified footballer in Scotland, but still I came back for more. Why? The reason is that this is where you find out what you have as a Rangers player and, in some ways, as a man; this is where you are tested to your limits as a footballer – in your body and in your mind. And it's against Celtic that I've experienced highs that almost defy description and lows that almost defy belief. That's what it means to me.

This book was never designed to be a diary of scorelines – I've read too many of those. I set out to try and get down on paper the emotions a player like myself brought up on one side of the Old Firm divide feels in these games. But 26 November 2000 does deserve to be etched in here. The scoreline? Rangers 5, Celtic 1, and for the first time my name was there underneath the result as one of those who had scored a goal.

There is so much spotlight now on the money players make and the lifestyles we enjoy that people forget that some of us started out simply as Rangers fans. I'm no different from any other punter before an Old Firm game. In the week building up to a derby match, I still sometimes sit and watch Rangers DVDs, like any Gers punter, to remind myself of the good days and pray there's another one coming.

Before the game in which I scored my first goal, my mind

kept flashing back to 1986 when Ian Durrant had taken Davie Cooper's unbelievable reverse ball before waiting for the right moment to slot the ball into the corner past Packie Bonner. It was eerie that when the game came round we should fast-forward to my time and my life and an almost carbon-copy situation – Claudio Reyna's pass was up there with the one Coop gave Durranty that day. You pause, your mind is clear and then you whip it in the corner. That is 100 per cent the best feeling in football that I've ever known. I've only scored two goals against Celtic in my life, but they mean a lot to me. How could they not? It's what I dream of.

In the 2002 Scottish Cup final, when we won 3–2, the free-kick we were awarded was in a place I loved, and I immediately scurried to get the ball. Then I glanced round to see Lorenzo Amoruso's tanned, shaved legs walking towards me. In his famous Italian accent, he said to me, 'OK, Barry. This is for me.'

I turned to him and said, 'Fuck off, ya fud!' I think that's where the *Only an Excuse* sketches started. Big Amo was a bit startled, but I had to let him know, in no uncertain terms, that I was taking this one because I'd had a vision. I knew I was scoring it. And I did.

There is a picture that hangs in my house with me in front of the Rangers end with my top off and my best mate Craig Moore on my back. It makes me smile every time I walk past it – just to remember the sheer joy of the moment. My brother Derek was in amongst all the fans, and he told me afterwards that he had fallen down ten rows of seats getting swept along in the celebrations.

I still laugh when I watch that game back and listen to the

Sky Sports commentary – it should have made Ian Crocker for life. Neil McCann gets the ball wide left at 2–2 with the clock ticking down. He is so direct, Neil, and when he scampered down the wing, I just felt something would happen. Crocker was yelling at that point, 'Could there be a twist in the tale? *Lovenkrands!*' It was a perfect ball – all Peter had to do was put his napper on it – and we all just lost it in the joy of the moment. We knew it was the last minute and it was over. I went off my head. It was a day I will always treasure.

My dad always remembers the Old Firm's 1973 Centenary Scottish Cup final when Tom Forsyth forced the winner over the line from about six inches. Well, I'll always feel that 2002 was like that for my generation. Alex McLeish had come in at a very difficult time, and we had given him two trophies against the odds that season. To be honest, it was the foundation for the Treble to come.

Celtic had scored early that day through big Bobo Balde, and even though we were twice behind in the game, we just kept coming back – I loved that. I felt that character was what Rangers are all about.

Winning trophies is always special, beating Celtic to do it doubly so. But when the biggest Glasgow derby for two decades arrived on 2 May 1999, I was stuck on the sidelines crocked, and I have to confess that the 6.05 p.m. kick-off on a Sunday night wasn't good for me never mind the Rangers and Celtic supporters. I'd injured my groin and missed out, and I was dejected. But I went as a fan that day, and I have to admit I had a few beers before we got there. It was some experience.

I was just willing my mates to win it, and once again Neil McCann was head and shoulders above the lot of them – the best player on the park by a country mile. He scored twice as we dumped them 3–0, and I was staggered by the intensity of it all. I saw sights I thought I'd never see. For example, the referee Hugh Dallas going down after a coin thrown by a Celtic fan hit him in the head and blood started to flow. That shocks you back to reality. Then I looked up and a *body* fell out of the Celtic stand. I just couldn't believe it. I actually saw this guy drop about 40 ft, and I thought, 'Dear Christ. He has to have died there.' He didn't. God knows how. Then I realised that was the section where my father-in-law Kaney sits, and I started praying it wasn't him!

That game cemented Neil McCann's name with Gers fans for ever – it should have done anyway. There had been a lot of talk of him being a childhood Celtic fan and that we shouldn't have signed him because of his Catholic roots. Me? I loved having him in those games because he thrived on them.

The Old Firm is one merciless arena. I watched Fernando Ricksen whipped off by Dick Advocaat after just 22 minutes in that 6–2 hounding we took at Parkhead. That could have killed him, because it sent out a signal not just to the team but to the fans. It's like publicly saying that the manager doesn't believe in you when it matters most. Fernando dug so deep to recover from that humiliation. I admire that in people, because I know from my own hurt in the game that splits the city down the middle just how long it can take to recover if you are cast as the villain.

When I came back from Blackburn Rovers, my first Old

Firm game was at Parkhead, and we won 2–0 to end five years
without a victory at their place. They say these games turn on
a moment of genius or a mistake, but that day there was only
one man being cast as the scapegoat: Rab Douglas. Gregory
Vignal's shot reared up off the turf, and Rab fumbled it in.
He looked as if he wanted the ground to swallow him whole.
But I'm not going to lie to you: at the time, I couldn't have
cared less. I was off to celebrate, and when Nacho Novo
sealed it, I was in dreamland. Then, at the end, I came down
from my adrenalin high, and I started to think about the cost
of something like that to a man's career – especially a guy I
respected and valued both as a pal and a Scotland teammate.
I was gutted for the big man because I knew so many Celtic
fans would simply never forgive him for his mistake. That's
why I say it is a game that can reward you or murder you.

That day meant a lot to me. I'd come home, but I knew
there were doubters who saw me as having betrayed Rangers
when I left. I've never been a badge-kisser – I've seen too
many foreign players on both sides of the divide do that too
early before they even know what the club means – but as
we partied in front of an ecstatic Gers end, I simply pointed
to the crest on my shirt, touched it and pumped my fist.
Back for good.

I came back for days like those. Being in front of the
Rangers fans at the final whistle meant a lot because I knew
what they had been through at Parkhead those last five years.
The gaffer, too, had gone through eight games there before
that without winning, and you start to question yourself.
Now he knew what it felt like to win an Old Firm match on
his rival's turf.

I felt that result was the reward for big Eck's good work in the January transfer window. He went through a lot, but I think, on balance, over the duration of his reign, he showed that when he had money to spend, he spent it wisely. For example, he landed Jean-Alain Boumsong on a Bosman and then sold him for £8 million to Newcastle United just six months later. Some deal. And that day I was so proud of the new players he'd landed with the proceeds of the Boumsong transfer, from Ronald Waterreus through to Sotirios Kyrgiakos and Thomas Buffel. I said in the build-up to the game that they had the passion for an Old Firm match, and they showed they did. It felt like having a team again. Every time I went in for a tackle, I had a mate behind me – that's what Rangers should always be about.

The influx of foreign players to our game sparks many debates. At Rangers, one question is always uppermost in my mind: 'Will he bottle it in an Old Firm game?' Call that narrow-minded if you like – I don't particularly care. That's how I judge new arrivals as players and men, simple as that.

Dick Advocaat understood the Old Firm by the time he arrived because he was given videos beforehand to begin understanding the passion and all that surrounds not just that one game but Rangers as a whole. Dick was an aggressive little bastard, and I loved that about him, but he was cool with the tactics board before a game. The shouting and the 'Let's get fucking intae them!' was left to me and the rest of the Scottish boys. It wasn't about the money with Advocaat: he bought into it all and just loved to beat Celtic. I love that in the foreigners.

But who was the most passionate Gers man of all the foreign imports? The answer might surprise you. It was Arthur Numan, my room-mate, who remains one of the best players I have *ever* had the pleasure of working beside. He was hellish to live with when we were on the road, though. We were like the Odd Couple. I'd leave a magazine lying on the floor, and he'd shout at me to tidy up. He was one helluva nag – worse than my mam. If we had breakfast at 10 a.m., he'd be up at 9 a.m. with the curtains flung open and the light streaming in, and he'd order me into the shower first! He was torture. But when it came to game time against Celtic, I loved having him beside me.

Just as I wanted Craig Moore alongside me, too. And not because Oz is one of my closest friends. I can see past our friendship to a mentally and physically tough guy who was so underrated as a player at Rangers. He would rip you in two in a minute if you were his rival on the park, and I love that in centre-halfs.

I miss him now. I wish he was still here at Gers, but life moves on, and he wanted to try something different. He has always been single-minded and is his own man. I think it was sad that his decision to go to the Olympics with Australia and be stripped of the Gers captaincy turned so many of the fans against him. I went on holiday with him and our sons – without our wives – to the Gold Coast and saw how much his homeland means to him, and I have listened to him talk about how proud he feels playing for the Socceroos. His passion for his country is genuine. He made that decision from his heart, knowing the stick that would come with it.

He's had his adventures with Borussia Mönchengladbach under Advocaat, played for Newcastle United and made it to the 2006 World Cup finals with Australia, which up to now is more than I have ever done with Scotland. Even still, whenever we go out to blow the froth off a few Buds, his first questions will be on the last Old Firm game I played and how our new boys coped and whether Celtic's can take a slap or not! He misses those games. Badly.

I feel a major responsibility when I play in Old Firm games. I have it inside my boots to either kill a guy's weekend or extend it into such an unforgettable time that he doesn't go to work on the Monday. I always think about how our fans will feel if we lose. They will be miserable, have a torrid time at their work and be slaughtered by the Celtic fans until the next Old Firm encounter. I carry that guilt with me if we lose a derby match.

I went into my first Old Firm game desperate to make a mark on Celtic's midfielders, but like so many on their debut in this derby, it just passed me by. It was a whirlwind, a mental game. I barely got a touch, and there was hardly any football played. That can happen in those games, even though I had nothing but quality surrounding me in guys like Arthur Numan, Giovanni van Bronckhorst and Gabriel Amato.

There had been a big build-up to the match, but the whole occasion just swallowed me up. I was well warned, but you cannot beat the feeling of walking out into that atmosphere. Those games surpass the Champions League and everything else I have experienced. You are there in the middle of it all, and it is just a rumble of noise. There are times when you cannot hear yourself speak to someone standing five yards away. It's not like a normal game, because normally sane people sit there hollering for the most ridiculous decisions, screaming their heads off.

Even in the reserves, when I played against Celtic teams that had the likes of Malky Mackay, Chris Hay and Brian McLaughlin in them, the games had such passion and could draw crowds of 20,000 fans. Those were great contests, and in those days we played at Parkhead and Ibrox, which I loved. But you just don't get gates like that for the second team anywhere else.

I've experienced times when we have been the lords of the manor and spells such as the 2005–06 season when it has been Celtic's turn to be the guvnors. Wiser people than me say that football goes in cycles, but that makes it no easier to stomach when your rivals are turning you over on your own pitch and you are having a nightmare.

The 1–0 defeat from Celtic at Ibrox, as our 2005–06 SPL title defence went so badly awry, was billed as Barry Ferguson v. Roy Keane. I knew it would be. I'd had a choice when the bombshell news came that Celtic had lured him to Parkhead after he quit Manchester United. I could give it the old 'No Comment' treatment when I was inevitably asked about him, or I could tell the truth. I chose the latter and admitted he was my favourite player. Looking back, I may have heaped some extra pressure on myself by doing that.

But I will never hide from the fact that Roy Keane was my favourite player. I always knew that his heart was with Celtic and he skippered the Republic of Ireland, but why should that change my opinion of him as a footballer? I didn't look at him like that. I looked at what he did on a football park for Manchester United – he was brilliant. He was a horrible bastard on the park with a nasty attitude, but I loved that about him. He had huge ability to go with his growling desire, and he was such a driving force as a player. His teammates reacted to the way he led. Look at the semi-final of the Champions League against Juventus in 1999. He'd been booked and knew he would miss the final, but he scored an inspirational goal, and all through the match he was the one roaring them on to get there.

Footballers always sit around at lunch and speak about who their favourites are – Murray Park is no different. Some would say Patrick Vieira, Wayne Rooney and all the rest of them, but there was only ever one man for me: Keane.

I was always desperate to test myself against him, and I did it at Blackburn when we went to Old Trafford and lost 2–1. Individual accolades don't usually bother me, but I was proud of my Man of the Match that day. So I suppose that and my admission of admiration is why his first Old Firm game was always going to be built up as Ferguson v. Keane.

Perhaps the Gers fans didn't want to hear me lauding Celtic's new hero; they wanted to see me stick the boot into him and put him in his place. Life is not as easy as that, though. Roy might have been in his veteran stages at that point, but he was as fit as ever, and he'd been in the jungle too long not to know when the ambushes were coming. He snapped into some tackles, got hold of the ball, kept it with Neil Lennon and they won the midfield battle. Hard to take and even harder for me to admit, but it's the truth.

We lost badly, and I played so poorly, but the defeat was not simply down to me – we were shit, and they were better. Simple as that. But the nature of the beast in Scotland is that a scapegoat must be provided, and this time it was me. After the match, I was hurting badly, and I knew I was going to get battered in the press, but I felt I had proved myself in this fixture before and done enough to have some leeway granted. Not in some minds. It is the worst game in the world when you lose it like that, but I spoke to those close to me, and I vowed to myself that what was happening would make me a stronger and better player.

That day, Celtic scored, sat back and won what became one of the ugliest, most horrible Old Firm games I have ever played in. In my opinion, Rangers v. Celtic is the best derby in the world, but the standard of football in that match was an embarrassment. Even so, the focus was on me afterwards. I was cast as a failure. The headlines in some of the papers were savage, and those are the times when the people who want to stick the knife into you have their day. It is the perfect opening.

Even an element of your own fans need someone to blame, because they are smarting so much, but there was still a part of me that railed at the injustice of it when I picked up the *Daily Record* and James Traynor's headline read 'Gutless – Keane doesn't give Ferguson a kick'. Have an opinion on the game if you want, but gutless? Me? I think it is gutless to write something like that. I will hold my hands up to the fact that I played badly that day – I like to feel that I always do that when I have a poor game. But I have never been gutless in my life. My dad read that article, and he was boiling inside. I wasn't brought up to be gutless. He raised me to have character and not to be a coward.

I'd gone through six games around then when I had toiled badly, and I knew it, but to say that I had hidden and not had the heart for it was wrong. I was seething. I have had to learn to accept it, though, the same as when my friends tell me that some DJ called Ewen Cameron on Real Radio has described me as 'the worst player ever to captain Rangers and Scotland'.

Even now there are times when I could take the bait, and I sometimes feel like having a pop at them in return, but it is at those moments that you have to take a step back from it all. After all, this is Scotland, land of hate mail. When I came home from the quiet of Blackburn Rovers and life in Lytham, there were days when it felt like I'd swapped a seaside village retreat for a timeshare in Beirut. I forgot how intense it all was when I was away from it, and it took a bit of getting used to again. I needed time to acclimatise to opening up letters and seeing one word staring back at me: reject. I still get them from fans of Celtic and other clubs. And I remember one that read, 'You're murder. You shouldn't be back.' I hope they keep sending them – it inspires me, all this talk that I'm a Premiership reject.

You'd have to ask the sensible Celtic fans where I stand with them now, but I hope as the years go on they will have some sort of grudging respect for me. I certainly don't have a problem with the Celtic players off the park. Every time I bump into guys such as Neil Lennon or Stiliyan Petrov in town, we will have a beer and a laugh, and I respect them. Stan is a gentleman. He had enough class in him when we drew 1–1 with Inter Milan to phone me and congratulate us on making the last 16 of the Champions League. I thought that was a quality gesture, but I expected no less of him.

However, there are others who get to you in the heat of an Old Firm game. During the 2005–06 season, we were going through a dreadful period with injuries and loss of form. Just the sort of time when you don't want an Old Firm double-header, but we faced one, and we got battered. Nightmare. We lost the league game 3–0 at Parkhead, and they were lording it. I accept that because I have been on the other side of it. But there was an incident in that game that really stuck in my throat. I made a break and Aiden McGeady sprinted back to get at me. I had a swipe at him. He went down, and I thought that I would try to pick him up to dodge the booking. Players sometimes do that, and if you're not hurt, you accept the hand, get up and get on with it. Not only did he not accept my hand, but he didn't even acknowledge it, and I was seething – in a fury. I know I was wrong in the first instance, but he didn't even raise his hand an inch, and I thought, 'I can't believe you've just fucking done that.' That's football, though, with all the little incidents that niggle you and live inside you.

There are always little mind games going on during Old Firm games that perhaps the fans don't notice. For instance, when Shunsuke Nakamura came to Ibrox with the £2.75 million price tag from Serie A and the big reputation I admit that I thought, 'Let's give him a wee dig and see if he fancies it.' He is a very talented footballer, but I didn't want him coming to my place and running the game. I was out to let him know I was there. It worked. We won 3–1, they went down to ten men, and he got swallowed up and was subbed.

I can look at players' eyes in the tunnel now and see if they fancy it. The first time I looked at Neil Lennon, I knew they'd signed a warrior born to play in those games. But if I was to pick out one Celtic player who stood out, it would have to be Henrik Larsson. His movement was superb, and he worked his bollocks off for that team. When you consider that he cost just £650,000 from Feyenoord, you have to say that it wasn't a transfer – it was robbery. I was happy for him that he got the move he wanted to Barcelona and then created the two goals that won them the Champions League final against Arsenal. He earned that medal, but I will admit that I was glad to see the back of him.

Like Numan, Larsson was calm and measured in everything he did off the field, but on it he loved the fray of the Old Firm. I think he realised, as I do, that so much rests on your shoulders in this country of 5 million people, especially when it seems as though 2.5 million of them care about the outcome of the game. That takes some getting used to, because this is a fixture that can ruin you. Win it and you will have the weekend of your life; lose it and you get in, close the gates and don't leave the house. I switch my phone off – I don't want to speak to anyone.

The feeling of what it really meant to the club had been battered into me from my youth team days when I faced the Celtic youth team at either their Barrowfield training complex or at Creamery Park in Bathgate. That's a juniors ground, but I loved it there. It was a massive pitch, and the people enjoyed the fact that Rangers youth team came there to play – they treated us like kings.

From the start, those games meant the world to me, and I remember us losing the Glasgow Cup because I missed a penalty, and I just couldn't handle it. I was sick to the pit of my stomach. I had let everyone down, and I couldn't even bear to watch them lift the trophy. At the end, I walked straight off the park and right down the tunnel, and John McGregor bollocked me in the dressing-room. He warned me that I had better start showing some dignity and behaving like a Ranger in defeat as well as in victory. I just couldn't do it that day, and I took the fine because I could not accept having to watch them celebrate.

We can dress this up, and we can dodge the issue, but I won't lie: I *hate* losing to Celtic – I detest it. I hope anyone can see from my private life that I am not a bigot, but neither will I ever hide the fact that I am a Rangers man and proud of it. It is for that reason that nothing else in my life hurts as much as losing to Celtic – it will always leave the bitterest taste.

The Helicopter is Changing Direction

'This is not over, Fergie, never. Keep believing.'
Alex McLeish tells his skipper the seemingly
impossible can happen – it did.

'Scott McDonald has done it again. The championship
trophy is on its way to Easter Road. The helicopter is
changing direction!'

Every time I hear Radio Clyde commentator Peter
Martin's trademark screaming commentary that described
perhaps the most dramatic day Scottish football will ever
see, a smile plays on my lips and my mind drifts back to 22
May 2005. The final day of the season dawned with us two
points behind Celtic. We were up on goal difference, but
did that really matter? They knew what they needed to do:
go to Fir Park and win as we chased three points at Hibs
and prayed they would come up short.

Our main focus that day was simply to keep up our
end of the bargain – just go out there and beat Hibs and
hope against hope that Motherwell did us a favour. If I am

honest, I just didn't see it happening, because I knew the mindset of those who mattered inside that Celtic dressing-room. Chris Sutton, John Hartson, Alan Thompson, Neil Lennon – guys like that just don't crumble when the chips are down. They may have been my enemies in Old Firm games, but I have respect for them. So much respect. They are the type of boys you'd want beside you in a team. I loved the attitude they carried with them, and I could always see why Martin O'Neill paid Premiership wages to bring them to the SPL. They were worth the money because they were just real nasty bastards who hated losing.

But it was Fir Park, one of the toughest places you can go to in the SPL looking for a result. We'd won 3–2 there in the run-in. I'd got suckered into a little flare-up with Richie Foran and somehow stared at a red card for it. The fans are right on top of you, growling, and like Tynecastle, it's the sort of bear pit where the opposition can get right in your face.

You need things to cling on to in run-ins like that: mine was what had happened on the closing day in 2003. The memory was still with me. And I hoped against hope that Celtic would come unstuck at Fir Park so that we could recreate that special day.

I'd come home from Blackburn determined to be the difference, vowing to myself I'd make up for all the hurt I had caused Rangers by bringing the title home, but then we lost what seemed like the pivotal Old Firm game 2–1 at Ibrox in the run-in. I was desolate. I can admit now that deep down I thought we were finished on the back of Craig Bellamy's performance that day – he tortured us.

Bellamy will always provoke controversy; he's that type

of character. He can't operate as a footballer unless he is needling people and getting at them. All that spiteful stuff when he told the Clyde players 'You'll be digging my garden next summer' when Celtic beat them in the cup left a sour taste in people's mouths. I would never utter words like that to a fellow pro. I'll elbow them, fight them and swear at them as I try to get an edge, but I would never belittle people because of the wad I have in my pocket. I wasn't brought up like that. But I've seen the other sides of Craig: his concern and compassion for me when I was lying with my knee in bits at Newcastle that day; and his blinding skill on a football park.

I don't care who knows it now, but I walked off the pitch at Ibrox that day wishing Bellamy played for Rangers. I cursed the fact that we had used up all our loan deals, otherwise we could have lured him to our side of Glasgow instead. Red tape killed that possibility, but I know it was on Alex McLeish's agenda. What an impact Bellamy made that season when he came on loan from the Toon. His goal against us summed him up as he got away from Soto Kyrgiakos and curled one into the far corner. Bellamy has great movement, and he made life so difficult for our boys at the back. I walked off thinking that it must be a joy for their midfielders to play beside a player like that. He is so clever; he spins into corners, and he can hurt you from those positions. Plus they had the players to find him. I could see beyond all the controversy that surrounds him to appreciate him as a player, and I would have loved to work beside him.

Celtic used the intelligence they had in midfield that day.

They knew how to mix it up, whether it be using Bellamy's pace or by playing balls up to John Hartson and joining him in attack. Fernando Ricksen and I had run the legs off them in midfield when we'd won 2–0 at Parkhead – we had made them look old and tired. Good players and proud men respond when you do that to them, and they came to Ibrox and dictated the match.

The final Old Firm game of the season was one I felt we had to win, and we'd lost it. Now I knew the *post mortem* and search for the scapegoats would begin, because it looked like the title was slipping away. The gaffer had shown courage to go with Marv at the heart of defence, despite the fact that the big Trinidadian had refused an operation on his cruciate injury. He instead insisted that his faith and trust in God would heal him. During the match, Stiliyan Petrov got in there ahead of the big man to bury a header for Celtic's first, and I knew the stick would come because we faced being left with only the CIS Cup to show for the season, while Celtic went for a second Double on the bounce.

We'd shown guts to claw ourselves back into the match at the end, and Steven Thompson came off the bench to lash one home late on. Deep down that goal seemed like an exercise in satisfying the diehards to me. We showed them we were still giving everything, and the fans chanted defiantly, but we'd been outplayed. That goal was cold comfort and only a crumb of consolation. The truth is that all three points went where they should have.

So, now the fingers were being pointed: at the manager for keeping faith in Andrews; at Marv for sparking the dilemma and not going under the surgeon's knife; and at

Nacho Novo, who was on a six-game streak without scoring. I hated seeing Nacho taking flak – he just didn't deserve it. He has fought so hard to make himself a good player, coming from a small club in Spain to Raith Rovers, Dundee and then to Gers. He'd shown guts and been worth every penny of the £400,000 Eck had paid for him, and he had repaid that fee with 25 goals that season. But people needed to translate their hurt by venting their anger on someone, and he was the easy target. Those are the times when you wish fans would take a deep breath and think it through before they start slating players.

Still, there was no question, the situation looked desperate. We were five points behind with four games to go, and it looked like the league was beyond rescue, it really did. That is when those who would snipe at Alex McLeish and underestimate him as a manager should have been at Murray Park. He could have let the situation drift, admit defeat and chuck in the towel, but he simply refused to. He was so positive in everything he did. He dragged our chins off the floor and almost single-handedly kept the momentum going. He was the glue that held Rangers together in the next three games. He looked to the big characters in the dressing-room, and he just kept chipping into me, saying, 'This is not over, Fergie, never. Keep believing.' He pounded away at me and ensured that I never once let my head drop in view of another player. You have to set a tone at times like that, and the manager did that. His optimism began to course through the place. Never once could a young player look to me and see that I had chucked it. I was down when I came home after that Celtic defeat. I just felt so hollow

– spent. But that was the only time and the only place I ever allowed it to show. At work, I just kept giving it the 'Gospel According To Marvin'. Keep believing.

I'd be lying if I didn't admit that I had lurking doubts, of course I did. Publicly, I kept making positive noises, but privately, at times, I would sit there thinking we'd blown it. But day by day, as McLeish's positive attitude seeped through the place, all that despondency was replaced by defiance and belief.

We tore out of the traps at Pittodrie, and I scored one of my best goals of the season as we won 3–1, then we beat Hearts 2–1 and murdered Motherwell 4–1 at Ibrox. Marv didn't help our nerves in those two matches, the big man having some bloody mad moments and scoring an own goal in each. You couldn't keep him out of the news that season.

The run-in was about who cracked first, and Celtic did, right after winning at Ibrox when they lost 3–1 at home to Hibs. I reckon that was the first time people started to talk about Ivan Sproule. He scored one of the Hibs goals, using that frightening pace of his, and I was sold on him as a player. And his is the sort of signing I admire so much. Tony Mowbray went to the Northern Irish league and got him for £5,000 from a club called Institute. If I was finished today and they made me a manager, I'd pester my chairman to buy him. And if he continues to develop the way he has, one day you won't get much change out of £2 million if you want to buy him.

Ivan helped us take the championship down to the final day, and Eck's last team talk of the season was one of his shortest ever. The big man simply stood up and said, 'You know what you have to do here. Just go out and win for this club. The rest is down to the Man Above – and today we have to pray he is a Rangers supporter.' There were a few nervous laughs, and we got ready to go out there. It wasn't a day for long speeches. We knew the mission; the gaffer got it right.

What happened next will live with every Rangers fan for the rest of their lives. It was surreal. We were on the pitch at Easter Road, and it was an awful game, just minging. I came down the tunnel at half-time in a bad mood and cornered a Hibs official: 'What's the score at Fir Park?'

He looked down and said, 'Sorry, mate, 1–0 Celtic. Sutton.' They'd got through the first half ahead. There were 45 minutes of the season left, and if the scores stayed the same, they'd win it by four points.

We had to drag ourselves into our own match, and when we came back out for the second half, Nacho got us ahead when he cut the ball across the face of the goal and it went in off Gary Caldwell. But still we waited for news from Fir Park. And through it all, Ian Murray – who'd already agreed to come to Rangers on a Bosman – was careering around kicking us black and blue! I was smiling and saying to him, 'Nid, get a grip. You're one of us now.' He just growled at me, slammed into another tackle, sent someone else five feet in the air and got himself booked. That sums up the type of player he is. He desperately wanted to show the Hibs fans he would never cheapen their jersey. He loves Hibs. Now their fans sing, 'Oh, Ian Murray. He used to be a Hibee but he sold his soul.' I can't agree. Nid never sold anyone short in his life, and he certainly didn't cheat on Hibs. He simply moved to try to better himself as a footballer, and for that crime he takes hellish stick at the club he supported as a kid. Listen, I know that is part of life, but it is still a crying shame to see him take the abuse he does when we go back there now, because I know how much it hurts him. But there are some minds you will never change.

The game that day was going nowhere: Hibs were happy at 1–0 down because that result meant they would qualify for the UEFA Cup. Then an ear-splitting roar went up when I was on the ball, and I remember it was as if the world seemed to pause for a thudding heartbeat. It was like slow motion. I looked around, and all the Gers fans were losing it. Delirium.

It was like I could actually hear the blood swooshing through my veins, and my head felt like it would explode. I thought, 'Naw, it can't be.' I put my hands on my head, and Alex Rae screamed at me to give him the ball. I knocked off the pass and looked to the bench, and they gave the signal: '1–1!' Still I was convinced it was a wind-up, but then, two minutes later, the whole place erupted again, and the bench were screaming '2–1!' I looked over, and Bob Malcolm was leaping around the technical area like a lunatic battering people. It was then that I started to believe it.

I have to say that a part of me still loves Scott McDonald to this day – even if he did opt for Celtic over us when his big move came. But the weird thing is, I've never seen his two goals. Afterwards, I was on party patrol for five days. The big reminder of that moment for me is that now famous Peter Martin commentary as the chopper made its way to

Fir Park with the trophy for Celtic. McDonald's second went in, and Peter bellowed, 'Scott McDonald has done it again. The championship trophy is on its way to Easter Road. The helicopter is changing direction!' I respected him so much for the professionalism he showed then. Let's just say that I have a sneaking suspicion he may be a Celtic man, but he still marked a historic moment with a brilliant bit of commentary. I've met him since and told him his phrase was now the ringtone for tens of thousands of Gers fans' mobiles. If he'd sold it for £3 a pop, he'd be on a beach in the Bahamas sipping pina coladas and not sweating away on *Super Scoreboard*!

That day will live with me until they put me in the ground. The scenes in the dressing-room afterwards were unbelievable, and we were throwing the champers down our throats. Hibs were nice enough to bring in crates of Carlsberg, their sponsors' brew, and that took a battering too, even though I hate the stuff.

Laurence McIntyre, our security chief, warned us that we had to stay in the dressing-room for 15 minutes because we were waiting for the helicopter to arrive with *our* trophy. By the time it arrived, everyone who got onto the pitch to see the Gers fans was half-cut! What a feeling. I looked at the crowd, and I could see all my pals amongst the sea of faces – so many of them were in tears. It meant the world to me to see how happy we had made them. Tears flowed that day from so many people I didn't expect to see them from: hardened physios, the doc and all the rest of them.

I had no problem watching Fernando Ricksen step forward to lift the trophy. This was his day as skipper. I had never once mentioned the captaincy throughout all the negotiations to get me back from Blackburn – all I wanted was to come home to the team I should never have left in the first place. I think people realised I hadn't tried to muscle my way back into the job, and, come that summer, Fernando himself came to me and said he felt I should have the armband back. That doesn't prevent the pub talk of rifts between us, but they never existed. He is a hyperactive pest, but I loved him for that – most of the time. New players who come to the club, such as Kris Boyd, were bewildered by Fernando and his behaviour around the dressing-room. You could be trying to have a peaceful shower, and he would be flinging buckets of ice and turning cold hoses on you or spraying soap at you.

I looked at him that day in a moment of quiet and just laughed: 'Old Mad Eyes' is back. He'd captained Rangers to a championship and been instrumental in our triumph. No one should ever forget that or take it away from him. He'd shown his own brand of courage, coming back after being subbed in the 6–2 hounding from Celtic to prove he had what it takes to be a Ranger.

I was happy for Fernando and the band of players the manager had bonded together. I get sick fed up of all the talk that Celtic handed Alex McLeish his two titles – it is utter nonsense. Whoever finishes top of the league deserves it. People try to snatch the credit away from him, but they should remember we were five points behind with four games to go in that second championship. He managed the club through that to glory, and in the January transfer window, he made signings like Ronald Waterreus, Soto Kyrgiakos, Thomas Buffel and myself. I think those signings were all key to us clinching the championship, alongside the likes of Ricksen, Pršo and Novo, who were superb over the course of the whole season.

The club had been sent into mourning when Stefan Klos did his cruciate on the training ground, but on an Arthur Numan recommendation, Alex got Ronald from Manchester City reserves. And he was superb: bad mullet and appalling dress sense, but some goalkeeper. Waterreus had that de Boer touch: he loved himself! He thought he had good reason, though, and he was right. Have you ever seen a keeper as two-footed as he is? There are midfielders earning a good living from the game without that sort of ability.

When Stefan came back from his injury, I knew it would become Klos v. Waterreus, and the manager was faced with a massive decision. Again, Alex faced charges that he lacked courage and conviction, but I think that goalkeeping debate surely killed them off. In many ways, it would have been easier to opt for Stefan between the sticks: he was the fans' hero and had been the skipper after I left. But the gaffer looked at the problem logically: Ronald had made very few mistakes, and, the truth is, it would have been an injustice to drop him. Why change if the keeper you have does not merit being dropped? Alex was there to make those calls, and that one took balls. It taught me that if I ever do go into management, I will have to make those decisions on my own.

Klos is top class, and he had earned his idol status, but Ronald could cope with the pressure of taking over because of his strength of character. He was replacing a man who is a god to the fans, but Waterreus *knew* he was good and had that unshakeable self-belief.

But his clothes were just awful – up there with Dado, who regularly walked in wearing a pair of Rupert the Bear trousers halfway up his shins. It was bizarre. I asked him about them one day, and he just shrugged and said, 'I love these. I have had them for 12 years.' 'Aye, that right?' I thought. 'You've got some money now, put them in the bin.' He couldn't care less, and he wanders about in a dressing-room where Hutton, Smith and Burke are all playing with gel, and I swear they're using straighteners on their hair.

Dressing-rooms can be strange places at times, full of different characters, such as José Pierre-Fanfan, who looked like he'd just come off the catwalk. Then there was Marv, who had 287 tracksuits and 485 pairs of trainers – he never wore anything else. Blinged up too.

I looked at all of my teammates that day at Easter Road before the party really swung into action, and I thought we'd all shared the sort of adventure you truly would tell your grandchildren about. This is a dangerous statement when you live life in the Old Firm soap opera every day as I do, but I don't think there will ever be a finish like that again.

We partied in style, and, for a while, life was a blur – so many memories will always live with me from that time. I will never forget Rangers being crowned SPL champions for 2005 – but I might not remember all of the celebrations! The title party lasted for *five days*. What I will always remember, though, is that by 6.30 p.m. that Sunday night we were back at Ibrox, and there were 30,000 fans there.

It was astonishing. I was already two bottles of champers down, but I'd have been drunk on emotion anyway.

Then there was the sponsors' dinner on the Monday night. We were all there in our dickie-bows, until big Bob started rampaging around the hall ripping people's black ties off. I was drinking red wine like it was Coca-Cola, and I remember standing at a burger van in a tuxedo signing autographs in the queue, then hanging out of the sunroof of a taxi on the way home giving it the Sky *Soccer Am* 'Easy, easy' at 5 a.m. Madness. Loved it.

It was the biggest party of my life. Only when I finished celebrating, could I truly appreciate what it all meant to me. Once I came out of party mode on the Saturday night, I had a night of sanity with my missus in a restaurant. I sat and quietly shook my head in disbelief. She was smiling at me, and I was sitting there grinning back like an idiot. I just slumped in my seat and thought, 'I have woken up now, and we really *are* the champions.' Only then did it truly sink in that we had done it.

For a time in my life I had lost sight of what was important to me as a footballer and been blinded by what other people thought was best for me. I still read the views of some people I respect who think I let Scottish football down in some way by coming home. That is their opinion, but mine will always be that I shouldn't have gone in the first place. Things happened between me and the club that shouldn't have – but now we are back together. This is about me and my gut feelings – I can't help my attachment to Rangers. I wish those who criticised me for coming back could experience what I feel about the club – and I also wish they would stop belittling the Old Firm. I've played Manchester United, Chelsea and Arsenal, and I genuinely don't think they are bigger clubs than the Old Firm. Yes, they have a better league, but I always used to say to my old mates at Blackburn that they should collect their boots and try it up here – they'd soon stop sneering. They'd be at Fir Park, Tynecastle or Pittodrie with someone up their arse every second wondering what the hell had hit them!

Those celebrations just proved to me that I had made the right choice when I moved back to Ibrox in January 2005. I could have gone to Newcastle United or Everton and faced another challenge in the Premiership, and there are times when I wonder what I would have looked like in their kit playing in front of their fans. Liverpool and Newcastle are two passionate football cities. Then again, when the call came from Rangers to come home, there had never been any question of me going anywhere else, and that day at Hibs dispelled any doubts that may have been lingering. This is my club, the team I support, and I got to play for them on a day like that. And the truth is that nothing Newcastle or Everton ever achieved would have made me as happy as Rangers winning the league that day did. The helicopter changed direction – and I was there.

13

The Season From Hell

'Don't worry, Barry. God will heal your nose.'
Marvin Andrews comforts Fergie after leaving
his battered hooter spread all over his face in
a sickening training-ground collision.

I was in the gaffer's office, and Murray Park was like a morgue again. It was the Tuesday after another bad afternoon at the Brox. We'd bossed Aberdeen at times, but Scott Severin had hit a poxy shot that had smashed off Julien Rodriguez's heel and flown in: 1–1. Two more vital points had been hurled away. Kris Boyd had been scoring goals for fun – he'd end the season with 37 and be top scorer for Gers and Killie – and he was pulling us out of holes, but even then, rescuing second place from that sorry excuse for a title defence was looking beyond us – it was now Hearts' property to lose. They would get a shot at the Champions League, not us. Christ, could that season have got any worse?

The answer for me, naturally enough, was yes. I knew the four words that had to be spoken. I was about to tell

Alex McLeish that I'd never play for him again. Our close relationship as manager and captain meant I also knew those four words would leave Eck totally dejected. Yet I had to utter them. I looked at the guy who'd faced all his trials and troubles that season with so much dignity and simply said, 'I can't go on.' Bruised and battered, my right ankle in bits, I knew that I had played through the pain barrier once too often for my own good.

When I told Alex I'd played my last game of the season, his face betrayed his emotions. It crumpled a little, and then he just sighed and said, 'You're right. I won't let you harm your body or the rest of your career.'

That was it. A thumping smack from Dons midfielder Gary Dempsey was the final withering blow for me. I'd been playing with a right ankle that needed to be totally reconstructed and also hiding the second fear of suspected cartilage damage in my knee on the same leg. It had to stop.

That meeting with the gaffer was one of the hardest things I have ever had to do in my football career. It was very emotional because he is someone that I have the utmost respect for both as a coach and as a man. And this wasn't me telling him that I would have to miss one game; this was me saying that I wouldn't play for him again as he prepared to walk away from Ibrox.

It was even harder to do that because of the way we had defended the title – it had hurt both of us. Jesus, we'd been languishing down in *fifth* place in the league at one point, and at Rangers, you can't be anything but ashamed about that. It's unacceptable. I had been desperate for us to make the Champions League qualifiers to somehow compensate a little bit for our poor performances, but we'd failed even in that quest. Now here I was telling Alex I just couldn't go on, and, worse still, I'd have to miss an Old Firm game, too. That was gutting, but there were no options left for me.

Six days after that Murray Park meeting, I was in the clinic of top surgeon Steve Bollen on the outskirts of Leeds, facing the knife once more and living in a world of worry. He warned me that if there was significant cartilage damage on top of the ankle op and the left kneecap that I'd already broken, then my career expectancy was going to plummet. He said I better start coming to terms with the fact that if the results revealed the worst-case scenario for me, then I might only have *two years* left at the top. At the age of 28, I was shocked to be told that I could be done at 30, but there was a determination that kicked in, and I thought, 'They told me I was 50–50 to ever play again after my knee was smashed up at Blackburn when I was 25, and I beat those odds.'

I knew my ankle was buggered, and I needed the surgery, that was critical to my future, but waiting for the knee scan almost did for me. It was mental torture. I was in pieces, and then the news came back that it was clear – just a stretched medial ligament. All I required was a procedure to flush my knee out and clean it up. They'd put in a scope to assess the cartilage damage in my knee, and it was discovered that it was just wear and tear. The news was sheer relief, because it had been such a freak incident that had caused it in the first place. I had stretched to block a cross in training and had felt it ping. It was the last thing I needed on top of all the worries about my ankle. I kept the truth about my knee secret for a time after it happened, but, eventually, when all the pressures of that season started to mount up, I couldn't escape from what my body was telling me.

I am now going to have problems later in life, it is as simple as that. I know it and so do my family. It is the price you pay for pushing yourself to the limit and beyond time and again. Arthritis, ankle replacements, plastic knees, they could all be on the agenda. After the operations, I looked down at the plaster that stretched up my leg, and at the bandages swathing my right knee, and reflected on that fact. Meanwhile, the painkillers had me drifting in and out of reality. I was phoning my mates to tell them how I was then forgetting I'd done it and calling back half an hour later.

When I hurt like that, I always have the same instinct: I just want to be home. I've been lucky that in the two major ops I've had to save my career, I have found straight-talking surgeons I could bank on and men who have understood my desperate desire to get away from them as soon as their work is done. Paul Rae rebuilt my kneecap, Steve Bollen reconstructed my ankle and our old club doc Ian McGuinness was there as the sounding board to help me through it all and explain every process. This time the toll was two pieces of bone shaved off my ankle to prolong my career and two screws inserted to hold it all together, and the total reconstruction of my ligament to repair years of damage.

The doc has been through so much with me. He'd been there to get me through the medical and calm my fraying nerves in the frantic signing deadline race against time to rejoin Rangers. Now, 17 months later, I was lying in the back of his people carrier once more after checking myself out of the Yorkshire clinic as quickly as I could. My ankle throbbed, and my brain was foggy with the drugs to keep the pain at bay. When my head cleared and the miles ticked by to bring me home wounded again to Margaret and the kids, I knew that this had been the overhaul I had needed. I was still only 28, and I vowed that if I could just come back from this one pain free, then I could return to Rangers a better player than ever.

Only those close to me know the nightmare I went through in the last month before I finally went under the surgeon's scalpel. I was wrestling with the shame of a season in which I was embarrassed to be the captain of Rangers. All I wanted was to somehow find a way to turn it around and give Alex some sort of comfort on his way out the door. But my body was failing me. I was told to stop playing five weeks before I did, but I wanted to keep going for the gaffer. Then when I heard that the experts were talking about shaved bones, rebuilt ligaments and screws to hold my ankle together, I suddenly realised that there was no alternative. That's when, in the cold light of day, I had to question my sanity. I thought I could keep going, but I was kidding myself, and for the final month, I wasn't even training any more. I'd turn up on a Friday for a loosener and a jog, then play at the weekend. I just couldn't keep going any longer. I tried so hard, but by the Saturday night after the Aberdeen game, I could hardly walk. I was like an old man getting out of bed on the Sunday morning, and I was in agony.

But on the journey home from Leeds, I had a vision of me running free from a marker from midfield, smashing a ball into the corner of the net and running to the Rangers fans to celebrate. All I wanted was to be able to play with that freedom again and not have my ankle niggling away at me. I knew the nightmare of rehab was ahead of me: four weeks when I would do nothing but climb the walls, driving Margaret mental. Then it would be four more weeks with a special brace fitted to my ankle, but at least then I could be on the bike, walk on the treadmill, do a little boxing training and dig some punches into the bag to release my frustrations. But despite the slog ahead, I knew deep down I had needed this. My body needed a rest, because I had been playing through a catalogue of injuries for so long.

When I switched my phone on after the operation, there was a message from the gaffer: 'Hope you came through it, Six.' He was always wryly smiling about my obsession with my jersey number and took to calling me Six as a wind-up. It stuck.

I have a bond with McLeish because we've been through so much together as football men. I will always owe him a debt, because I know how personally hurt he was when I decided to try the Premiership and go to Blackburn. He was big enough to bury that, man enough to keep slugging it out with Rovers to bring me home. I'll never forget that. I wanted to make up for my mistake, but I couldn't have without him putting his neck on the line.

Alex was on a hiding to nothing when he came to Rangers because of the finances of the club at the time. But he knew the circumstances – the £68 million debt – and still he wouldn't turn his back on the job. It was an offer he couldn't refuse, and do you know why? Alex McLeish is a Rangers man, just like me. Don't listen to all the nonsense that Rangers are not in his heart. Those accusations have as much credence as the jibe about him being tactically naive. Bollocks. He knew he was walking into that sort of flak, but let me ask you a few questions: who sussed out Martin O'Neill's Celtic first? Who put Peter Lovenkrands through the middle first to use his pace to devastating effect? Who won five trophies on the bounce? Eck did all that, and in the time he was up against Martin head to head, he won 7–4 on the trophy count. Do people forget that?

Yes, I take the Seville factor into account, but we still won the Treble. It wasn't handed to us or gift-wrapped, we won it, and the name of Alex McLeish deserves to be up there beside Bill Struth, Scot Symon, Jock Wallace, Walter Smith and Dick Advocaat as the only Gers bosses to have done that.

By the time he walked out the door after four and a half years, he had *earned* Rangers £13.6 million in the transfer market, and in the David Murray era, during which the chairman has backed his managers with so much cash, that is unheard of. And despite all the financial constraints, we still won two leagues and made history by reaching the last sixteen of the Champions League.

Those facts will always be my case for the defence with Eck, but I think we're both man enough to realise there was *no* defence for trying to retain the title like we did in the 2005–06 season. For a spell, I felt that both Dado Pršo and I could inspire the side and drag us back to the sort of form we would need to keep our crown. I was deluding myself. My ankle was a constant source of pain and worry, and Dado was taking injections of oil into his knee to help keep the European run going. I'd see him limp into the treatment room after another punishing shift the night before and take a jab of an oil called Synvisc to stave off the pain and get his knee moving again. I felt for him, because the big man had been exceptional since he had come to the club. In the end, his body was giving up on him, too, and the Rangers fans were all but giving up on us. I knew just where they were coming from.

I remember the pain of losing 3–0 at Celtic as perhaps the lowest ebb of my career. I honestly felt then that the mental agony I was going through was worse than the physical pain I'd experienced, lying in hospital with a busted kneecap. I was so focused that day at Parkhead, vowing that we wouldn't fold like a house of cards again. I went out and battered myself through the match, but we lost an early goal. I then caught a cross on the sweet spot, but Hamed Namouchi missed the header. At every key moment in that league season, we just didn't step up to the plate.

In the aftermath of that game, we had to somehow try to find a way to get a result in Porto on the Wednesday night in the Champions League – unbelievably, we did, securing a 1–1 draw – but on the Sunday after cowering to defeat against Celtic again, I had never felt more down. We were stuck in a horrible rut, and it was getting deeper and deeper. Life had become about clutching at straws. I was listening to all these excuses being put forward by people inside the club – that we'd done well in the first half, for example – and

I thought it all sounded pitiful. Pathetic really. The truth was we'd hurled away another cheap goal to John Hartson and rued misses from Franny Jeffers, Namouchi and Dado, while Bobo Balde and Aiden McGeady completed the scoring to give Celtic another easy win. I couldn't stomach it any more. For 45 minutes, we played well enough, but all that matters in Old Firm games is the result – the rest is window dressing. We'd come out trying to play football and keep it simple, but we'd given them another goal out of nothing. Once again, we'd played badly, and we had to live with the consequences.

We just couldn't get ourselves settled down in games. Every time we were on the brink of winning, we'd lose a goal. The gap was huge in the league after the loss to Celtic – up to 15 points – and it was a joke. Too many of the players were hiding. At Rangers, you are under the microscope constantly, and the fact was that we were not performing at the level we should have been.

When I look back, I realise that the pressure on the gaffer at that time was almost unbearable. He had been given a stay of execution until the end of November 2005, and I prayed that we could save his job. I felt torn up, and the only way I can describe the depth of my feelings is to tell you that at the end of matches I began to feel physically *sick*. I know what it means to the supporters: I'm a Rangers man and a Rangers fan myself. I looked at our fans at Parkhead defiantly singing their hearts out on the day we lost 3–0, and it cut me to bits. They were belting out 'Rangers till I die', and I was gutted for them. They pay so much money to watch us, and they deserve a lot better than we gave them that season.

When I was at Blackburn and lived in Lytham, few people knew me, and I could walk down the sleepy seaside streets without being recognised. Now I was suffering as a footballer, and it was being played out in the goldfish bowl of Glasgow. However, there will always be a way to keep life in some sort of perspective.

On that Old Firm weekend, I led my teammates to the Anthony Nolan Bone Marrow Trust's ball to help leukaemia sufferers. The old doc has been a long-time supporter of the charity, and he had vowed his players would be there. God knows that a night on the town was the last thing I wanted, but I put my head above the parapet and went out to help when I least felt like it. I knew the parents of the late Johanna MacVicar, a leukaemia patient who had campaigned so hard in Scotland for the charity and had died at just 27 having gone through true pain. I watched a video at the charity ball about a boy called Neil Redpath, who had come back from leukaemia and run a marathon – it was so inspiring and taught me that football must have its proper place.

For all the professional anguish I was going through at that time, there was one thing I was sure of: even when the club was being pilloried and my own reputation as a player was being torn to shreds, I still didn't regret coming home, not one bit. That thought has never entered my head. Rangers is about passion and belonging, and this is definitely where I belong. This club is about winning, and when we lose the way we were that season, it hurt like hell.

Those were easily the worst days of my career, but I needed to take a step back and try to come out of the experience stronger. They say you learn more about yourself in defeat, and I vowed that night I would recover, but I couldn't escape from how it felt to be the Rangers captain at that time. It was hellish. On a scale of zero to one hundred, I felt as if I was at zero.

I can't hide from the fact that the mix wasn't right during the 2005–06 season. When it mattered, we didn't have the togetherness you need to be champions, and everyone has to take the blame for that. As captain, I was desperate to bind the team together, but defeats drain people of their belief, and the grinding pressure that comes with playing for Rangers can destroy players at times like that. Too many of the players were disappearing inside their shells, and my frustration mounted. I was angry with myself, angry at everyone else, angry about my ankle, and just angry at life and what was happening to us.

I couldn't rid myself of the fury I felt about the state we were in, and I can admit now that it boiled over in the wrong way on the training ground with Olivier Bernard. There are mornings when a little spite seeps into your work during the training games. Players sometimes have issues with teammates whom they feel may be letting them down on match days, and a sly kick or an elbow in the ribs makes you feel better – it's human nature. That morning, the tackles were flying in training, and Olly rattled into me right on my bad ankle. He wasn't to know the pain he had just caused – not everyone inside the club knew the extent of the ankle damage I was toiling with at that point – but I leapt up and shouted, 'What the fuck are you doing, ya idiot?' He wasn't happy. He walked over with menace in his eyes, and I went for him. The punches started flying, but we were split up.

Then it continued twice in the dressing-room, and we were ripping into each other until the gaffer dragged us out the door into the corridor and shouted, 'Get a fucking grip.'

Do I regret it? No. The bad feeling when you are losing always comes out somehow, and it just happened to be us that boiled over that day. Every player has done the same in training, don't let them lie to you. I know the nine-in-a-row team fought in training almost every day because I saw some of their scraps – they were legends but they could still be at each other's throats every day they went to work. I may have fought with Porrini and Bernard, but Gough and McCoist battered each other almost every morning.

The best one I have ever seen was in Scotland training when Steven Thompson volleyed Christian Dailly in the balls! We were playing fives when all of a sudden an argument kicked off. I looked up and Thommo whacked the big man in the stones – it was a classic. And they are two of the intelligent ones.

There have been other incidents that still make me smile. For example, the time Michael Ball landed one on Bajram Fetai. The kid was from Macedonia and a bit heavy – I don't mean his weight, I mean he had a background that told you to go and mess with someone else – and he said to Bally, 'You have made big mistake. I will have you killed.' Bally crapped himself for a week thinking that gangsters were coming from the Balkans to kneecap him.

These days, we work each day in the seclusion of Murray Park, behind electric gates and away from prying eyes, apart from the 15 minutes each week when the snappers are allowed in for training shots. But, somehow or other, every story still leaks out – that's Glasgow for you. It might not be the right story, but they get a version of it. We have spent years searching for the Murray Park mole but haven't found him yet – the journalists protect him too well.

The best story was when I broke my nose after a training-ground tackle with Marvin Andrews, and it was suggested that we had been fighting! Me and Marv? I'm telling you, I would have to blow up his church for him to hit me! We went in for a tackle, he came in 110 per cent as usual and I went up in the air. When I fell, my nose battered off his knee – it was spread across my face. He was distraught, and I was raging, but afterwards he came into the dressing-room as the doc was wiping the blood from my coupon and said, 'Don't worry, Barry, God will heal your nose.' I told him to fuck off.

However, I do respect Marv's religion. I tried to catch him out, but his faith gives him an answer for everything. He enjoys his career to the full, cherishes every day and he is one player who appreciates what we have in this life. He has taught me to enjoy my own life more and relish being a footballer more than I ever did. I will always be the richer for having known him.

In the season when the helicopter changed direction and we won that title on the final day, he had kept chanting the mantra 'Keep Believing'. It was even written on a big banner at Easter Road when we clinched the championship. And when we won it, I remember thinking that maybe he was on to something. It is also staggering to think he had done his cruciate knee ligament yet used his faith to keep playing, insisting simply that the belief he had in God had healed him. There were some mornings in training just after the injury when he would wince then grit his teeth and get out there again. I'd say, 'Do you have a screw loose? Get the operation.'

He would turn to me and say, 'My master will look after me.'

When the doc told me Marv's cruciate had gone, I was devastated for him and made sure he got to see Paul Rae, the surgeon who sorted out my knee when I was at Blackburn Rovers. Marv went down to visit him, and I know he was told for definite that his cruciate was damaged and would have to go under the knife.

Stories swirled around Murray Park about what would happen next, but, if I am honest, I always thought he would wake up one morning and see some sense – know he had to face the scalpel. That morning never came. Instead, he spent two weeks visiting his church, speaking to his mentor Pastor Joe and getting advice and healing. Then he returned with a bottle of a potion or liniment which he now rubs on his knee before every training session. I was forever telling him that Pastor Joe had given him a bottle of Fife tap water, but he just smiled at me knowingly and said, 'I told you, Barry, my master will look after me.'

He worked on strengthening the muscles around his knee, he took his lotion, or whatever it was, and he got back playing. It was without doubt a footballing miracle. And, after a while, I just shrugged off the fact that I was sitting beside a man who was defying medical science. He was just Big Marv.

The year we won the title on the final day at Easter Road, Marv's career should have been finished. His should have been a sad story that season, but, instead, he was a big part of it all, and one of the best photos I have of that day is of Marv with his head bursting out of the sunroof of his car with a Rangers scarf wrapped round his napper. I love that picture. There's a car sticker on his windscreen that bears the two words I'll always associate with him: keep believing.

He came through that injury, and no one ever poked fun at his beliefs in the dressing-room after that – we respected them. He explained a lot of it to me one day: how the former Raith Rovers and Hibs winger Tony Rougier had introduced him to Pastor Joe and how the church had changed his life. And his knee wasn't the first injury that he thought God had healed for him. He once had a pelvic problem and was told that he needed pins in it if he was to keep playing. He went for healing, and it worked. Again, he cheated the knife, and that's why he has so much faith in the man.

Marvin is a remarkable man who has gone from once working in the Carib beer factory back home in Trinidad to where he is now. He has done the drinking and womanising, and lived on the wrong side of the tracks, but he has changed himself for the better, and I respect that so much. Fight him? Never. I think I can count myself as having a record of two fights, two wins, but I'm sure Porrini and Bernard would want a rematch.

Training-ground scraps make good headlines, but they are a necessary evil. When you have 24 men cooped up together for too long, an occasional fight is inevitable. The red mist has enveloped me more than once, but what is in me, is in me. I can't help myself, even if I try and count to ten. It should be the last resort, and I have learned in the main, but sometimes I still snap.

I have to admit that I actually like to see fights in training at times because it shows people care. I would rather have that than folk slinking out the door and backstabbing one another. After that bout with Bernard, we walked away together laughing, and that's how it goes. The problem with Rangers in 2005–06 was that we didn't show enough of that sort of fight *on* the park – that's what had to change.

14

Taking Flak and Making History

'What was I fucking thinking? What have I done? Sorry.'

Dado Pršo in the dressing-room after his handball gifted
Villarreal a penalty in the last 16 of the Champions League.

'Jesus, it's like Magaluf on a Saturday night.' I looked out the window of the Rangers team bus as we edged down a dusty, cramped street in the little Spanish town of Vila-real. It was a sea of blue. The street was filled with fans singing their hearts out and willing us on to give them a good performance. I was staggered after a season when we'd gone ten games without a win at one point and slumped to an unheard of fifth position in the SPL. There were times when I felt ashamed of myself, and I was left searching for some answers to explain what had gone wrong, but still those diehard Rangers fans believed in us.

In the last 16 of the Champions League, we drew the first leg against Villarreal at Ibrox 2–2 and had to give every ounce we had in us just to stay with them. But we were so up for the return leg in Spain, even before we got to the stadium. If I am truthful, I think we all knew that something was ending on that trip. That was it: drinking in the 'Last Chance Saloon'.

It had been confirmed that Alex McLeish was on his way out, and Paul Le Guen was on his way in, and I could sense the dreaded word that always accompanies a new manager and a fresh regime at any football club was in people's thoughts: clear-out. Who would stay, and who would go? It was in our minds that any one of us could be for the chop – we would be lying if we said it wasn't – but I'd like to think that what we gave that night was about more than saving our own skins. That night was what Rangers are all about when they are at their best: defiant and together. If the new manager wanted a base to build from, then that game was all the evidence he needed that there were strong foundations at the club.

I'll never forget the moment when we got to the outskirts of Vila-real. We were stopped by the motorcycle cops, and I was impatient because I couldn't understand why. Then we turned the corner of the street going towards the El Madrigal stadium, and I saw that our punters had taken the place over – it sent shivers down my spine and brought a tear to my eye, and that's not me going all Hollywood on you. I looked at the boys and said, 'Look at what this means to these people.'

I knew what it was costing the fans. I'd scrambled round Ibrox, badgering every source to scare up tickets for my mates – they were setting me back £53 a pop. That's before you pay for the flights, hotels and, of course, drink. But there were fans everywhere. It was a sea of blue, and the minute we got into that dressing-room, I knew we were going to see the *real* Rangers on the park. There would be no charges that this was a team of overpaid impostors this time.

We did see the true Gers, too. We dominated the match, keeping the ball when we had it and hounding them in snarling packs when we lost it. Riquelme couldn't get possession to do his magic, and they were hating it. I could see it in their faces: we had them.

I thought the tone had been set from the off when the gaffer decided to bring every player on the trip, whether they were injured or banned, as Dado Pršo was. It was a great touch, and the togetherness was there again. It is hard when you have foreign players in the team because the tradition of bonding by going on the bevvy is not part of their culture. I would love 11 Scots in the side one day, but that is not the way the game goes, and I have grown up enough now to learn the lessons of this football life from great men such as Arthur Numan and Dado. It is hard, therefore, to create the special sort of chemistry that teams need, but we had it that night – the will to go even further in the best tournament of them all. We should have.

It seemed like we had waited all winter long for that first game as the title defence began to collapse around our ears. And there had been a build-up like never before, because this was a chance for us to save ourselves and rescue a season that had turned sour. Then, within six minutes of the first leg starting, the atmosphere fell flat on its arse with an incident that showed how the fearsome intensity of these games can affect players.

Big Dado has played in the Champions League final for Monaco against Porto; he's carried Croatia in the finals of major tournaments. But when someone floated in a corner, he flung up his arm and punched the ball away. You could have heard a pin drop. Penalty, Riquelme, 1–0. I can't explain moments like that. It's a reaction – a mad, crazy reflex you regret the second you have done it. He was distraught.

Dado was a guy I grew to respect and trust so much. We were often sent to get our rubs in the morning together, and we'd talk about everything lying stretched out in the masseur's room. Pršo loves Rangers, and even though he's gone now he always will. Not in a kiss the badge, thanks for the wages, see you later sort of way, but genuinely. I laughed so many times at his big daft pony-tailed head and mental singing as he slaughtered one tune after another before training.

But at half-time in the Champions League last 16, we were 2–1 down. Diego Forlan had booted us where it hurt after Peter Lovenkrands' equaliser. Forlan was an education that night. I have to admit that when he was at Manchester United I thought the dodgy South American agents had stung Sir Alex Ferguson – £7.5 million for him? I wasn't having it. Then I played against him in the flesh, and he was brilliant. He never stopped roving across the line, giving his midfielders angles and making bad passes into good balls. I wished he played for Rangers.

At the break, Dado was shaking his head at the floor and mumbling, 'What was I fucking thinking? What have I done? Sorry.' His words weren't needed: he had dug us out of enough holes before, but we were in the brown stuff, and it needed a lucky own goal off Thomas Buffel's cross to take us to Spain level.

Despite all the dark predictions and people saying we were going there just to save face, I really began to believe we would do it. After the keeper saved at my feet early on, Peter again scored in Europe. And no one can tell me that we didn't dominate that game. All we did wrong was get sloppy for ten minutes when we lost the Rodolfo Arruabarrena strike that put them through on away goals.

Afterwards, the dressing-room was a scene of devastation, and I felt so deeply for Kris Boyd, who'd missed a golden chance to put us through. Chris Burke got half a yard on his man and whipped in a dream ball to the near post. Boydy was born to make those runs – his movement in the box is magnificent – and for a split second I was ready to take off and celebrate like never before, but he didn't get the contact he wanted, and the ball trickled harmlessly past.

I needed a room-mate when Stevie Thompson left for Cardiff City, and I inherited Boydy. I soon sussed that shyness would not be a problem for him! He's big and brash, and loves the banter, but he started looking a little unsure of himself in training just after his move. His touch wasn't there, and he was getting nutmegged for fun. He was toiling, and I wound him up. I told him that every time I passed to him it was bouncing back like he was a brick wall. He wasn't too happy about that, and he got worse when I muttered, 'We should never have sold the big man. Bring back Thommo!' But it all helped him to settle, and I know he now realises that he must add to his game by improving his movement outside the box. But inside that area he is one of the best I've ever played with – a natural. Scoring 37 goals that season was in McCoist territory.

That was why I was banking on him to take that chance, but he will miss worse, and it should never be allowed to haunt him. I won't let that happen. After the game, Kris just sat there in his strip, staring at the floor and blaming himself, but he shouldn't have. Since he'd come in the January transfer window from Killie, he had done little else but score.

The Champions League is all about fine margins, though. We were out, and the dream was sadly gone again. It was there for us: we were a midge's bawhair away from the last eight. That's a fact. As performances go, that was 100 per cent the best European performance I have been involved in as a Rangers player. In a way, I was dejected and angry that the same team that had failed for most of the season in the SPL, which should be our bread and butter, could then hit those heights.

Privately, Alex McLeish had decided early in the campaign that it would be his last season in charge, but we had put him through hell by underperforming. He had been forced to leave by the side door when there were 200 seething Gers fans out front at Ibrox calling for his head after a 2–2 draw with Falkirk, and he had to endure that soul-destroying 3–0 battering at home to Hibs in the cup. How had we come to be a team who left their manager in the lurch like that? If I could put my finger on how a team can underachieve the way we did domestically yet be such a success in Europe, I would be a coaching genius. You can use injuries and suspensions as your way to hide, but they are nothing but excuses in the end. When I looked at our squad at the start of the 2005–06 season, I thought we really had something, but there were flaws in the make-up of that team that I couldn't see.

What happened during the 2005–06 season was not for a lack of trying, and nor was it down to the manager, but so much flak was directed at Alex McLeish for the team's failures domestically. Well, if people felt that criticism was justified, then the praise for the European run should have been given out in equal measure.

For eight months, I'd lived with the dream of success in Europe in my head again. It was my first season back as skipper, and we were at the heart of the tournament I love the most. And being in that competition had played a big part in bringing me home; the Champions League is not part of the vocabulary at Blackburn Rovers. They had one campaign after they won the Premiership but had never been back. With Rangers, I'd been to the brink of the second phase before, and I was desperate to make it this time around.

Ibrox can cut you to ribbons in the dark times, but when it's going right, it can be the best place in the world, and it was where our 2005–06 European journey started. We'd just beaten Celtic 3–1 in the first Old Firm game of the season, and I couldn't have imagined at that point the strife that was to follow. I remember I made sure that it was the shortest derby celebration party. Whereas the bash had lasted five days the season before when we won the title on the last day, this one lasted only five minutes. We put the lid on it because we had Anorthosis Famagusta in the Champions League qualifier to think of.

Back then, I was still looking around me and thinking that we had a squad that could defend our title, even though we'd already lost a league game 3–2 to Aberdeen. I could see genuine shock on some players' faces that day. They were in a daze afterwards because they had been hit with something they hadn't experienced before. However much you warn players from France or other countries about the pace of our game and the battering they might get, you can't prepare them until they've taken a few dull ones. Julien Rodriguez and José Pierre-Fanfan struggled at Pittodrie, but looked safe in Cyprus, and that gave you food for thought.

Elsewhere, I'd always thought Ian Murray was a good player, but I didn't realise how good until he came to Gers. He wears his heart on his sleeve and gives every shred he has. He is exactly the type of player we need at the club. I think many would have looked at him and thought 'Squad player', but he became far more than that. Sometimes you don't know the worth of a man until you are wearing the same jersey as him.

Money dominated the talk in the build-up to the game against Famagusta. Our bonus of £45,000 a man to qualify had leaked out, and it was being compared with the situation of the opposition players, who worked a day job then played football part time. I was getting sick of it. They had Giorgi Kinkladze, who doesn't play for washers, and I've been in the game long enough to know all that chat counts for nothing when the match starts. My first wage at Rangers was £72.50 a week, but football is not about wages, and it's not played at a cash point. It's about what you do on the park, and Famagusta had just knocked out Trabzonspor. I knew their players would be fired up and motivated, right up for it, but we are paid to be professional and overcome that.

Famagusta is the sort of team against whom Gers have slipped up in the past, but we won 2–1 in Cyprus. Fernando Ricksen was superb that night. I knew then that we just had to stay on our feet at Ibrox, and we would be in the group stages that I savour so much.

The group we were drawn in was tough, and it made me laugh when people said it wasn't. Inter Milan are one of the biggest clubs in Europe, and Porto had won the Champions League just two years before. They'd broken up the team José Mourinho had built but had spent a fortune trying to create another one. And although no one had heard of Artmedia Bratislava before they battered Celtic 5–0 and then lost the return 4–0 at Parkhead, they went on to beat Partisan Belgrade in the final qualifying stage.

Our adventure started in earnest at home to Porto, and we won 3–2 with big Soto Kyrgiakos clinching it late on. He flicked on my free-kick with his head, and it seemed to take for ever and a day to loop in off the post. I couldn't believe the negative reaction from the press after that result. Yes, we'd been outpassed at times, and they were class on the ball, but it was a victory for spirit and togetherness that night. I didn't touch a drop of my Man of the Match champagne. I signed it and placed it behind the bar of my mate Aki's Indian restaurant Spice in Hamilton where we celebrated after the match. It's still there; I go back to visit it every week.

The section unfolded, and we only lost once to a deflected free-kick from Inter's David Pizarro in a silent San Siro. That was one of the most bizarre nights of my career, because the flares their fans had thrown at AC Milan keeper Dida the season before had cost them dear, and the game was played behind closed doors. That helped us. They couldn't raise their game, and they only won from a freakish goal that actually went under our wall then reared up and over Ronnie Waterreus.

Against Artmedia home and away, I was left with the same feeling both times: frustration and regret. Both times I felt we should have beaten them, yet both times we drew. The away match was particularly bad. We were ahead twice through Stevie Thompson and Dado Pršo but managed to hurl it away, losing two ridiculous goals. The gaffer's job was on the line, and that was preying on me, but the main thing I kept thinking about was that we had a chance to make the second phase and secure a place in history, and we were throwing it away again.

It came down to matchday six and Inter at home. Once again, we lost an early goal to Adriano's header, and that silenced the place. Then Peter Lovenkrands sped away and equalised, and we got the 1–1 draw we needed. We just had to wait for Porto's result at Artmedia.

Standing on the pitch waiting for news from the other game was sheer agony. I was swearing at the doc, shouting, 'It has to be fucking finished now. You are winding me up.' Then, finally, we got the nod that we were through, and I just exploded. Those two minutes had felt like twenty.

It was one of the greatest nights of my career; we had made history. And that was what it was about – not money or bonuses. We get paid good enough money as it is, and I don't throw the toys out the pram over bonuses. I find it hard to believe when some players grumble about incentives, because some of my mates work all year and don't earn what we can for qualifying the club for the Champions League. I would have played that game against Inter Milan for *nothing*, not one penny. You can't buy the way I felt that night, because it may never happen again.

I will always be grateful I shared a game like that with the gaffer before he left because he deserved it. It meant so much to him, especially after he'd had to take all the criticism from the press: he was a dud; he was tactically naive; he was out of his depth. It was all disrespectful bollocks. Alex looked completely drained at the end, but he still had the energy to lift me off the ground in a bear hug that almost broke my back. In a jumping dressing-room, I saw just how much making the last 16 of the Champions League meant to him. He looked at me after the hug and muttered four words that summed up how he felt: 'Thank fuck for that!' I knew deep down that it was the beginning of the end for his time as manager, but Rangers means so much to him, and I couldn't dwell on him going at that moment.

It was a measure of the man that he refused to milk us going through after the match; instead, he went straight down the tunnel. I think it was partly that he recognised we had been in the toils, and he couldn't shout from the rooftops too much. The other reason was sheer nerves. There always seemed to be about four minutes left in Bratislava, no matter how many times we checked, and he wanted to go and hide in a cupboard!

There is real pressure at this club all of the time. From wee Mary, who does our laundry, to Jimmy Bell the kitman, there are constant demands on everyone. But there was never a sense of desperation or the feeling that this was Alex's last team talk in the hotel before we left for Ibrox for that Inter game. Instead, there was a statement at the end of his talk when he just said that as a group we had been under pressure, and we had to show we could now cope with it. The message was: show them you're not bottlers. We did just that for a manager who I believe always showed what a fighter he is – never more so than against Inter. We were told not to shy away from what it means to play for Rangers, and I felt we did that.

I will always hold my hands up and say that I did not play to the standard I should have during the 2005–06 season. That run to the last 16, though, was for a manager who was under so much pressure but never once transmitted that to us. Every morning, I'd look for signs from him at Murray Park, but they were not there – he was always upbeat. If we'd seen him on a downer, it could have seeped through to people, but that just didn't happen. People forget that in 2003, after the Treble, he had to sell so many players. To come back and achieve what he did showed tremendous character in my eyes.

I wear a mask now with some of the media, and I just give them stock answers to their questions. I won't lie about that. Most journalists are genuine football fans who, like me, love the fact that the game takes us onto aeroplanes and around the world. It also allows them to visit great stadiums, and provides them with the opportunity to have nights out before games and, when the guard comes down on both sides, some shared nights out on the bevvy with the players. But there are some journalists who should be ashamed of the way they behaved in Alex McLeish's last days at Rangers, because they were working to an agenda.

I looked at some of their faces the night Ross McCormack came off the bench to score when we somehow snatched a 1–1 draw in Porto that kept us alive in the competition. It was a heist: we were wearing an away strip, but we should have been dressed as highwaymen! We nicked it after they'd murdered us, but the press should all have been happy for us. However, after the match, I walked out of the stadium, still shaking my head in disbelief at our Dick Turpin job, and I saw some of them sitting on their buses with their faces tripping them – they were actually gutted we hadn't lost because it meant that they couldn't stick the knife further into the manager. That sickened me.

It's in situations like that when you get worried about how every single word will be taken in the media, and you start trotting out the 'One game at a time, 11 v. 11 out there' bullshit. So, as the pressure mounted on Alex, and I did interviews about his future, I'd say, 'It's not my decision; it's not up to me.' Looking back now, that sounds as if I didn't care – but I did. Deeply. The man gave me a chance to rectify the huge mistake I made in leaving Rangers in the first place. He more than anyone showed the belief that was needed to bring me back, and, for all the highs and lows, I will never forget what the gaffer, David Murray and Martin Bain did for me at that time.

All through that European run I heard accusations of

tactical naivety being aimed at the boss, and I'd smile, because we went through everything so thoroughly before each match. For instance, in the Inter game at Ibrox we were well warned about the quality of Siniša Mihajlović at set-pieces. Sadly, we got caught out at a corner – but it was the players who made that mistake; it was not because we were not aware of the threat.

When Adriano's header flashed in, I'll admit that I wondered if we were going down the drain again. But there was a split second of silence, then a massive roar from our fans – and the players responded to that. So many flags were held up at the start of the match that night – including two Union Jacks and a Saltire made up of cards provided by the club – which made the hairs stand up on the back of my neck. The atmosphere was as if an Old Firm game and the great Euro nights I have had in the past, such as beating Parma, were all rolled into one. It was just electric.

Thomas Buffel made such a difference to us, even though his legs buckled when I played him in with 20 minutes left! He was only just back from injury, but he camouflaged those 11 games he had been out so well because he has a great football brain. Thomas constantly makes little angles for me, and he's always in the right position. It is a joy to play behind him.

It also meant the world to me that we got through with Bob Malcolm in the team. Bob eventually left for Derby County seeking more game time, but I know a little piece of his heart went with him. I wish those who growled when he got the ball at Gers could see how much he cared. I have seen Craig Moore and Maurice Ross go through the same at Ibrox – it's an unforgiving place at times. But we are very close, and Bob will always be part of the Rangers family – he, like me, is steeped in the club. He took so much stick at times, but he refused to hide, and I love that about him. Bob is a far better player than he is given credit for. He knows how to celebrate, too, and that night sparked one of the great parties as I dodged a police caution and almost lost my reformed image!

Mr Singh's restaurant in Glasgow has long since been a haunt for footballers with a love for curry, and that was our venue of choice after the Inter game. After the feast and more than a few Buds, we went to where the cars had been dumped for the night, because I still had a huge garden firework in my boot from Guy Fawkes Night for some reason. This thing was the size of a car wheel, and us lunatics, who had just qualified for the last 16 of the Champions League, lugged it to the front of the restaurant with the owner Satty now looking out of the window more than a bit worried. 'Light the blue touchpaper and retire.' The explosions began in the night sky, and they seemed to go on for ever. I looked up in wonder at all the colours like a little kid. I was still wearing my club suit, but the tie had long since been scrunched up in my pocket, and I was laughing like a madman. We'd made it: the last 16; history. I thought, 'This is what it is all about.'

European football has always flicked a switch inside me. At the time of writing, I'm one short of John Greig's record of sixty-four ties for Gers on the Continent, and I have loved every single one.

I remember that when Graeme Souness arrived for his

first season and Derek was at the heart of Rangers' midfield, the club played Boavista in Portugal but were not fancied after the first leg. My brother screamed one in from 25 yards that night, and when I saw it on telly, I just loved the fact that he'd gone to someone's backyard a long way from home and had had the balls to play his own game and win it for Rangers. So, when I set out on my own career, I was aching for a taste of European action.

Now that I am 28, I sense that I have four more tilts at the tournaments I love. I've never disrespected the SPL – I fought for its honour every day in the dressing-room at Blackburn – but Europe just makes you do everything that split-second quicker. For example, my mind was buzzing from the first whistle of the game against Villarreal. 'See the pass quick, or Tacchinardi's on you; don't throw possession away, or Riquelme will kill us.' Thinking, always thinking.

Being involved on the European stage has made me a better footballer than I ever would have been if I had just played domestically. And it does strange things to people, too. I have a great photo from the UEFA Cup campaign before Dick quit to go upstairs. I'd scored the winning spot-kick in the shoot-out against Paris Saint-Germain, and Dick was running down the touchline going mental in his Crombie coat! It's a magic shot. He has just lost it.

People always ask me about my favourite European game, and they quote winning at home to Parma, that penalty shoot-out in Paris against PSG or beating Bayer Leverkusen away, but the truth is that every one is special. I have so many memories – like being poked in the eyes by Bayern Munich's Lothar Matthäus in 1999 when we came so close to the second phase of the Champions League. At the time, I was raging about what he had done, but then, after the game, I just smiled and thought it was all a bit surreal. During Italia 90, I had been a 12-year-old kid sitting cross-legged in front of the telly watching him burst forward from midfield for West Germany and smash shots into the corner of the net – I thought he was immense. Now he was getting the hump and sticking his fingers in my eyes because I was outplaying him!

I still feel today that we would have won that night had Michael Mols not shattered his cruciate knee ligaments. When I saw him walk onto the training ground for the first time, I had wondered who he was – who exactly was Michael Mols? And who were FC Utrecht? I have to confess, I wondered why we were shelling out £4 million on this guy, but within 20 minutes on the training field, I knew why. He was electric.

He scored 13 goals in his first 19 games, and he was flying. It still upsets me that he was injured against Bayern because he was too *nice*. Oliver Kahn came careering out of his goal to the touchline, and if Michael had the nastiness in him that I have, he would have gone through the tackle and the keeper. I'd have followed through, no question – you have to protect yourself. Instead, Mikey hurdled the collision to avoid hurting Kahn, and he ending up wrecking his own knee. You have no idea how many times after that I wished God had put more spite in him, but he just wasn't that type of boy. He was a gem.

Rangers are a club built on the tradition of being a somebody in Europe, not no-marks who get dumped out in the qualifiers. I see the status the Barcelona Bears have, and stories are still told of their 1972 European Cup-Winners' Cup triumph over Dynamo Moscow, despite the fact that it was 35 years ago. John Greig's nickname 'Legend' – 'Ledge' to every one of us inside the club – has partly been given to him because of what he did captaining that team. I was brought up on Bobby Russell's goal in Eindhoven when the Gers became the first team to beat PSV in a Euro tie on their own ground. I know all the tales.

Maybe when I quit I'll get around to having a look at where the ones I have been involved in should stand, but one thing I know is that for all the hell the 2005–06 season brought at home, it deserves an honourable mention for what we achieved abroad. That night in Munich in 1999, part of me felt that we would never make the second phase, but we have done it now – we made the last 16, and no one will ever be able to take that away from us. And those 15 seconds when the Champions League music starts up still make the hairs stand up on the back of my neck. All I can do now is pray there is more of it to come.

15

Love Across the Divide

'I can honestly say that it has never once
crossed my mind that it should be a problem
that I was a Rangers player dating a Catholic.
Why should it?'

Barry Ferguson.

James Kane stood stern-faced at the door, clad in his Celtic
jersey, holding the family Alsatian Shane. His lip was curled up,
and he was growling. Shane's, not his owner's. I stood at the
garden gate, a 16-year-old apprentice footballer at Rangers,
and thought that deciding his daughter Margaret was going to
be my girlfriend hadn't been one of my best shouts.

That went on for the first three months that I was going
out with the girl who is now my wife, but it had nothing
to do with bigotry, the West of Scotland curse. Instead,
it had everything to do with the guy I now know just as
Kaney when we go out for a few beers on a Sunday being
fiercely protective of his daughter and wanting to make sure
the boy who was taking her out wasn't just another smart-

269

arsed toerag from the scheme. So I took it. He wound me up with the Hoops and the guard dog, and I stood at the garden fence and whistled up to Margaret's window until she looked out. Then she'd come down, and we'd go out, with her old man glowering at me in the background and warning me we'd better be back on time.

In the 13 years since then to the life we have now, with our sons Connor and Kyle and daughter Cara, Margaret and I have come through such a lot together. I don't like to analyse our relationship too much; I just know we bounce off each other and that it works. We have had our ups and downs like any couple – the arguments, the break-ups, the make-ups – and I'm sure there have been times when she has wondered whether I am worth all the grief that comes with being married to the captain of Rangers.

Looking back, I was naive to think that religion wouldn't be mentioned when we got married. All the stories were dragged up from the dim and distant past. For example, how Alex Ferguson had felt victimised and shunned as a Gers player when they found out that he had married a Catholic. It was said that the way he was treated had always lived with him, and that's why he had turned down the chance to manage the club when they came in for him. Sir Alex, though, had been a player in the '60s and was then offered the chance to be the gaffer in the '80s after he'd lorded it over us with Aberdeen. This was a new millennium; surely the same wouldn't apply to me?

The sad thing is that in some eyes it did; it really mattered to people where Margaret went to school, not that she made me happy. But I can honestly say that it has never once crossed my mind that it should be a problem that I was a Rangers player dating a Catholic. Why should it? Sure, her dad Kaney knew that I was an apprentice learning the ropes at Ibrox and that I came from a Rangers-daft family, and I suppose on a football level he wasn't that happy. But that just led to some great banter between us, and he'd set me little tests to prove I was serious about his daughter. Now, we go through all the wind-ups before and after Old Firm games, and it is strange when I run out of the tunnel at Parkhead for an Old Firm game and glance up to the left corner where he sits and know that he is up out of his seat screaming at our team and giving his son-in-law dog's abuse!

The personalities Margaret and I have always meant the road to marriage would be rocky. Sometimes we'd fight like cat and dog. But without getting all Mills and Boon on you, I just felt like a better person when she was with me – always. Sadly for her, I'm no romantic. I proposed when we were out on a walk somewhere one day, and I certainly never got down on one knee – that's not me.

She keeps me in check, and it is nice to have someone there sometimes to kick my arse when I go over the score or calm me down when I am losing the rag about something that is not worth bothering about. Getting married just seemed like the next logical step to me when I got to the stage that I couldn't imagine what my life would be like without her in it.

When the stress of planning a wedding began, I think we both started to worry that what should be our special day was going to turn into something out of an episode of *Dream Team* or *Footballers' Wives*. Thrones and crowns and Beckham weddings were not for us, and we certainly weren't going to sell our pictures to *Hello!*. That's some people's choice, and I'd never criticise them for it, but it's just not us.

We were going to have a big wedding at first, but then we started to think that it was not the right way to go during the build-up. It should be a private time, so we decided that the thirty of us in the family party should go to St Lucia for ten days instead. It was worth it. We loved having that time together in the Caribbean away from prying eyes, and it was special. I'll never forget it.

I was nervous as a kitten on the day but not as bad as I had been when I was a 14-year-old kid trying to make a speech at Derek's wedding. That day, I stood there shaking like a leaf and bumbled through my words. Now he was beside me as my best man and was there for advice and laughs. There was no media presence, and it was all just perfect. I'll always be glad we did it the way we did. There are parts of your life that shouldn't be public property.

There was a time back in the day when I was being built up and put on a pedestal as if the media in Scotland wanted me to be our answer to David Beckham. Transfer prices had gone mental, and every time it was mentioned that another club wanted to take me away from Rangers, it was said that they wouldn't get much change out of £10 million. It was nuts. The thirst to have our own celebrity footballer like Beckham naturally led to me, but my face just doesn't fit that photofit, sorry. Neither does Margaret's.

I've played against Beckham, and I admire him so much because I know as a fellow player how hard he has worked on

he technique that has made him rich. You only get as good
as he is at taking free-kicks and delivering crosses by staying
behind for hours when every other player has buggered off
home. Ask Shaun Maloney. But Becks also works on his
image off the field, and the PR machine behind him and
his wife has managed their life to the stage that it is now
a brand worth over £100 million – not to mention that
contract at LA Galaxy that will land him a reported £128
million! Good luck to them; I just know that Margaret and
I couldn't survive the life they have.

These days, we're lucky that our house is in grounds
behind gates, away from prying eyes. It is our own space.
When I lurched into the nightmare that was the Battle of
Bothwell Bridge, I stayed on a nice estate in Hamilton, but
it was open for the press to camp out on my doorstep the
morning after the fight before. I looked out my curtains,
and it was like something out of a movie. All those camera
lenses were pointed at me, desperate for a shot of the shamed
Rangers player and his battered face before he went into
Ibrox to face the music. I felt hunted. That was my taste of
having the paparazzi setting up shop outside my house, and
I hated it with a passion. If that's the way David Beckham
lives his life every day, then I have even more respect for
him now than I ever did.

I once watched a documentary in which Tim Lovejoy from
Soccer AM followed Beckham around Madrid during his Real
days, and while I am nowhere near his league, I could see
some parallels. He's a London barrow boy, and they slaughter
him for the way he speaks and call him thick; I'm painted as
a ned from a scheme. But we have made money beyond our

wildest dreams doing a job millions would swap their own lives for. And we've been able to indulge our passion for cars and buy motors we never thought we could possess. So just who is thick?

I see some comparisons between us, but the fame and constant spotlight on him is not for me. For example, there was one cameraman who lived outside Beckham's house in Spain from the moment he moved to Real Madrid to the day he left – how sad is that? And the comparisons between us end with his OCD, or Obsessive Compulsive Disorder. Apparently, he tidies up all the time and has to straighten the tins in the cupboards so the labels all point to the front. He also only wears each pair of boots once. Me? You only have to ask Margaret, and she'll tell you that I've got MBS, Messy Bastard Syndrome!

I don't know the guy, but he seems grounded, and for all the stick Victoria Beckham takes, she seems to be a genuine anchor in his life with all the madness that surrounds him. I got married when I was 22 to have that same grounding and I love it that Margaret hates football and will only come to cup finals when she is forced. She doesn't care about Barry Ferguson the footballer, only what we do with the family, and I respect that.

It has helped me to have my separate world with Margaret and the kids, and I don't care about her religion. I am a Protestant and a Rangers fan, and I am proud of both, but so many of my pals are Catholic and Celtic fans – I just couldn't care less. I judge them as people, not where they go to church. I suppose I knew all of this would be examined when I became Rangers captain, but I hope now that every little statement I make about this situation is listened to by the kids who look up to me. The next generation are the ones who matter the most, and I pray that we can chip away at it all and bring a little more tolerance.

I'm not a politician – who would want to be? – and I'm not a churchman or a journalist; I'm a footballer. It's not for me to examine sectarianism or try to cure Scotland of all its ills. I don't have the right words to combat it, and I'm not great in debates. All I can do is live my life and try to show people that the Old Firm rivalry should be intense and passionate but never about life or death. There is a difference between being proud of your roots as a Rangers man and being a bigot.

I find it difficult to make the link from a fiery rivalry to people being stabbed in the street. That is the part I will never get straight in my head – how it comes to matter that much. After the game, go to your Celtic pub and drown your sorrows, your Rangers boozer and celebrate, but don't take it to the extreme. How can it matter that much that you pull a knife on someone? It's a game of football, for Christ's sake.

But let's not take the heat out of the derby altogether, because it is the ferocity of the rivalry that makes it the game it is. I remember the first time I took that 30-yard walk from the Rangers team bus into the safety of the Parkhead foyer, and the abuse rained down on me. I was turning round and shouting, 'Who are you lot talking tae?' but the more experienced players behind me pushed me into the stadium. These days I listen to my iPod, pretend I'm on my mobile, look at my shoes, smile nicely, anything to just walk in there quietly.

I grew up with this rivalry as a major part of my life, especially because Derek was starring for Rangers at the time, and I learned to deal with it. I know what the club means and realise that Rangers is at the centre of many people's lives, because it means that much to me too. But as you grow up, your family becomes what matters most, and when something threatens your kids, it puts everything into focus.

These days, I watch Kyle tear around the place in whatever strip he has on that day and smile. I go to his games, and although he is only six, I can see he's a good player. But I bite my lip and don't shout too much, just encourage him to use his booming shot. Then I think back to the days when there was a shadow hanging over him before he was even born and remember the nights when I lay awake staring at the ceiling thinking we would lose him. It still makes me shudder.

The last month of Margaret's pregnancy with Kyle was hellish. She had a low-lying placenta, and I came to learn how dangerous that can be. There was a lot of bleeding and constant problems. She was in and out of hospital so the doctors could monitor her, and they warned us that both the mother and the baby were at risk when it happens as late in the pregnancy as it did with us.

Throughout all of this, I was trying to play for Gers and keep my head on football. I found that so hard. It was touch and go whether he would survive the birth, and I will never forget when the doctor was good enough to be straight-talking and said to me, 'There could be a major problem here.' Money counts for nothing at those times – neither does fame or reputation. I was just like any other young parent: worried sick, hoping to God everything would be all right and trying to sort out all the medical terms they were firing at me. And I have never been so relieved as when he came into the world unharmed. We owe so much to the staff at Bellshill Maternity Hospital.

The birth of my children will always be the most important thing in my life. And they are becoming their own people now: Connor's a typical kid with his music, computers and secret messages to his pals on MSN Messenger; Kyle rampages around the house trying to use up all his excess energy, desperate for his next game of football; and Cara's just my wee princess.

This chapter was, in many ways, a hard one for me to write because my family's privacy is a precious commodity. But it is going to become harder to keep them out of the spotlight, especially as my boys are Rangers daft, and they desperately want to go to every game at Ibrox – it would be an easier life if they supported the Accies.

Kids are great, though. There have been times when I have come out after a match, and I've had a poor game. I'll go to the Players' Lounge to meet my guests, and my mates all say I did well, because they want to give me moral support. Then, when I get in the car to come home, Kyle will say, 'Dad, why were you crap today?' I love that. I want to clip his ear, but I love it. He brings me down to earth. Kids speak the truth.

I can't hide from the fact that the money I now earn means that my children will grow up in a different environment from the one I did. But they're not living with Posh and

Becks here. If Margaret and I get a spare couple of hours together in midweek, we go to Marge's Café in Larkhall for a fry-up and bring home some of their cakes for tea. I can't imagine that David and Victoria crave for a box of empire biscuits too often. And my kids won't be cosseted or mollycoddled. They go to state school, even though I'd never criticise anyone who put their children through private education. That's one of the most important decisions a parent can make, but Margaret and I wanted them in an environment where they must stick up for themselves and grow up the right way.

I don't spoil them: they have to do their homework, tidy their rooms and clear away their plates. I am lucky to have money now, and it is hard not to indulge them at times, but I want them to respect their parents and their grandparents. And when they grow up, they won't sponge off me. They will have their fees paid when they go to university, or whatever, but they will work. They won't be the idle rich.

I guard my family jealously, and I always have done. I like to keep them separate from my football life. Some players like their wife and kids to be part of their public profile, but Margaret hates that, and I have never wanted it either. I can be Barry Ferguson captain of Rangers and Scotland to the outside world, but behind closed doors I'm just Dad. Being like that has meant I can still do all the things that I want to do: I still go to Toys'R'Us and JJB Sports and get the kids their new trainers. I take them to McDonald's for a treat, watch the boys playing football and all the rest, and I love it. And most of the time people in Scotland respect that.

But there are times when Celtic fans will shout, 'Ya Orange bastard' or whatever, and it still makes my blood boil when my kids are with me when that happens. I hate it. I'll take the abuse if it is just me, because it goes with the territory, but I don't see why it should happen when I have my children with me. Thankfully, it has only ever been a minority of Celtic fans who have given me the vile stuff. Most of them are willing to have a laugh and a sly dig, and when I am injured, they will genuinely wish me well.

However, when I am confronted with the younger ones with the smart mouths, I have learned to keep the red mist away and control myself, because they are just looking for a reaction. These days, they're shouting at a different guy from the one they think they know.

People judge me when they don't know me: I'm a bigot, I'm a ned, I'm thick. But I'm not ashamed of the way I speak. I'm not going to change. I come from Hamilton not Holyrood! They don't do elocution lessons where I come from, and if they did, I wouldn't sign up. So I sound how I sound on radio and TV, and if people want to slag me for that, then fine. I am comfortable in my own skin.

Another accusation I sometimes hear is that I am a flash git. When I hear this, I cringe, and then I get angry. Flash? Never! I might take a table at a charity dinner or a box at Hamilton races and invite all my mates from time to time, but I'll pay for that quietly. It's my present to them for all the things they do for me in my life.

One of my close pals now is John, whom I met when he fitted the security cameras and alarm system at my house. I have other mates who have kitted out my cinema room or sold me a car at BMW. They're just guys I've become friendly with over the years. Then there's Aki, who owns a brilliant Indian restaurant called Spice beside Hamilton Park racecourse, where we spent long hours doing the interviews for this book and playing pool. And when I shoot the breeze over a few beers with Col and Tam, self-made businessmen but normal guys, I have never once pulled out £2,000 and said, 'Look at me.' That's not my style. If I'm paying, it is done quietly.

My indulgence, ever since I was able to afford them, has been cars: a Bentley DB7 or a BMW M6. I'm addicted to them and interested in them, but I'm not ashamed of them. I dreamed of having them when I was kid, and I have grafted to have them. Is that flash? Not in my book.

I have sniffed out the hangers-on over the years. The friends I have now are people I want to spend time with away from the game. I have people I can trust around me, and I have mates who are my age, such as my childhood pals Ian, Phil and Nicky, and others who are 40 or older. They are all guys I hope would still be my friends even if I didn't have the Rangers armband. You learn that some people just want to cling on to you because of who you are; it's not about friendship but about status, and there are bloodsuckers like that throughout the game. They are users, professional mates, and they are only interested in what standing next to you brings them, not what is best for you. Therefore, I only have the family and friends around me now who can provide the support network I need for the next part of my story.

I think I have six years left at the top. My ankle feels

stronger than ever after the operation, and my body can keep me going at the top level until I am 35. And I'm still driven on by the things I have been deprived of in the game. Missing out on the 2006 World Cup simply increased my desire to make it to South Africa in 2010. I want to get to a major finals and stick two fingers up to those who say I don't want to play for Scotland or even that I'm not good enough to play for my country any more. That theory began to be kicked around after the last World Cup qualifiers when we won 3–0 in Slovenia without me. Everyone is entitled to their opinion, but I'm telling you that I will make sure that those who say Scotland are better without Barry Ferguson eat humble pie during the 2007–08 season.

I have three years left at Gers, if my current contract is not renewed, and I want to get through 500 games for the club and 50 caps for Scotland. I should be in the Hall of Fame by now but injuries have bitten big chunks out of my international career, which is a major regret.

Football will always be a part of my life after I hang up my boots, and I sway from the idea of youth coaching to thoughts of trying to become a manager. I've had a good think about the latter, and I already know whom I would have next to me. My old Ibrox reserves mentor John McGregor has been lost to the game for far too long. He is an honourable man and a superb coach, and he could guide me if we got the chance.

For now, though, I have a lot of ideas, first and foremost being the Barry Ferguson Soccer School. I want to build it in the community I came from so that kids can learn the game. And if there are youngsters struggling to get the right gear and their mums and dads are scraping for a living, then I will try to hand something back. I know what a week training in the right place with the best coaches can do for a kid and how football can help you feel better about yourself. That's my goal, and I've already looked at sites and examined the figures. The business plan is there, and it will work. I can see the building rising out of the ground in my mind's eye, and the thought of opening day is something that inspires me now.

I am well down the line with the soccer school partly because I am involved with the Rangers Charity Foundation and have seen the good work that they do. Charity is high in my thoughts now, and I'll develop that side of my life more in order to be able to give something back.

My last ambition will make people laugh, and I'll take more dog's abuse, but stuff it. The truth is I have always wanted to be a *fireman*. I don't know what it is, but I loved the idea long before *Rescue Me* was on the telly or *Ladder 49* was a hit movie. I'm deadly serious about it. There is something about the job that attracts me – the thrill of danger maybe. If I don't stay in football, I will maybe look to pursue that part time.

One thing is for sure, I couldn't sit here counting my money, twiddling my thumbs and playing the property market like a rich playboy no-mark. That's just not me.

16

By Royal Appointment

'I now pronounce you a Member of the Order
of the British Empire.'

Her Majesty The Queen. Enough said.

This is it: the final word on the story of my life so far – a PS that I can't believe is going at the end of this book. This unplanned chapter began when I sat at my kitchen table sifting through the mail on 12 May 2006, trying to shake the morning fog out of my head. I yawned – another morning of rehab ahead. Same old, same old.

I will remember that date for the rest of my life. I woke up and hobbled into the kitchen on my crutches, cursing the ankle operation that had ended my season prematurely. My scar was itching like hell and driving me crazy, and I knew it was a fortnight until they would saw the plaster off and let my leg breathe again. I was feeling grumpy, as usual. Then I started shuffling through the post, searching for my plane tickets and confirmation of my itinerary from the club for the beano to San Francisco for the North American Rangers Supporters Association Convention.

I'd promised the club that I would go as our ambassador. I was to take Bob Malcolm with me and introduce Kris Boyd to the Rangers family abroad, letting him see just how much his goals meant to people across the world. It would make him realise just how big a club he'd joined. Last but not least, I wanted to say goodbye to Alex Rae, a true Rangers man whom I'd come to respect during the two years since he had come home from Wolves to the team he'd supported as a kid. Alex had taken the player–manager's job at First Division Dundee and, at the age of 36, was on his way in his new life. He deserved a send-off from us, though.

So I was thinking about all that, pondering a way to keep Boydy under control on the plane, when I saw an official seal on a weighty letter – it was from Downing Street. As I read through it and scanned it line by unbelievable line, I was overcome with a sense of astonishment. My missus says my face looked like a character in a kids' cartoon. My jaw literally dropped. They wanted to tell me that I had been recommended for an MBE – and they were asking if I was willing to accept it. Accept it? I don't know too many boys from Striven Terrace in Hamilton who have turned them down!

I burst out laughing when I got that letter. I just couldn't believe it. To be honest, I thought it was all some kind of complex wind-up. I was looking for my mates hiding under the kitchen window to pop up and deck themselves laughing in a *You've Been Framed* moment. But there was no one there – it was real.

What an honour. They said they were giving it to me for

services to football, and even after it was confirmed in the Queen's Birthday Honours List on June 17, it remained very hard to take in. It is the biggest achievement of my life and one that I will savour for ever. I look at people at Rangers who have been recognised like this – for example, John Greig and Ally McCoist – and it knocks me out that it has happened to me. I feel genuinely humbled. There is a statue of Greigy in bronze outside the stadium – he is the greatest-ever Ranger – and Coisty scored 355 goals in 581 games for the club and is, as he keeps telling me, our greatest-ever striker. (The minute Ally got his medal, he had Jimmy Bell make sure that MBE was printed on all his training gear so he could run out and give the snappers the shot they wanted. Always understated, Coisty.) To be ranked up there alongside the likes of Greig and McCoist and be given an MBE leaves me speechless. Rangers are a club with 134 years of history, and it scares me that I will now always be part of it all after receiving this award. John Greig is the Ledge partly because he has an MBE, and to have been awarded one of my own at the age of 28 left me bewildered.

This chapter was originally written on 26 May 2006, two weeks after I got the news, and even then, only Margaret, my mum and dad, my two best mates, and my co-author Kingy knew. Every one of them was sworn to secrecy. News of these awards always leaks out, but I was paranoid. It seemed like a dream, and as much as I wanted to shout about it from the rooftops, I didn't want Downing Street to have an excuse to snatch it back from me.

I'd thought that just like all the sports stars I'd seen in

the papers getting this honour, I would also experience the dream of visiting Buckingham Palace. I drove past the palace on a weekend down in London once, but the last time I saw it Batman and Robin were hanging off a balcony in a Fathers for Justice protest! The crying shame was that I didn't get to meet Her Majesty because the next communication I received from the palace asked me down to London on 11 October, the very day that Scotland played a Euro 2008 qualifier in Ukraine.

I was given the award in Scotland by the Lord Lieutenant of my local area in Hamilton. But it didn't change the fact that I had been honoured, and the letters 'MBE' can be placed after my name for the rest of my life.

I knew in the wake of the award there would be criticism from some quarters, and the bad things I had done in the past would be dragged up again. People questioned whether I merited an MBE, but, for once, I truly couldn't care less what others thought. I hope it proves that over the six years that I have been captain of Rangers, since Dick Advocaat took a chance on me just two months after I brought shame on the club, I have learned my lessons and conducted myself in the right way. The Battle of Bothwell Bridge has haunted me at times, but all the problems I have come through since and all the things that I have achieved have made me stronger. The journey has brought me from a council scheme in Hamilton to becoming someone that the Queen felt worthy of recognising. I hope people see that I am a different person from the boy of 22 who got sent off against Celtic and ended up on the front pages branded a thug. That was a low point in my life, but I'd ask anyone reading this to consider if they have ever come to a point of regret in their own lives, a time when they have needed a second chance?

I have read countless words written about me over the years, and I have ranted about the injustice of the opinions of some when they have sharpened their knives in times of trouble: I shouldn't have the Scotland armband; I was gutless and so weak-willed and insecure that I was scared of Paul Le Guen coming in. The last accusation resulted from an innocent radio interview when all I said was that the new manager might not fancy me, and if he didn't, he'd sell me, and I would take that on the chin. I saw that as grown-up footballing logic. Next thing I knew, there was a screaming headline in a paper and people were writing columns about it calling me a coward. Unreal. It is at times like that when stuff gets to me because my dad will be up a roof working and his mates will ask him about what is being written about me. My mum also hears about it and gets upset. I will always understand criticism when I play badly, but that was just bollocks. I'm a mile away from being perfect, but I'm not weak, gutless or a bad captain. That's why the MBE means so much to me. It vindicates me in so many ways.

I will never forget being able to walk into my mum and dad's house armed with the news of my award and knowing how happy I was about to make them. My mum burst into floods of uncontrollable tears, and my old man burst out laughing. A roofer's son being recognised by the palace? You just couldn't make it up.

I thought of many ways to end this book, but I could never have imagined that it would be like this. The strange thing is that the award came at the end of a season to forget, which included coming third in the league, undergoing an ankle operation and the loss of my manager. After all the pain we went through, to finish it all with a letter from the Queen overwhelmed me.

From battling the demons inside my head as a ten year old to the tears when they said I was too small to play for Scotland and the street brawl that left me forever tagged a thick ned, I've had to overcome a lot, and I think for all the mistakes I have made there are enough reasons for me to take pride in myself, too.

I've had so much luck in my life – signing for Rangers, scoring against Celtic, playing for Scotland, leading my country, marrying Margaret, the birth of my kids – but this was some Hollywood ending. Scratch that – you couldn't have scripted it like this in the movies. They would have thrown it back at you as too far-fetched.

I looked down at the letter and all the faces of those who have helped and inspired me flashed before me: my dad, my mam, Derek, Margaret, Danny Cunning, John Chalmers, John Brown, John McGregor, Walter, wee Dick, the chairman, Big Red, Souness, Craig Brown, Berti, Arthur Numan and the rest. I said a little silent thank you to everyone who has touched my life and my career and put up with me striving to get to where I wanted to be in one helluva hurry.

Then I had a quiet smile to myself and thought, 'At least Rangers won something this season.' Barry Ferguson MBE: not bad for a kid they said would never make it.

17

Manchester and the Edge of Greatness

John Greig emerging from the door at the top of the steps
of the plane and thrusting the European Cup-Winners' Cup
into the air: I'd seen that picture of Greigy in those 1970s
shades with his goatee beard a thousand times – the leader
of the Barcelona Bears. I envied him that moment. I always
wondered what it must have felt like.

Now it was 1 June 2008, and I was lying by the swimming
pool in sweltering Portugal, sipping from a cold bottle of
beer after a game of golf with the close-knit group of pals I
trust most. It was the calm before the storm; our big boys'
night out on the lash in Vilamoura beckoned. We'd been
looking forward to it for weeks.

The troops were in the garden of our villa playing
keepy-uppy with a ball we'd bought for four euros at the
supermarket, and they were slaughtering each other. Their
control was shocking. I looked up and grinned at them,
this band of mates who share in my good times and lift
me when I'm down: Macca, property expert and manager
of junior side, Royal Albert; Col, big businessman and
even bigger Rangers man; Phil, pal and agent; Big Tam,
another self-made guy who couldn't spell golf but loved
the holiday anyway; and Aki, Indian restaurant guru and
shortest driver in the game's history. My jaw was still sore

from laughing at the patter on the flight over to Portugal for my summer break.

But the truth was that I was drifting away from them that afternoon, my mind whirring back to the month before, to the City of Manchester Stadium. To the UEFA Cup final against Zenit St Petersburg. To the chance to become an immortal in the history of Rangers Football Club. I used to deck myself at a line in *Only an Excuse*: 'Aye, he was one of the immortals. He's dead now.' Now I was staring up into the perfect blue sky, and that's when it truly hit me for the first time. If we had not lost 2–0 to Zenit, that's what we would have been: immortals.

I would love to think I will get a second chance before I hang up my boots, but it had taken Rangers 36 *years* to get another shot at winning a European trophy. The guts of four decades had come and gone since Greigy's side had beaten Moscow Dynamo 3–2 and become the side who mean as much to Rangers men as the Lisbon Lions do to Celtic fans.

Now for one last time I let the games we had come through play through my memory banks: beating Werder Bremen when Allan McGregor came of age as a keeper up there with Andy Goram and Stefan Klos; Nacho Novo's winning penalty against Fiorentina in the semi-final. Yes, that run would live with us for ever, but I wanted more. I wanted to know what it felt like to come home on the plane with that big trophy on the seat beside me.

I'm not going to lie. I had dreamed of that – fantasised about what it would be like to hoist the trophy aloft at Glasgow Airport the way Greigy did. Then we'd go back to an Ibrox full to the rafters and show the UEFA Cup off to the fans. I could see it all in my mind's eye.

It didn't happen. If I am honest, we lost to a better team, one with the brilliant Andrei Arshavin in it. My old boss Dick Advocaat's side had a little too much craft in the end. Yet when they open the history books in the future, the 2–0 scoreline won't tell the whole story – the story of how I ended up walking out to play the biggest game of my life bursting with pride and boiling with anger.

The UEFA Cup final, 14 May 2008, City of Manchester Stadium: Zenit St Petersburg skipper Anatoliy Tymoschuk was standing a yard away at the mouth of the tunnel, keyed up and ready. His team were buzzing. They'd had a fortnight to prepare without any games, just thinking about that day. One game from destiny. Me? My boys were up for it all right, but *seven* of them were carrying injuries into the final. That was the toll of the SPL's refusal to call off games or extend a season interrupted by the awful weather and the nightmarish death on the pitch of Motherwell's Phil O'Donnell to buy us some breathing space. Even when I think of it now, it makes me furious.

I couldn't give a toss if people think I'm petty. I can't forget the decisions made by the SPL hierarchy during the run-in to the end of the season. And I'll never forgive them. It was the biggest game of my life, of any of our lives, yet we got no help. Even for a legend such as Walter Smith, that was it. It was a defining game, and I will always feel that not enough was done to help us.

I was angry then, but now there is just a lingering disappointment that Rangers' biggest game in 36 years was played with that sort of preparation. The truth is that we walked out into the stadium that night with those seven starting players carrying niggling injuries. You can't tell me that would have been the case had we had even just a couple of days to rest and prepare better. I was bitterly disappointed in the SPL, and I always will be. No matter how fit you are and how well you do the recovery programmes, you just can't cope with the schedule we had.

I understand the circumstances of the Russian League were different, because their season had only just started, but Zenit got a fortnight free to prepare for the biggest game in their history. Our rulers couldn't see fit to give us a week. Instead, we played Wednesday against Motherwell then Saturday against Dundee United before we could even think of Manchester.

I wanted us to prepare in the right manner, even for a couple of days, but it wasn't to be. We lost running on empty. Some fans rioted in the centre of the city. The memories were not what they should have been.

The aftermath washed over me: all the stories in the news, the fights, the baton-wielding cops and the big screens showing the match to people without tickets breaking down. I just felt those Rangers punters deserved more from a side who were so obviously low on gas when it mattered most.

Look at the atmosphere and the numbers we took down to Manchester. It disappoints me that I knew we weren't as sharp or as fit as we could be. When I saw people shelling out over £1,000 for a ticket, I wanted us to have everything in the locker for them, but we didn't. I saw so many of our fans making the journey, and I wanted to give them our very best. I can't go back and change it now, though. All I can do is carry the reception they gave us at the end of the match with me to my grave.

Even mentally, we couldn't focus on the UEFA Cup final with so much riding on the Dundee United game we were forced to play on the Saturday. Look, I'm not saying we would have beaten Zenit had we been given that extra time, but we'd have had a better chance. Ask any player and they'll tell you they always carry niggles, but at the end of a long season a week of rest would have meant so much.

Rangers had been slated for not even being close to reaching a European final after Celtic reached the UEFA Cup final and lost to Porto in Seville in 2003. Now we had matched that, and I wanted the SPL to recognise the achievement, but they gave us nothing. They keep saying they want their teams to do well in Europe, but in our case the actions didn't back up the words.

This is not sour grapes as a new season rattles on, with new rows and new heroes, but there was sheer disbelief in our dressing-room when the fixtures were made public. We made a decision within the four walls of Murray Park not to whine at the time. Yet there were players inside our dressing-room from abroad – guys such as Carlos Cuéllar and Jean-Claude Darcheville – who were just astounded. They were used to the hierarchy in Spain and France helping their teams. They were staggered that our own league would treat us like this. There was a lot of anger among our players, and they couldn't believe what was happening. But as one decision after another was made, we never expected any help.

No one should *ever* again have to play four games in seven days to try to win a title as we did. It was ridiculous. I kept hearing people saying that they do it in the juniors all the time, but with no disrespect to them – some of my best mates play at that level – this is not the juniors. And look at the games we had before that week. The SPL knew what we'd been through, and still those decisions were made.

That will always live with me.

By the time we toiled past First Division Queen of the South to edge the Scottish Cup final 3–2 and at least finish the season on a high, we were a shell of a side. Now I think lessons must be learned in the corridors of power after what they put us through.

Yet for us the season was an epic. Losing the UEFA Cup final and the league will always hurt me, but when we returned to Ibrox after the final, Walter Smith said something telling to me. Our party was going on around us, and he said, 'Every competition we ended up in, we took to the last day.' I'll take that every season. We set a standard that must now be bettered. When you look at where we were under Le Guen – exiting cups at the hands of Dunfermline and St Johnstone – it was some turnaround.

I will always maintain that defeat in the UEFA Cup final was no excuse for losing the title to Celtic – none at all. The scheduling was, though. The SPL placed demands on us that were totally unacceptable. They let us down. I don't care how fit and mentally tough you are, you *cannot* do that. They were massive games, and there was no way we could play to our full potential in them. I and many people at Rangers will always be bitter about the way we were treated.

We ended up with two trophies but not the ones I wanted most, and there is no question the powers that be had a big hand in that. Carlos Cuéllar was up to 58 games, and he kept saying in his broken English, 'Fergie, what the fuck is happening? Why won't they help us now.' The most he had played before in a season with Osasuna was around the 40 mark. Now he was facing a punishing schedule, and I just smiled: 'Wake up. You're in Scotland now.'

The number of games we played was a sign of our success that season. It's just that in my eyes the timing of our run-in at the end of it all was a sick joke. We were playing two seasons rolled into one, and we needed help; instead, the last week they inflicted on us was way beyond harsh.

Up until then, I could handle the heavy workload, but in the end, they broke us, and when the new season started, there was a price to pay. Since the February of the titanic 2007–08 season, I'd been toiling. My ankle had gone in the CIS Cup semi-final win over Hearts, and I was struggling. Badly at times.

The first half of the season when I was 100 per cent fit, I was flying. Then came the injury. But I wanted to play so much, so I decided to keep going. It's not false heroics with me, this playing through the pain stuff. I'm not looking for headlines or praise for doing it – it's just what I do. It would need a broken leg to stop me, because if I can still contribute, I'll play. Walter Smith would have binned me if I hadn't still been giving something to Rangers during those last three months of the season.

When you are on crutches and in rehab, you get a lot of time to reflect on whether you made the right choice, and perhaps I am my own worst enemy sometimes. But I'm out there living a fan's dream, and when you play for Rangers, you keep going.

Pre-season is about getting fit, but the failure to win the league costs you so much, because you have to play in those dreaded qualifiers for the Champions League. They were looming over all of us in the summer, and as I pushed myself, my ankle was agony. I knew the surgeon's knife was beckoning. Again. When the news came that I would be out for four months, I took it better than I would have done in the past. I was sick of covering up, sick of playing when I wasn't 100 per cent. Now I could get it fixed, even if the timing was a nightmare. And I had the Champions League to look forward to when I came back – to another European adventure. Be careful what you wish for.

To hit your peak as a modern player, I believe you need around twelve games, but now you have four or five friendlies then you play a European tie that is worth £10 million to the club. No one is ready or sharp enough, but it frames a season, and we walked into the FBK Kaunas tie with me injured and a side still crunching through the gears. I watched us going out, and I was just devastated. We were UEFA Cup finalists and now look at us: out of Europe altogether without a parachute.

Life at Rangers, though, is about how you react to the bitter setbacks that come your way. From the club, the manager and the chairman, I felt the reaction was the right one. Sir David Murray put his hand in his pocket, and the manager spent the dough shrewdly. I think this is the best squad I have been involved in since I came home in 2005.

There was so much crushing disappointment around the place after what happened in Lithuania, but I think things are looking up now. I understood the grief and anger of the fans after Kaunas, because we should beat teams such as that. But no one hurt more than Walter did, believe me. The gaffer is a Rangers man through and through. The headlines mocked us and the phone-in fans called for his head, but Walter swallowed it all and got to work again.

Under so much pressure after the start from hell, we went to Celtic Park and won the first Old Firm game of the season 4–2. I thought the second half of that clash was the best we have played for a very long time.

Pedro Mendes is a player I have watched and admired in the Premiership with Spurs and then Portsmouth. He scored a fantastic goal against Celtic, but it was the other stuff he did that I seized on. It thrills me to see clever players, the ones with the guts to take the ball in tight situations and play a pass. He is quality; I saw it right away. He is an effective midfielder who keeps it when you need him to but can play someone else in, too.

You also know what you are getting from Steve Davis – he's an intelligent footballer – and 'Magic' Bougherra has been rock solid at the back. I loved that 4–2 win. You know what I look for in those new boys? What they have upstairs. By that I mean mental toughness, and they all showed it that day – showed that they have what it takes to be Rangers players. I thought, 'I can't wait to play beside all of them.' Those are the boys you want in your corner. Proper footballers. With guys such as Pedro in the team, we are looking good. He has helped the club to react in the right way following our premature exit from Europe. We could have slinked off as a team and hid in a corner, but we were top of the league soon after, standing up to be counted. It has been the right reaction. I pray I'm fit again by Christmas 2008 and at the heart of another title battle.

Winning the league on the final day of the season when I came back from Blackburn in 2005 was such a massive high. But Celtic winning three in a row? It *can't* go on, and everybody at Ibrox knows that. I don't care what anyone says, I would rather have won the league than the UEFA Cup last season. That's our bread and butter. If we'd won the title, then the hellish Kaunas mess would not have happened.

We have not won the title for three years – those are the facts. And league tables don't lie. Yet I sense a determination around the place to make sure this ends here. Look at the top of our club: the manager who won nine in a row, the striker who was there for every one of those titles, the midfielder who was the fans' favourite player through the bulk of that time. There are no bigger Rangers men than Smith, McCoist and Durrant. Do you think that losing the title in 2007–08 didn't cut them to the quick? We all know what it means at this club, and strong characters such as Madjid Bougherra and Pedro Mendes will buy into that and feed off it. They'll help us.

Rehab: the hardest time for any professional athlete. My hatred of watching and not playing is well documented, and few games have been harder for me to sit through than Scotland's opening 1–0 World Cup qualifying defeat in Macedonia.

Skopje was a nightmare. I was dejected, although I would have taken a draw before that game if I am honest. Better teams than us have struggled there before, but to come away with nothing put so much pressure on us. However, the reaction in the 2–1 win in Iceland that followed was great. I would have taken the worst performance in history if it meant we could come away with three points. Instead, the boys played really well in the first half and hung on for the win.

The campaign to get us through this section as winners or in the play-off slot means so much to me now. I am 30, coming off another major operation, with a crescent-shaped scar on my right ankle, and this is my last kick at a World Cup finals. I know that. We were so close to making Euro 2008, but the absence of Scotland from the big tournaments will always play on my mind. I'm just desperate to make it and on the way to get the 50 caps that will take me into the Hall of Fame. That would mean so much to me. As I've said before, I want my kids to be able to go there in the future and see their old man. Injuries have stolen a lot of caps from me, but 50 is a realistic target.

We need to kick on under George Burley. It's a shame I wasn't there for him at the start of his reign. He came in with some act to follow – the European Championship qualifying wins home and away to France took us to the brink. The reaction then taught even someone steeped in football since he was a kid something new. I felt as though we brought the whole country together.

As ever, there had to be a stomach-churning end to it all in the showdown clash with Italy at Hampden. We pitched away a stupid goal to Luca Toni before the place had even drawn breath, I scrambled one in to level it, Faddy nearly nicked it, the ref then gives a scandalous foul against Alan Hutton and we lose it at the death. Fucking typical.

I could almost taste my first major finals, then it was ripped away from me. Just like that. Now I know that the clock is ticking. Much as I pride myself on my fitness, I have had a busted kneecap that threatened my career and two major ankle ops. Can I keep going on both fronts now that my 30th birthday, the one footballers most despise, has slipped by? For now the answer is yes, because it means too much to me to do anything else.

Just like Greigy at the top of those aeroplane steps, I also remember Colin Hendry leading Scotland out to face

Brazil in the France 98 opener. How does that feel? Another question that needs answering before I hang up my boots.

My 30th birthday didn't slip past without me being duped in one of the best wind-ups ever – up there with Margaret sneaking Neil Lennon into the house to record a tribute to me winning the MBE! The Gaffer was at the centre of it. He told me I had to accompany him to a Saturday-night dinner date at Glasgow's Alea Casino. He said, with a deadly serious look on his face, that our chairman had some investors from America on the hook. They were high-rollers, and the presence of the club captain might just clinch the deal. He looked me right in the eye and said, 'Fergie, you're always fucking moaning about us being stingy in the transfer market. Now we can change it – and we'll buy midfielders, too.'

I was gone. I sapped it all in, even though I was raging that my Saturday night was being wrecked. So I went, phoning a few mates and whining about how I had club business and couldn't join my pals and their wives, who all seemed to be heading out on the town.

I got to Alea and headed upstairs to the private function room. When I threw open the door, instead of Rangers' Yankee version of Roman Abramovich, 150 of my closest friends and family were there, yelling, 'Surprise. Happy Birthday.' Bastards.

I have faced so many accusations of disloyalty when I have missed Scotland squads that the storm that surrounded my close pal Lee McCulloch's decision to quit international football in September 2008 didn't surprise me one little bit. I'd known since the Italy game that Lee was thinking about retiring from the international scene, and we talked about it way back then. Yet just 48 hours before the clash in Iceland, the news leaked out dressed up in a way you could never have credited: 'I'll Never Play for Burley Again' screamed the headline.

Well, I knew Lee was on the brink of going, but I also knew it was because he wanted to spend more time with his family and was worried sick about the niggling injuries he was picking up, costing him his Rangers place. It had sod all to do with George Burley. To suggest it was because of George was bang out of order, as the Italy match is how long ago it was in Lee's mind.

As the dust settles, people have to respect his choice. Lee believes it is best for his career, and whatever some people might say, he *agonised* over the decision. He knew he would get slaughtered, but he still believed he had to do what was right for him and his family.

The timing of the story just killed him, and he has been filleted for it, but that is not his fault. Lee wanted to cement his Rangers place and knew that not playing for Scotland would give him time to recover from knocks. He didn't make the decision lightly. For ten months, he debated it with his family and those he trusts. Now he should be left to get on with his football. He didn't wake up one morning and think, 'I'll quit Scotland today.' The whole episode ripped him up, but it's over with now, and I think people should draw a line under it and move on.

For all our passion for this game we love, there are more important things in life. Dear God, if we haven't learned that now after having had Phil O'Donnell, Tommy Burns, Colin McRae and Jamie Dolan taken from us before their time, then we never will. The year since I was last asked to reprise this book has brought so many tears, so many times when I have asked myself the question that can never be answered: why?

T.B. – a true gentleman and football man – gone at 51 after battling skin cancer.

Colin McRae, the rally legend and my pal and neighbour, killed in a helicopter crash along with his little son, Johnny. Tragic is way too mild a word.

Phil dying of heart failure on the Fir Park pitch with his beloved nephew, David Clarkson, looking on.

I'll never be able to fully describe how I felt when we made the journey to what had become a shrine to Phil at Fir Park. Humbling. That is perhaps the only word for it. I stood alongside Stephen McManus, the Celtic skipper, as we laid floral tributes in honour of Phil.

I'd watched a stadium I know so well become a shrine after the fateful events of the Saturday before. I just couldn't get my head around the sheer outpouring of emotion attached to every jersey, scarf or teddy bear that had been left there. I was overwhelmed by the depth of loss people felt.

A great player, a thoroughly decent man, a doting father and husband – just a top bloke – gone. I can't come to terms with it even now. When I look back on 2007, the controversies and confrontations of my own football career seem so small and insignificant.

Phil O'Donnell and Colin McRae: two sportsmen, two right good Lanarkshire boys who grew up to be heroes whether they were in a Motherwell strip or behind the wheel of a rally car. They have been snatched away in the prime of their lives, and that is what I find so very had to take.

I was privileged to be at Fir Park that day in the company of the Well number two, Scott Leitch. I was among Phil's people, and I could see just how much his death had shattered the club. They were devastated, because their captain had touched the lives of everyone around the place.

I came to know and respect Phil through my friendship with his brother-in-law, John Henderson. I made the journey to the ground – a journey I was dreading – alongside John and top ref, Eddie Smith, another of Phil's brothers-in-law. It always has been – and remains – a family steeped in good values and a love of the game, and that has brought us all together. Yet as I walked among the tributes that day, I kept wondering how what they call the 'Beautiful Game' could be so cruel.

Inside the stadium, Leitchy told me how Phil had seemed to have at last overcome all of his injuries. This was the fittest he had been. He was flying, and Scott reckoned being the father figure of Mark McGhee's young side was something he revelled in. I just had to look at Scott's face to see how this had affected him – the toll is still there for all to see. I also saw David Clarkson at the ground. How can you come to terms with what he has been through as a player? He has lost a teammate, an uncle, a friend and a mentor. It is harrowing. Yet Phil would have wanted him to come back from this, and I pray he does.

It was right that big Mick and I stood side by side at Fir Park. The decision to call off the Old Firm game is for others to debate. It is not for me to comment on. All I know is that the loss of a man such as Phil puts everything in perspective. Our wives, Eileen and Margaret, are close, and I thought Phil's missus was incredibly brave to visit the ground and see how much her man meant to people.

Only three months before, I'd watched Alison McRae show that same courage at Colin's funeral. It hammers you, the loss of men with so much left to live for. It guts you. I came home feeling utterly numb. I just wanted to put my arms round Margaret and the kids and feel safe.

I've been taught some lessons about life and how you have to seize the day and cherish it. Tommy, Phil and Colin did that, only to be stolen from us way before their time. When the initial feeling of total loss seeped away, though, something remained that is hard to explain. I thought of all those different strips at Fir Park – Rangers, Celtic, Hearts . . . even the Accies. The way Phil played the game, how he conducted himself, it struck all those people the same way. They might not be Well men, Celtic men or whatever, but they recognised what he was and what he stood for. And I felt proud to be a part of Scottish football, proud that for all the rivalries we still have the decency to say goodbye to one of our own in the right way.

My heart goes out to Eileen and the kids now as the headlines fade and the game roars on. It breaks for them. These are just words, and they can't heal or change anything. In the end, all I can do is say one final thing to add to all those tributes I walked among. Phil O'Donnell was a true football guy and a gentleman who brought pride to his family – and I'm proud I knew him.